Doing Your Qualitative Psychology Project

SAGE has been part of the global academic community since 1965, supporting high quality research and learning that transforms society and our understanding of individuals, groups and cultures. SAGE is the independent, innovative, natural home for authors, editors and societies who share our commitment and passion for the social sciences.

Find out more at: **www.sagepublications.com**

Doing Your Qualitative Psychology Project

Edited by

Cath Sullivan, Stephen Gibson
and **Sarah Riley**

Los Angeles | London | New Delhi
Singapore | Washington DC

First published 2012

SAGE Publications Ltd
1 Oliver's Yard
55 City Road
London EC1Y 1S

SAGE Publications Inc.
2455 Teller Road
Thousand Oaks, California 91320

SAGE Publications India Pvt Ltd
B 1/I 1 Mohan Cooperative Industrial Area
Mathura Road, New Delhi 110 044
India

SAGE Publications Asia-Pacific Pte Ltd
3 Church Street
#10-04 Samsung Hub
Singapore 049483

Library of Congress Control Number: 2011935564

British Library Cataloguing in Publication data

A catalogue record for this book is available from the British Library

ISBN 978-0-85702-745-0
ISBN 978-0-85702-746-7

Typeset by C&M Digitals (P) Ltd, Chennai, India
Printed by MPG Books Group, Bodmin, Cornwall
Printed on paper from sustainable resources

MIX
Paper from
responsible sources
FSC
www.fsc.org   FSC® C018575

CONTENTS

ACKNOWLEDGEMENTS

This book has grown from work done by a working group on the teaching of qualitative research methods at undergraduate level (TQRMUL) which was established by the UK Higher Education Academy Psychology Network (HEAPN) in 2005. The authors and editors of this book have been members of this working group for a number of years. This book would not have been produced without the support of the HEAPN, and in particular, we would like to thank Annie Trapp and Marina Crowe for their valuable work in support of the TQRMUL group over the years. We'd also like to thank the other members of the TQRMUL group who are not authors in this book, as they too played a significant part in its development.

NOTES ON CONTRIBUTORS

Michael Forrester is a reader in the School of Psychology at the University of Kent, UK. His teaching and research interests are in early child development and qualitative methods. He is co-editor (with H. Gardner) of *Analysing Interaction in Childhood: Insights from Conversation Analysis* (Wiley-Blackwell, 2010) and editor of *Doing Qualitative Research in Psychology* (SAGE, 2010).

Nollaig Frost is a senior lecturer in Psychology at Middlesex University. She teaches qualitative research methods at all levels from undergraduate to doctorate and has produced an edited book on combining core approaches in qualitative research. She uses qualitative and mixed methods approaches to pursue her research on second-time motherhood and on issues of mental health and mental illness.

Stephen Gibson is a senior lecturer in Psychology at York St John University. He is a social psychologist with research interests in areas such as peace and conflict, citizenship and national identity, and dis/obedience. In addition, he has been involved in numerous projects concerning the teaching of qualitative research methods. Between 2008 and 2011 he was chair of the TQRMUL group, and is co-editor (with Simon Mollan) of the forthcoming volume *Representations of Peace and Conflict* (Palgrave, 2012).

Siobhan Hugh-Jones is a lecturer in Health Psychology at the Institute of Psychological Science, University of Leeds. Her main research focus is on health and well-being in individuals, families and societies, and her research draws upon interview, media and visual data. She predominantly uses discourse analysis in her work. She has forthcoming publications on healthy eating by children, well-being in siblings and the educational well-being of teenagers with cancer. She currently serves as a committee member of the Qualitative Methods in Psychology section of the British Psychological Society and has a longstanding interest in the scholarship of learning and teaching.

Nigel King is Professor in Applied Psychology and Director of the Centre for Applied Psychological Research at the University of Huddersfield. He has a long-standing interest in the use of qualitative methods in 'real world' research, especially in community health and social care settings. Recently, he has carried out several projects in community palliative care, focussing especially on roles, relationships and identities. Other interests include the experience of chronic illness, psychological aspects of contact with nature, and ethics in qualitative research. He is well-known for his work on the 'template' style of thematic analysis, and more recently the development of a visual technique known as 'Pictor'.

Kathryn Kinmond is a chartered psychologist and accredited counsellor. She currently works as a senior lecturer at Manchester Metropolitan University where she teaches social psychology, abuse studies and qualitative research methods. Her main research and publications have addressed self, identity and experience within a range of topics, including self-harm, spiritual abuse and the use of imagery as intervention following stroke. Kathryn is also a counsellor with Mencap and a women's refuge.

Sarah Riley is a senior lecturer in the Psychology Department at Aberystwyth University who uses and teaches a range of qualitative methods. Recent projects include looking at clubbing and dance cultures as forms of social and political participation (Economic and Social Research Council) and using cooperative inquiry to explore 'dilemmas of femininity' (British Academy). Her books include an edited collection: *Critical Bodies: Representations, Identities and Practices of Weight and Body Management* (PalgraveMacMillan, 2008) and *Sex, Identity and Consumer Culture* (with Adrienne Evans, Open University Press, forthcoming).

Cath Sullivan is Senior Lecturer in Psychology in the University of Central Lancashire's School of Psychology and her research interests mainly relate to the social psychology of gender, discourse and social constructionism. Cath was an active member of the Higher Education Academy Psychology Network working group on Teaching Qualitative Research Methods at Undergraduate Level from 2005 until 2011. In 2012 she took over as Chair of the newly formed Higher Education Academy 'Teaching Qualitative Psychology' Special Interest Group. In addition to this work supporting and training psychology lecturers who teach qualitative methods, Cath has over 10 years experience of teaching qualitative methods to undergraduate and postgraduate students. Her published articles and book chapters include empirical qualitative papers and pieces about qualitative methodology.

1

INTRODUCTION AND AIMS OF THE BOOK

Cath Sullivan, Stephen Gibson and Sarah Riley

In this chapter we provide an overview of the book and how it can be used. We also consider three key underlying issues, which come up repeatedly in later chapters. The first two issues are decision making and critical thinking; these underpin many activities that you need to do when undertaking a research project. Our third issue concerns methodology. It can be useful to think of your method as a tool you use in research. For example, you could use an interview as a tool to create a person's life history. However, methods are always used with an underlying philosophy – this underlying philosophy is called the 'methodology'. Considering some of the foundations of methodology will help you to get to grips with your research project (and the rest of the book), which is why we focus on it in this chapter.

Aims of the book

In the chapters that follow, we take you through the process of completing a student qualitative research project. This will be useful for students of psychology, sociology, criminology, education and other related disciplines that use qualitative methods. It will be most useful to those completing an undergraduate final-year project (often called a 'dissertation'), but it will also be helpful for students completing other undergraduate qualitative projects earlier in their degree, and conversely, for postgraduate students, especially those who feel like they need a more solid foundation to their understanding of qualitative research before they continue with their studies.

In a nutshell: aims of the book

- To provide a guide to the decisions you need to make at key stages of your project, including:
  - o choosing a topic and designing research questions;
  - o reviewing literature;
  - o designing and managing the process of your project;
  - o collecting and analysing data;
  - o writing up and evaluating your work.

- To provide useful tips and strategies for your project, including how to deal with challenges and difficulties when they arise.
- To give ideas of ways in which you can build upon and extend your project – for example, as a way of demonstrating your skills when you apply for jobs or courses in the future.

Our main focus is on helping you to plan and execute the stages of your project, so we deal extensively with issues such as research questions, planning, supervisory relationships and writing up. Various methods of collecting and analysing qualitative data are considered and we provide overviews and key information to help you to select appropriate methods. We also provide many suggestions for further reading and information so that you can read up on your chosen methods of data collection and analysis in more depth.

Before we go any further, we would like to spend a little time considering what your research project means in the context of your course.

Your research project

Your research project allows you to apply and develop the research skills learned earlier in your course, and allows your lecturers to assess how well you can apply them to an independent piece of work. It is a complex piece of work that involves many stages. For most students it is the largest single piece of assessed work that they will do and it is a time-consuming, challenging and rewarding journey. Many people regard the final year (or master's) research project as a key indicator of a student's ability and it often has a very large contribution to make to the overall marks on a course. Because of this, and because it is a big step towards independence for many students, it can be a daunting prospect. Part of what is rewarding about doing a research project is its challenging and independent nature.

It's important then that before we start talking about the specifics of doing a qualitative research project, we take a step back and talk you through some of the core principles of good academic work, from which you can build. First, we consider decision making, as this has a central role in your research project at every stage.

Decision making

As you work on your research project, you will need to make a series of decisions. Throughout this book we aim to identify those decisions and to provide you with information and ideas that will aid you in making them.

Decision making involves a series of steps, skills and processes. In order to achieve your aims, you have to make practical decisions about what to do, when to do it, how to do it and where. At times when we find making decisions hard, such as when we are stressed or when the outcome is very important to us, it can be useful to break down the decision-making process into a number of components.

In a nutshell: what is decision making?

Decision making can be defined as the process of identifying a course of action that will allow you to overcome obstacles and move towards a goal in a context of uncertainty or risk (Thomas, 2008).

To make a decision we must figure out what our objective is, collect information about it, identify possible options for moving towards it and evaluate those options so that we can make a choice (Thomas, 2008). We then also need to try and evaluate our course of action to see if it is working or whether our decision needs to be reviewed (Thomas, 2008).

In a nutshell: decision making in your research project

Examples of some of the kinds of decisions you will need to make include:

- deciding on a topic area for your project;
- selecting literature to include in your literature review;
- identifying appropriate methods of data collection and analysis;
- deciding on sub-goals and deadlines as you work towards your final deadline;
- selecting material to include in your research project write-up.

Much of the research on decision making has focused on creating and testing models of how the best decisions are made. There is also research that examines how people make decisions and this can help us by providing tips for those situations when we're finding it hard to work out what to do next.

Decision-making tips

Take ownership

Remember from the outset that your project is an independent piece of work, your chance to show that you can really shine when you work on your own. Your supervisor will help and guide you, but the sooner you begin to own your decisions the better off you will be in the long run. When you decide something, it is you that will have to write a justification for it in your project. So, even if your supervisor can think of 10 good reasons for you to use, for example, grounded theory (see Chapter 7), you will be the one who has to construct a good argument in your write-up for that choice. It's therefore very important that you know why you made it.

Focus on your goals

When we make decisions, it is usually for a reason – that is, we have some long-term purpose in mind. Imagine that you are trying to choose between a number of potential methods of recruiting participants. It is easy to slip into a state where the only goal we can see is that we have to make the decision. Often, there is no problem with this, but when you are finding it hard to make a decision it can be useful to think about what your ultimate goal is. This will help you to really think through what criteria you should use to evaluate the options you have. Your ultimate goal, the reason you are making this decision, is that you are trying to identify a method that will allow you to get the kind of data you need, from the people who are likely to have it, and in a way that is practicable and achievable for you. As you can see, thinking about the ultimate aim here instantly gives us a set of criteria that you can use to judge the different options.

Find a reason

Research (for example, Shafir et al., 1993) has shown that when people are choosing between two options, they tend to try and look for reasons to accept one possible course of action and reject the others. This means that decisions can be especially hard when a clear reason to do something, or not do it, doesn't really stand out. This can lead to us feeling paralysed and not actually making a choice (Ayton, 2005). Imagine, for example, that you are struggling to see which of two methods of analysis you should use, and obvious reasons for rejecting or selecting options do not immediately appear. In this instance, one thing that you could do to help yourself is to find out as much as you can about these methods and any underlying methodologies associated with them. Try and ask yourself critical questions that can help you find a reason for a decision. Information is key here, so try to:

- Read as many relevant sources of information about these methods as you can.
- Talk to your supervisor about the suitability of different methods.
- If you are working in a group – either informally or formally – speak to your fellow students, as 'peer researchers' can be good sources of information, as they have to negotiate similar issues to your own.
- Consider the practical consequences and feasibility of each option, such as how much time it would take and whether you have the training and resources you need.
- Write lists to get yourself thinking in concrete ways about the advantages, disadvantages and key features of the various options.

Remember that, in a situation where there don't seem to be any particularly salient or obvious reasons, you can help yourself by gaining more information.

Don't sweat the small stuff

Designing and conducting your project involves many decisions and, inevitably, some of these are more important than others. One way to help you put your energies where they will bring the most reward is to try and distinguish those decisions that are the most important. This can be challenging, especially at the beginning, and this book, along with the other things you read, and discussions with your supervisor, should help you to do this. Some tips that can help with this are:

- Consider the consequences. Some decisions are very important because they have big consequences for other stages of the project. For example, the method of data collection that you choose will have big implications for the kind of analysis that you can do, and how well you can do that analysis (see Chapter 6 for more on this). Try and identify the big decisions that have many consequences.
- Think about the justification. The most important decisions that you make will tend to be those that need to be fully justified in your write-up. Your research questions, for example, will need to be fully and convincingly justified in your write-up.

Efficiency or outcomes?

Many decision-making models rest upon the idea that certain choices have greater 'utility' – that is, will bring a more positive or valued outcome. However, one thing that you need to consider is that you may often be in a situation where there are several possible options that are equally as good. Or, at least, where the differences in how positive the outcomes will be are so small as to make little practical difference.

Often students get bogged down at the early stages of their project in particular because they find it hard to make decisions. Understandably, given the importance of the research project, students worry that they will make a wrong choice. This can often happen in relation to the choice of a topic area (see Chapter 2). However, at this stage, you are probably going to be faced with a huge array of potential research areas that are all equally interesting and equally suitable from an academic point of view. It's important to make a relatively informed choice at this stage, but remember that making a choice too late and getting behind is probably more of a risk than making the wrong choice when your choices are between three equally suitable and equally interesting topic areas. You may find that it is useful to set yourself firm deadlines for key decisions in order to keep yourself from getting behind (see Chapters 3 and 4 for more on this).

In a nutshell: help yourself to make decisions

- Be aware of when decisions are needed and of when you have made one.
- Gather information and talk your decisions through with your supervisor, other lecturers or fellow students.
- Consider at every stage whether you will be able to justify your decisions and how you will do it – this is crucial for doing a good write-up.
- Record your decisions in a research diary; it can be easy to forget what you did, and why, at an earlier stage.
- Be aware that sometimes your choice is between several equally good options, and at times you will need to just force yourself to choose rather than risk falling behind.
- Ensure that you represent your decisions effectively in the appropriate section of the write-up (see Chapter 9 for more on writing up).

Decision making involves judgement (about the expected outcomes of options, for example, or their likelihood) and the appraisal and processing of information. It is therefore related to another foundational skill that underpins the research project; that of critical thinking, and we will consider this in the next section.

Critical thinking

Critical thinking is a term used a lot in relation to good work done by students. In this book for example, many of the contributors talk about critical thinking, and the institutions that you and they are part of will have critical thinking as part of their marking criteria. Indeed being able to think critically is a core component of undergraduate and postgraduate education. But despite so many people saying that critical thinking is important, actual definitions of what it is and how to do it are rather thin on the ground.

In a nutshell: critical thinking

Critical thinking involves developing the ability to:

1 Evaluate other people's academic work according to appropriate criteria, and being able to make links between other people's work, other relevant literatures, and your own work.
2 Present your own work in a way that convinces your reader (including the markers) that you are knowledgeable about the topic of your project and the research methods you've used.
3 Demonstrate to your reader that your knowledge has been applied so that your research project meets the quality criteria for an excellent project.

The emphasis on the importance of critical thinking, without guidance as to what it involves, can make the idea of critical thinking a daunting one. However, critical thinking is a skill you can learn and it's one that you may be more familiar with than you think. Music reviews, for example, can demonstrate a range of critical thinking techniques. A music review will often describe the music by highlighting important features of it, and discussing how these features distinguish it from previous work by the band or other similar bands. Reviews often locate the music being reviewed within a particular genre, and then give an evaluation of the music in relation to this genre. Such analyses allow reviewers to make evaluative judgements about the pleasures (or not) of listening to the music and how the music develops or represents a genre.

The processes involved in writing a music review are similar to those you need to go through when critically reading an article or developing your own project so that it will stand up to scrutiny. These processes involve locating the research project within relevant research methods literature or previous research on the subject; and evaluating the study both in terms of the contribution it makes to this literature and the persuasiveness of the argument (in music review terms, the equivalent of whether it develops the genre and how it sounds). To do this kind of academic critical thinking in relation to qualitative research projects you need to have an understanding of:

- quality criteria in relation to qualitative methods in general;
- quality criteria in relation to the specific methods you're using (or that the article you're reading is using);
- argumentation, rhetoric and persuasion.

We discuss qualitative research methods in general in Chapters 6 and 7 and refer you to books on specific qualitative methods for the detailed discussion you need for method-specific criteria (for example, Forrester, 2010). Here, then, we focus on argumentation, rhetoric and persuasion, while discussing the other quality criteria when relevant.

Argumentation, rhetoric and persuasion

Sarah once went to a museum of fashion with a builder friend. Knowing his interests didn't lie in clothes, she was surprised when he seemed happy to spend time there. All was revealed though, when they left and the first thing he said was 'did you see how they'd built that glass staircase?' While Sarah had been looking at the museum's content, he'd been looking at the museum's structure. But, together they'd evaluated the whole thing. In the same way, critical thinking requires you to evaluate the content of a research report and the way its arguments are constructed.

We need to consider how arguments are constructed because poor thinking can be dressed up in ways that make it seem plausible. Psychological research has shown that people can be persuaded to believe all kinds of things that are not particularly rational. So good quality thinking involves developing the skills we need to rationally judge the quality of research by evaluating the logic of the arguments it uses.

Applying critical thinking means that we can be persuaded by good quality arguments and have the skills to reject claims of poor quality ones. To develop this aspect of critical thinking, try asking the following questions about a report you're reading, or if you have already started yours, about your own project.

- Are the arguments given supported by evidence? And has this evidence been accumulated through appropriate methods such as exhaustive literature searches or systematic data collection and analyses?
- Is it a balanced analysis of the evidence? Do the authors examine alternative viewpoints fairly, but when relevant also show when there is strong support for a consensus?
- Given that all research comes from a specific standpoint, does the report recognise its standpoint and how that affected the study, or is the standpoint implicit and not addressed? (See the discussion of 'reflexivity' in Chapter 8 for more on this.)
- Is the ordering of the points logical so that gradually a complete and consistent account is built up?

- Was the study justified and explained in 'watertight' rhetoric (that is, persuasive arguments)? For example, if you follow their arguments to their logical conclusion do they still stand? What are the implications for their arguments? Are there absences that would allow you to question the logic (such as not reporting studies that take a different approach)? Do they play a 'numbers game', where the authors report a bigger number of participants or hours of analysis from a larger data set than the data set that they actually analysed, so making their present study look bigger than it is? Do they use precise terms that can be easily defined and studied or do they use vague concepts that can't easily be evaluated? Do they make false analogies or unwarranted leaps in the logic, such as arguing that one thing leads to another when it may not?
- Is the document consistent? Does the report draw on the same theoretical or methodological framework throughout? Does information on participants or other procedures remain the same throughout?
- Do the authors demonstrate that their work meets appropriate quality criteria? For example, do they demonstrate a good understanding of the methods and procedures they've used? Does their work make a contribution to the literature they're addressing and demonstrate rigour or transparency?
- Does the outcome of the work generate new ideas or ways of implementing others' ideas in new and potentially useful directions?
- Is it written clearly? Good writing is clear and concise and takes the reader on a journey that is so well articulated and signposted that the reader focuses on the content of the message and not the delivery. Conversely, poor academic writing often 'hides' behind big words and uses overly complicated sentences or obtuse writing that obscures ideas rather than clarifies them.

With time, asking such questions can become second nature for experienced researchers. However, for a student developing their skills it can be hard to know when or how to ask them. If you thought about each of these questions overtly for every paragraph you read or wrote you'd soon lose focus on the actual study. So take your time to become familiar with them and practice using them gradually. To help you get started, we finish this section with a table that identifies some of the common problems students have with critical thinking, with some suggested solutions.

Critical thinking challenges

When you are learning and developing your critical thinking skills, there can be challenges and difficulties. We have outlined some of these in Table 1.1, along with some suggested solutions for you to try.

Want to know more about critical thinking?

Cottrell, S. (2005) *Critical Thinking Skills.* London: Palgrave MacMillan.

Table 1.1 Common critical thinking challenges and some suggested solutions

Challenges	And possible solutions
Feeling overwhelmed by what you have to do	• Read though the questions previously listed regularly so that you are familiar with them and they can be in the 'back of your mind' when you are reading or writing. • Remember it is a skill that takes time to develop so you will not be able to do everything at once. • At the end of a paper or a significant section that you have written, go through the questions given previously and see if you can answer them easily. If you cannot, ask yourself if it is because you have not read closely or consciously enough or is it because there's a problem with the article? • When you read an article, make brief notes summarising the key points (for example, research question, topic studied, method used, findings, what you liked or disliked about it, how it might relate to your own work, or to other literature). This writing should develop your thinking, it will give you a summary of the articles you have read so that you can build up a database you can use for your literature review and it will allow you to develop links across the papers more easily.
Finding it difficult to do a balanced critique of a study, perhaps because all the points made seem good, or you can criticise easily but find it hard to see positives.	• At the end of each main section (for example, introduction or method) write one advantage and one disadvantage about the decisions made there. • Think of different options the researchers could have taken for each decision they made. Considering the advantages and disadvantages of your suggestions might help you either identify better ways of doing things or better realise the logic behind the decisions made. • Consider what level of knowledge you could develop that may help you. For example, would it help if you knew more about qualitative research methods in general, the specific method used or the topic being discussed? If you can work out which then you can find the right supplementary reading to help you. • If you cannot change your cognitive assessment, consider your emotional response. How do you feel when you read it? Your 'heart' may tell you something your 'head' has missed. For example, you may read something and feel that it is odd or it makes you feel uncomfortable. Do not ignore these feelings, but work out why. For example, you might develop an ethical critique because when you read the method section you felt 'I wouldn't like that to happen to me'.
Having difficulty making useful notes that do not just repeat what the authors are saying.	• Develop your critical thinking by trying to make links across the papers you read; note the author's position as succinctly as possible; how they tried to make their argument sound plausible; and any assumptions in the work. • Put the paper to one side and have a short break, such as making a cup of tea. When you come back try to write your notes without referring to the paper itself. The break may allow you to mull over the key points without having to rely on the exact words used by the authors.

Challenges	And possible solutions
Finding it difficult to identify what is important	• Read the article through once so you get a sense of the main points, then go back through each section, summarising each subsection and writing one advantage and one disadvantage for the decisions made there. • Compare the abstracts of different articles. Since abstracts summarise the key points of a paper they can help you identify what is important.
Not feeling motivated to do more than read an article.	• Develop your critical thinking by joining or starting a reading group. Reading groups let you learn techniques for critical thinking from each other and can help motivate you to do the work if you have to discuss it with others.
Being unsure how to develop self-awareness to know what your standpoint is or what implicit standpoints other researchers may take.	• Do the findings resonate with what you believe or don't believe, and could this be affecting your evaluation of the study? • Read more on principles of qualitative research methods to get a better sense of what standpoints are out there and which one resonates with you and the implications for taking that position and not another.

So far, we have highlighted the importance of decision making and critical thinking. The third key underlying issue relates to our understanding of methodology, which means dealing with some weighty issues concerning the nature and purpose of research, the nature of knowledge (in contrast to beliefs, for example) and the nature and role of evidence. The next section considers some key aspects of these issues that are relevant to your research project.

Methodology

The chapters in this book cover the full range of issues involved in conducting your qualitative research project, from managing the relationship with your supervisor to writing up your report. At the heart of any research project, however, is *methodology*, and many of the chapters cover various methodological issues about which you will need to make important decisions. Although most of these are presented in stand-alone chapters (for example, Chapter 2 on research questions and Chapter 6 on data collection), you will notice as you read the book that many of the issues involved are interconnected. For example, the decisions you make concerning data collection will be related to the decisions you make regarding your research question, your analytic approach, and so on.

Key definitions: method and methodology

It is useful to think of your method as the means by which you go about collecting data (for example, interviews or focus groups – see Chapter 6). Your methodology, however, can be thought of as the wider approach you adopt in your project which will inform your decision making about your research question, data collection and analysis (for example, discourse analysis or grounded theory – see Chapter 7). Your methodology can be thought of as the philosophy of research, or the underlying assumptions behind knowledge creation, that informs the use of your methods. This means that taking up a particular methodology often determines the kinds of methods you can use.

The decisions that you make in your project will be influenced by your methodology. Also, developing and refining your own methodological standpoint (that is, working out for yourself what your methodology will be) involves important decisions too.

In a nutshell: key methodological decisions

- What is your topic?
- What do you want to find out about your topic? (Research Question)
- What data are you going to collect? (Method)
- How will you analyse your data? (Analysis)
- What assumptions will you make about reality (ontology) and what it is possible to know (epistemology)?

The trick is to make these decisions in advance, while allowing sufficient flexibility to adapt to unforeseen problems or opportunities. In order to try and emphasise the interconnectedness between the key methodological decisions that you need to make, you could think of your project as being like trying to fly a kite on a blustery day. Thinking about these key methodological issues as different points of your kite highlights how they all depend on each other (see Figure 1.1).

In order for the kite to fly, all four points need to be connected firmly to one another. If any of the links are missing or loose then the kite is liable to fall to the ground, or not even get airborne at all! This also highlights how the decisions you make about each aspect of your methodology can't simply be made in a straightforward, linear fashion. Instead, try to plan how each element of the kite fits together at the outset (see Chapter 3 for more on planning your

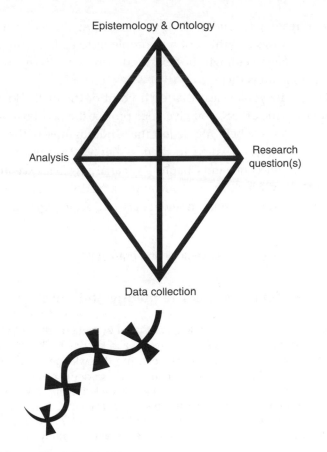

Epistemology & Ontology

Analysis

Research question(s)

Data collection

Figure 1.1 The methodological kite

project). This doesn't mean that things are completely set in stone, but if you think you're ready to begin collecting data simply because you've decided on your research question and how you're going to collect your data, then you will almost certainly be storing up trouble for yourself! When you come to think about how to analyse your data, you may well end up wishing you'd done things rather differently.

Although some authors (for example, Howitt, 2010) suggest that you should start with a problem, and then select an approach which allows you to address that problem, things are not necessarily as straightforward as that. Other researchers (for example, Potter, 1998a) have argued that the way in which we conceive of the problem we want to investigate will already involve a range of (possibly tacit) assumptions about the nature of the world, what it is possible to find out, and how we should go about doing that. One of the key points of this book is therefore to encourage you to think about these assumptions at the outset. Rather than thinking of a problem and choosing a methodology to address it, your reading around qualitative research might lead you to conceive of problems in new ways, to think of new problems to address, and to recognise that 'problems' themselves might not exist independently in the world, waiting for researchers to address them.

So, by making sure you're clear that each point of the methodological kite is connected up with the others, you give your project the best possible chance of success. This book aims to help you do just that. Indeed, three of the points of the kite have whole chapters devoted to them (Chapter 2 on research questions; Chapter 6 on data collection; and Chapter 7 on analysis). The exception is epistemology and ontology, which you will encounter at various points throughout the book. It is therefore worth taking a moment or two to get to grips with these terms.

Epistemology and ontology

Key definitions: epistemology and ontology

Epistemology: A theory of knowledge that specifies certain criteria by which we can answer questions such as 'What counts as valid knowledge?' and 'How do we know what we know?' From the Greek episteme (knowledge) and logos (word, account; and as the suffix –ology, branch of knowledge). At its simplest then, epistemology deals with questions concerning knowledge about knowledge.

Ontology: A theory of existence that specifies certain criteria by which we can answer questions such as 'What is real?' and 'What exists?' From the Greek on (being) and logos, ontology is therefore quite literally the study of being.

There is every chance that you may not really have come across detailed discussion of epistemology and ontology in other parts of your course. However, all research, whether qualitative or quantitative, involves making epistemological and ontological assumptions. The dominant position within many disciplines (including psychology) is one based upon a modified version of a philosophy known as *positivism*. This suggests that we can uncover the nature of reality through observation, and that which we perceive is that which exists. Ultimately, few researchers of social and behavioural aspects of the world would consider themselves to be straightforward positivists, with its implication of rather naive faith in the reality of what we observe. However, research that uses experimentation (or quasi-experimentation, as in field studies that manipulate variables with questionnaires) can be thought of as occupying position which has been termed *post-positivism*. This position (associated in particular with the philosophy of Karl Popper), acknowledges the limitations of pure positivism, and instead suggests a much more cautious approach based around the principles of *falsification* and *hypothetico-deductivism* (McGhee, 2001).

Key definitions: positivism

Positivism is a philosophy that suggests that all that can be known is that which we observe.

Post-positivism is a philosophy which suggests that in order to ensure that we can give ourselves the best possible chance of trusting the observations we make, we should test our ideas using the principles of hypothetico-deductivism and falsification.

Hypothetico-deductivism is the idea that we should make formal theories about the world, from which we can then derive testable hypotheses.

Falsification is a principle that means that we should never seek to prove our hypotheses, but that we should always seek to falsify them. When hypotheses derived from a particular theory withstand repeated attempts at falsification, we can be more confident that the theory reflects some feature of how the world really is.

Ultimately, what this leads to is an approach (which has been dominant in many disciplines) that accepts that our goal as scientists is to deploy a neutral and unbiased approach to making observations to give ourselves the best possible chance of uncovering reality, even if we are often cautious about what we may observe directly. Such an approach is therefore *realist* in both an epistemological and an ontological sense. In short, this means that we can assume that the world objectively exists, and we can have objective knowledge about it. This position is represented in Figure 1.2.

Figure 1.2 The realist approach – we can have direct access to the world, provided we have the right tools. (Reproduced with the kind permission of Sarah Riley and Richard Brown.)

Realism: a philosophical position which assumes that there is an objective reality out there (ontological realism) and that through the use of the appropriate scientific techniques, we are able to increase our knowledge about it (epistemological realism).

In contrast, many researchers have increasingly been drawn to alternative positions that emphasise the limitations of (post-)positivism and suggest that the goal of achieving objective knowledge about the world is much more problematic than is often assumed to be the case. Broadly speaking, these alternative positions can be characterised as *phenomenology* and *constructionism* (see Figures 1.3 and 1.4).

Figure 1.3 The phenomenological approach – neither researcher nor participant has direct access to reality, but we can make sense of people's subjective experience of the world, so long as we bear in mind that this will always be mediated through language. (Reproduced with the kind permission of Sarah Riley and Richard Brown.)

Phenomenology: The study of how phenomena (such as events, objects, emotions) appear to us in our conscious experience.

For an example of how phenomenology has been drawn upon by qualitative researchers, see the discussion of Interpretative Phenomenological Analysis in Chapter 7.

Figure 1.4 The constructionist approach – neither researcher nor participant has direct access to reality; rather understandings about what 'reality' is are socially and culturally produced. Researchers look at the meanings people use to make sense of themselves and their social and natural world. The focus is therefore on how reality is constructed through language and in people's interactions with each other. (Reproduced with the kind permission of Sarah Riley and Richard Brown.)

Constructionism: A position which challenges the notion of objectively existing reality – and even of any notion of 'real' experience – and suggests instead that 'reality' depends on one's cultural and interactional context. Often referred to as social constructionism. For an example of how constructionism has been drawn upon by qualitative researchers, see the discussion of Discourse Analysis in Chapter 7.

A further contrast which is relevant here is that between realism and *relativism* – a thoroughly constructionist position involves the adoption of a relativist approach. Relativists assert that we can no longer ground our knowledge or action in terms of what is 'real' or 'true' in the way that this is usually understood. Instead, they suggest that knowledge and reality will always be relative to the historical, cultural and social context.

Key definition: relativism

'A form of more or less systematic doubt about the possibility of objective, socially independent foundations to knowledge' (Hepburn, 2000: 93).

Some authors suggest that relativism means that all perspectives must be treated as equally valid. A common objection to such extreme versions of relativism is therefore that it results in a morally problematic view of the world as it appears to suggest that 'anything goes'. However, this position is not typically adopted by relativists themselves. For example, the exasperation is palpable when Jonathan Potter (1998b: 34) argues, 'No! Please! How many times does it have to be repeated that "anything goes" is a realist slur on relativism.' In contrast, Potter and his colleagues have argued forcefully that relativism compels us to confront the absence of timeless hard-and-fast rules underlying our moral positions. We thus have to make value judgements on social and political issues without the comfort blanket of 'reality' to keep us safe and warm (see Edwards et al., 1995). As you can perhaps see, what may initially seem to be a somewhat esoteric philosophical debate can lead some researchers to get rather agitated!

Some researchers do, however, accept many of the central claims of social constructionism about the inevitably constructed nature of the world and of our knowledge of the world, but without also adopting a relativist position. This has led to the development of a position known as *critical realism*.

Key definition: critical realism

A position that acknowledges the social construction of reality, but suggests that there are nevertheless realities existing independently of human activity (for example, social structure and/or human experience). For more on the relationship between social constructionism and critical realism see Sullivan (2010).

Phenomenological approaches can be understood as critically realist in the sense that they assert the reality of experience, while acknowledging the difficulty of achieving objective knowledge of it (Shaw, 2010), but more typically critical realist work within psychology adopts a position which asserts a particular political position (for example, feminism, anti-racism and/or some variety of Marxism). This has been a source of lively debate (see the 'Want to know more?' box below), and highlights the importance of the politics of research.

Politics and qualitative research

All research decisions are ultimately political in the sense that they have impli-cations for how we might think about and act upon the world. Even the main-stream scientific position of neutral disinterested inquiry is a fundamentally political position insofar as social scientific enquiry has important implica-tions for how people might live their lives. Research is political in the sense that it suggests to us what is possible in the world and, often, what might be the right or wrong course of action. Whatever decisions we make they are likely to involve significant political dimensions; as Billig notes, 'neutrality in the midst of conflict is every bit as much a position – and a controversial one at that – as is partisanship' (1996: 173).

Many of the relevant debates on this issue have been played out in particular in the social psychological literature, and so a basic familiarity with some of the key concerns of what has become known as 'critical social psychology' may be particularly useful to you as you begin the process of thinking through these issues (see the 'Want to know more?' box below).

It is also worth noting that there is nothing intrinsic to qualitative methods that makes them a force for good. Many students and researchers (ourselves included) have been drawn to qualitative methods over the years as they see them as providing tools for challenging the more troubling and oppressive aspects of mainstream practice. However, at times this has arguably tipped over into assuming that qualitative methods are *by definition* politically more prom-ising than quantitative methods – this is not the case (see Parker [2005] for some relevant arguments; and see Martín-Baró [1994], for a quite brilliant – and ultimately tragic – use of quantitative methods in the service of emancipation).

Want to know more about methodology?

Howitt, D. (2010) *Introduction to Qualitative Methods in Psychology*. Harlow: Prentice Hall. (Especially chapters 1 and 2.)
Stainton-Rogers, W. (2011) *Social Psychology* (2nd edn). Maidenhead: Open University Press.
Sullivan, C. (2010) 'Theory and method in qualitative research', in M. A. Forrester (ed.), *Doing Qualitative Research in Psychology: A Practical Guide*. London: Sage. pp. 15–38.
Tuffin, K. (2005) *Understanding Critical Social Psychology*. London: Sage. (Especially chapters 2 and 3.)

And if you want to know even more, then try dipping into some of the debates among discourse analysts in the 1990s (for example, Edwards et al., 1995; Gill, 1995; Hepburn, 2000; Newman and Holzman, 2000; Parker, 1998a, 1998b,

1999a, 1999b, 2000; Potter et al., 1999). Some of these might be heavy going at times if you're new to these issues, but the lively and sometimes even entertaining (no, really) way in which they're conducted makes them a great way to get to grips with the key differences between positions.

Now that we have introduced you to these three central issues, we will conclude this chapter by briefly explaining some of the central features of the book, and briefly introducing its contents.

This book and how to use it

In a nutshell: useful features of the book

Each chapter contains coverage of the key issues of the topic area being covered, together with some or all of the following features.

- Top tips: useful practical advice for maximising quality.
- Success stories and cautionary tales: examples of triumphs and obstacles in student projects supervised by the authors.
- Definitions: brief explanations of key terms. You will find defined terms for which indicated in the index with the page number highlighted in bold representing the page on which you will find the definition.
- 'In a nutshell' boxes: these highlight key points and summaries of concepts, approaches and chapters themselves.
- Decision flow charts: these are used to represent the key processes you need to go through in order to enable you to make the decisions that are right for your project.
- Where can I find out more? boxes: these provide suggestions for further reading.

We recognise that not all readers will want the same thing from this book. Some may want to read it from cover to cover before they begin their project; others may be coming to it at a later stage in their project for guidance on a specific issue; others still may want to supplement their reading around qualitative methods by dipping into particular chapters or sections. We therefore don't want to suggest that there is only one 'right' way to use the book. There is an important conceptual reason for this too – the nature of qualitative research is that it tends to be cyclical. This means that rather than beginning with a research question, and then working through the design of the study, data collection, analysis and writing up in a linear fashion, you may find yourself returning to earlier stages to revise your ideas. For example, you might find yourself revising your research question following the initial stages of your analysis, or refining your analysis as you write up your project.

Ultimately, of course, a book is presented in a linear fashion, with different topics presented in a specific order as the contents unfold. However, in putting together this book we have tried to ensure that each chapter constitutes a useful resource in its own right, and have included links to other chapters in which specific issues are covered elsewhere in the book. Similarly, we have included plenty of suggestions for further reading. For example, the book is not intended as a complete introduction to particular forms of data collection and analysis, and we have therefore constructed our chapters on these topics in order to provide a guide to the literature. You might therefore think of the book as a map of the terrain, rather than a vehicle to carry you across it. The hard work, ultimately, will be yours, but however you decide to traverse the landscape of your qualitative research project, we hope that you will find this book to be a useful source of ideas, inspiration and practical advice.

The book begins with Kathryn Kinmond's chapter on research questions (Chapter 2). Kathryn distinguishes between knowing what your research topic is and having a research question (something you want to find out about your topic) and introduces you to the importance of devising a good research question, or set of interrelated questions, for your qualitative project to address. The flexible and cyclical nature of qualitative research means that you will need to treat the development of research questions as something you review and refine throughout the project. The importance of consistency between your type of research question and the methods you use is highlighted and tips are given to help you through the process.

In Chapter 3, Cath Sullivan and Sarah Riley take you through the process of planning your project, with a particular focus on ensuring that your plans are informed by appropriate ethical principles at every step of the way. In particular, this chapter emphasises the importance of planning to ensure that your data collection and analysis runs as smoothly as possible, and shows you how to put together a project plan that you will be able to refer to throughout your project.

We then turn to the management of your project, and outline strategies for conducting the various stages as smoothly as possible. In Chapter 4 Sarah Riley and Nigel King consider three major areas of management in detail, which are: time management and planning; the student–supervisor relationship; and the dynamics between you and your research participants.

In Chapter 5, Michael Forrester explains how to do your literature review. As well as providing practical tips on issues such as how to search for literature and review abstracts to tell if a study may be relevant to your research question, this chapter also includes guidance on weaving your review into a coherent narrative when it comes to writing up your project so that your review doesn't merely describe previous work in your area, but provides an argument for why your particular research question is worth addressing.

Next we consider the processes and decisions involved in selecting an appropriate method of collecting your data. In Chapter 6 Siobhan Hugh-Jones and Stephen Gibson consider a number of key methods of data collection – including various forms of interviewing, diary methods and naturalistic data (such as naturally occurring conversations and Internet data). They highlight the importance of considering the assumptions and capabilities of different methods in order to help you select a method that is consistent with your research question(s) and method of analysis.

The aim of Chapter 7 is to help you to select an appropriate and practical method of analysing your data. First, Stephen Gibson and Siobhan Hugh-Jones review the assumptions and technical elements of a number of commonly used analysis methods: thematic analysis; discourse analysis; interpretative phenomenological analysis; grounded theory; narrative analysis; and conversation analysis. You will find useful hints to help you select a method that fits with other aspects of your project (such as your method of data collection and your theoretical approach). The chapter also considers key issues in transcription, describes some common challenges for qualitative analysis and offers suggestions for how to meet these.

In Chapter 8, Nollaig Frost and Kathy Kinmond explore the ways in which quality research can be evaluated. Essentially, this involves learning how to tell good qualitative from not-so-good qualitative research, and making sure that your project doesn't fall under the latter heading! The chapter introduces a range of quality criteria that can be used to evaluate various approaches to qualitative research, and focuses in particular on the important issue of reflexivity.

In Chapter 9, Sarah Riley explains how to go about writing up your project report. Beginning with a consideration of the aims of report writing, this chapter introduces the structure of qualitative research reports, and provides detailed guidance on writing each section and subsection. Particular emphasis is placed on the 'analysis' section, which typically includes substantial quotations from your data together with your analytic commentary and is thus usually the longest part of any qualitative report. The chapter concludes by providing some tips on how to write clearly and concisely.

In Chapter 10, Cath Sullivan explores a range of ways in which you might extend your research project. These include the possibility of publishing your work and/or using it as the basis for developing a proposal for further study. In addition, this chapter also highlights the transferable skills you will have developed during the course of your project in order to demonstrate how you can draw on the experience of undertaking your research project when it comes to applying for jobs.

References

Ayton, P. (2005) Judgement and decision making. In N. Braisby and A. Gellatly (eds) *Cognitive Psychology*. Oxford: Oxford University Press. pp. 382–413.

Billig, M. (1996) *Arguing and Thinking: A Rhetorical Approach to Social Psychology*. Cambridge: Cambridge University Press.

Edwards, D., Ashmore, M. and Potter, J. (1995) Death and furniture: the rhetoric, politics and theology of bottom line arguments against relativism. *History of the Human Sciences*, 8, 25–49.

Forrester, M. A. (2010) *Doing Qualitative Research in Psychology: A Practical Guide*. London: Sage.

Gill, R. (1995) Relativism, reflexivity and politics: Interrogating discourse analysis from a feminist perspective. In S. Wilkinson and C. Kitzinger (eds) *Feminism and Discourse: Psychological Perspectives*. London: Sage. pp. 165–86.

Hepburn, A. (2000) On the alleged incompatibility between relativism and feminist psychology. *Feminism & Psychology*, 10, 91–106.

Howitt, D. (2010) *Introduction to Qualitative Methods in Psychology*. Harlow: Prentice Hall.

Martín-Baró, I. (1994) *Writings for a Liberation Psychology*. Cambridge, MA: Harvard University Press.

McGhee, P. (2001) *Thinking Psychologically*. London: Palgrave.

Newman, F. and Holzman, L. (2000) Against against-ism: comment on Parker. *Theory & Psychology*, 10, 265–70.

Parker, I. (1998a) Against postmodernism: psychology in cultural context. *Theory & Psychology*, 8, 601–27.

Parker, I. (1998b) *Social Constructionism, Discourse and Realism*. London: Sage.

Parker, I. (1999a) Against relativism in psychology, on balance. *History of the Human Sciences*, 12, 61–78.

Parker, I. (1999b) The quintessentially academic position. *History of the Human Sciences*, 12, 89–91.

Parker, I. (2000) Critical distance: reply to Newman and Holzman. *Theory & Psychology*, 10, 271–6.

Parker, I. (2005) *Qualitative Psychology: Introducing Radical Research*. Buckingham: Open University Press.

Potter, J. (1998a) Discursive social psychology: from attitudes to evaluative practices. *European Review of Social Psychology*, 9, 233–66.

Potter, J. (1998b) Fragments in the realization of relativism. In I. Parker (ed.) *Social Constructionism, Discourse and Realism*. London: Sage. pp. 27–46.

Potter, J., Edwards, D. and Ashmore, M. (1999) Regulating criticism: some comments on an argumentative complex. *History of the Human Sciences*, 12, 79–88.

Shafir, E., Simonson, I. and Tversky, A. (1993) Reason-based choice. *Cognition*, 49, 11–36.

Shaw, R. (2010) Interpretative phenomenological analysis. In M. A. Forrester (ed.) *Doing Qualitative Research in Psychology: A Practical Guide*. London: Sage. pp. 177–201.

Sullivan, C. (2010) Theory and method in qualitative research. In M. A. Forrester (ed.) *Doing Qualitative Research in Psychology: A Practical Guide*. London: Sage. pp. 15–38.

Thomas, N. (2008) *The Best of Adair on Leadership and Management*. London: Thorogood.

2

COMING UP WITH A RESEARCH QUESTION

Kathryn Kinmond

Qualitative research is exciting because it asks questions about people's everyday lives and experiences. As a qualitative researcher you will have the privilege of exploring the 'significant truths' in people's lives (Bakan, 1996: 5). That is an amazing prospect, but if you are delving into people's lives and asking questions about real experiences, you need to get those questions right. This chapter will help you do just that.

In a nutshell: research questions

This chapter will look at:

- Why it is important to come up with a sound research question, or set of inter-related questions.
- How to decide upon a research area.
- How to identify a research topic or issue.
- How to formulate your research question.

Clear questions are important

A clear and appropriate research question, or set of interrelated questions, forms the foundation of good research. But excellent research questions are not easy to write. This is why we have devoted an entire chapter to exploring how to come up with a good research question.

A good research question forms the basis of good research because it allows you to identify what you want to know. As Payne and Payne note, 'in research we work from "knowing less" towards "knowing more" (2004: 114). So, identifying what you want to know more about is vital. However, at the beginning of a project students can be vague about what they want to know, and vague questions can lead to an unfocused project. Your aim therefore is to write a clearly articulated question, or set of interrelated questions, which allow you to go about finding answers in a focused and coherent way.

One of the reasons why writing a good research question is difficult is because there are potentially an infinite number of research questions that might be asked. Deciding upon 'the one for you' can be time-consuming and potentially stressful. Without a research question it is impossible to know how or what to research. Most students realise that if they do not know what they are asking they have little hope of finding any answers, but this may only add further stress to an already tense situation.

Common problems that you may also encounter when coming up with a research question include:

- Deciding which area to look at from a range of issues that have interested you in your degree.
- Not being able to think of any area or topic you find sufficiently interesting to focus a major piece of work on.
- Knowing which area you want to focus on (for example, health) but not a specific topic.
- Knowing what area and topic but finding it difficult to clearly articulate a question.

For many students, then, coming up with a research question is challenging, but this chapter will guide you through the processes involved and make this experience easier. To do so, I'll look at some of the pitfalls and problems in choosing a research question and offer suggestions for producing a good one.

Deciding on a research area

The first step in deciding on your research question is to identify the area (such as health, childhood or crime) in which you want to research. You can decide which area to focus on by considering areas that you enjoyed in your course, and what the staff members in your department are prepared to supervise.

Choosing to look at an area you already have some familiarity with is useful because it gives you some knowledge of the sorts of issues that are covered, and ideas for relevant research to read to develop your ideas. This will then help you to identify the topic you wish to explore in your project.

Deciding on an area to study involves a match between identifying an area you find sufficiently interesting to study and an area that a member of staff in your institution is prepared to supervise. Choosing an area that's already taught means that you're likely to find a supervisor with an interest in this area. Another way to match your interests to a supervisor is to use your departmental webpages to explore staff research interests in your department. It is often to your advantage if your project fits in with the interests of your supervisor, and in some departments you may be expected to undertake a project closely allied to the interests of a member of academic staff. Just make sure that you give serious consideration to the area you choose to base your research in – and make sure that a qualitative project is relevant and possible.

Top tips: choosing a research area

Ask yourself the following questions:

- Which area of psychology am I most interested in?
- Why?
- What is it that interests me about that area?
- Is qualitative research relevant to that area?

Identifying a research topic

Having identified a research area, your next step is to identify a topic within that area that you are interested in or care about. Do not make your choice frivolously. You are likely to be working on your research for several months, it will require intensive periods of focus, and it will probably be the piece of work that you feel you have the most ownership of. Your topic needs be able to hold your interest for some time.

For some students choosing a topic is easy – they have a burning ambition to research a specific issue and they know how they're going to do it. For these students – possibly the enviable few – suggestions for help with choosing a research topic may be unnecessary. Nevertheless, even for this group consideration of the appropriateness of the research topic is relevant. If you don't know unequivocally what you want to research, then the following suggestions may help.

Perhaps most straightforwardly, your chosen research topic might spring from something you have studied on your course, or that you have read about. There may be a particular topic that grabbed your attention when you encountered it on your course and which you did not have the opportunity to investigate fully at the time. If this resonates with your experience then in all likelihood your research idea will be grounded in relevant academic literature from the start, which is important in most qualitative research. The only exception to this is research using grounded theory methodology, which advocates reviewing the literature later in the research cycle rather than at the outset. Even here, however, Strauss and Corbin (1990) recognise that if you have experience as a researcher you are likely to be influenced by previous knowledge and research throughout the research process (for further help and guidance on different methodological approaches in qualitative research see Chapter 7).

In contrast to the situations described above, if you have not yet studied any topics that really inspire you, then think about the topics and issues that distract you when you are supposed to be reading for an assignment, or that engage you in conversations, discussions and debates with colleagues and peers – or perhaps your tutor. Check out any ideas you have with your supervisor as something in one of these areas may be appropriate to research. Or, it may lead to a discussion with your supervisor that plants the seed of an idea you are keen to pursue.

Another potential vehicle for finding a suitable research topic is everyday experience. You may have encountered a specific problem or situation you feel is worthy of further investigation in which case a research project would perhaps be appropriate. If you have undertaken any relevant work experience then this too may be a useful source of ideas, as would any voluntary work you've done. If you've worked for a voluntary organisation you might find it useful to ask staff there if they have any research needs. For example, they might be interested in the experiences clients have of the service/organisation.

A further possibility is that your research topic may come from 'suggestions for future work' listed at the end of a research paper you have found interesting; though in this case it is advisable to undertake some literature searching and/or contact the author of the paper to see what 'future work' they have already undertaken. You will then be aware of any additional work undertaken by the researcher that is linked to the published research.

Top tips: identifying a topic

- It is important to derive research questions from the literature, rather than simply from 'armchair speculation' or anecdotal musing.
- It is therefore important to take account of the research that has already been conducted in the area. In this way you do not run the risk of asking a research question that has been addressed and answered already!
- The only exception to the tips noted here is grounded theory (see Chapter 7) which advocates delaying the literature review until after data collection has started.

However, there are also a few words of caution to consider when choosing your research topic. Some students hone in on a research topic simply because it is of personal relevance to them. Although the topic may retain your interest and you may be committed to undertaking such a study, it is important to recognise that some topics of personal relevance may also be deeply significant and difficult to research.

Activity 1: topic ideas

Make a list of possible topics and issues you might like to investigate. Consider how and why you arrived at this list. Note any personal links with any of the topics and issues and consider how these may affect you and your study.

A final word of warning is that you need to ensure that your chosen topic is one that can actually be researched within the constraints of your project. This may sound obvious, but I am referring here to the need to consider the level at which you are working. For example, undergraduate research is generally not as complex as postgraduate research, and the time frame in which students have to work often limits what they can do. If you have an idea for a project that is too ambitious for the stage you're at, talk to your supervisor and see if you can find an aspect of the idea to focus your research project on.

To explore this further, we can consider the following example of an undergraduate project which has now developed into postgraduate study.

Success story: working at different levels

Julie completed an undergraduate research project exploring a woman's experiences of being told that her two sons had learning disabilities. Julie used interpretive phenomenological analysis, which is suitable for exploring such significant experiences (Smith et al., 2009). In her undergraduate project, Julie explored her participant's experiences of realising there were problems with her sons' developmental progress and then having this confirmed by doctors. This project focused on that specific experience and was therefore a well-defined project that was achievable within the time and resources available.

After graduating, Julie went on to do an MSc and for her project she built on her undergraduate work by conducting a more complex project on three women's experiences of parenting children with learning disabilities. The development in complexity between undergraduate and postgraduate level was not, however, due to the larger sample size! Rather, it was because the postgraduate project was more complex in a number of ways. It was a much more wide-ranging project, which explored the impact of the children's disabilities on the participants' sense of identity. (For further information on interpretive phenomenological analysis see Chapter 7, and for more on how to develop ideas for future research from undergraduate projects see Chapter 10.)

Choosing a research topic requires you to go to the library and read, but do not become 'stuck' in this phase. You will find that you need to return repeatedly to the library and to published work throughout the research process. So, familiarise yourself with the available research but do not get bogged down. If there is no previous research this could be an indicator of an area 'ripe for study' or that the area may be difficult, or not relevant, to study (as illustrated by Sampat's experience, discussed below). For more on literature reviewing see Chapter 5.

Success story: refining and refocusing the research question

Sampat was interested in doing her undergraduate project on how British men in their 70s experienced and coped with the loneliness resulting from their sons leaving home for the first time. Sampat went to the library to search for relevant literature, and was surprised to find there was virtually no published academic research on this topic. Coming from India, Sampat's personal experience indicated that this was a major psychological issue within society. However, in the UK most young men leave their parental home when their parents are younger than 70. Indeed, the changing demographics of family life in the UK mean that many sons do not live with their fathers at all. So, an issue that is pertinent to life in India did not appear to be much researched in the UK. Possibly this is because it is a concern that is relevant for a relatively small proportion of men in their 70s in the UK. It is possible that social change in the UK means that this is increasingly becoming an issue, and it could therefore be a topic that is ripe for study. But, given the time constraints of undergraduate research, Sampat's supervisor helped her to explore the possibilities of developing a research study in a related area such as 'empty-nest' syndrome, loneliness and the ageing process.

In a nutshell: choosing a topic

So far, I have identified the following key points about developing research questions.

- It is important to formulate a sound and appropriate research question.
- There are a number of ways to identify your research area.
- Within this area, you will need to select a research topic.
- When developing your ideas you need to be aware of what is appropriate for the level of study that you are undertaking.

Developing your research question

Can the topic be researched qualitatively?

So, having decided that the topic you have chosen can be researched at the level at which you are working, the next thing to ensure is that it can be researched qualitatively. Discussions of research methods and research methodology often centre on the differences between quantitative and qualitative approaches and there have been many attempts to define qualitative research and to differentiate it from quantitative research (Silverman, 2006). However, there is still no consensus as qualitative research cannot be neatly pigeonholed because it includes a number of different approaches. Yet, in practice, as researchers we must – and do – make a decision as to whether or not the topic (and research question) we wish to investigate can be researched qualitatively. So the question then is – on what basis do we make that decision?

Quantitative research tends to focus upon things such as measuring a number of variables against one another and it often focuses on research topics in overarching and general ways. If you wish to explore the meaning of a topic or issue then qualitative research is more appropriate. Qualitative research enables exploration of dimensions of the social world: features of everyday life, the understandings, experiences and imaginings of research participants, the ways in which social processes, institutions, discourses and relationships work, and the significance of the meanings they create.

In determining whether your project is one where qualitative methods are suitable, it is really your research question that is crucial. Many topics are suited to qualitative and quantitative research but it is the research question that tells us which of these two will be most suitable for any given project. For example, the topic of interventions for stroke patients can be investigated using a quantitative approach (Chatterton et al., 2008) or by exploring the qualitative experience of that intervention (Ewan et al., 2010). It is the research question that makes the difference, not the research topic. Although qualitative and quantitative methods do share features (for example, methods in both traditions involve systematic and detailed analysis of data with the aim of addressing a specific aim or research question) they tend to be suited to different things.

In a nutshell: what are qualitative methods good at?

- Qualitative data tends to be in the form of texts or images, which are analysed in their 'raw' form without coding them numerically.

(Continued)

(Continued)

- Qualitative projects tend to be focused on how participants make sense of things, and what their perspectives are.
- Qualitative methods are often most useful for examining a range of perspectives within data and are good at picking out inconsistencies (rather than smoothing them out by using mean scores).

The most important point here is that different methods tend to bring different assumptions with them, and tend to do different things, which means that they will vary in how suitable they are for addressing any specific research question. These differences are just as apparent between different qualitative approaches as they are between qualitative and quantitative approaches (see Chapter 1 for more on this). So, as your research progresses it will be important to keep checking whether your question fits with the methods you have chosen. In later chapters (particularly Chapters 6 and 7) we will give you more information and guidance on this; the key thing is to keep returning to the issue of whether your research question is a good one for qualitative research and to remind yourself to keep reviewing this as you progress, modifying your question as necessary.

Want to know more about philosophy and research?

For useful explanations of the philosophical assumptions relevant to different research approaches see:

Sullivan, C. (2010) Theory and method in qualitative research. In M. A. Forrester (ed.) *Doing Qualitative Research in Psychology: A Practical Guide*. London: Sage. pp. 15–38.

Activity 2: can the topic be researched qualitatively?

Ask yourself, which of these topics and issues can be researched qualitatively?

1 The link between playing violent computer games and violent behaviour in children aged 10–15.
2 The link between living near to someone and being friends with them.
3 The experience of living with an autistic child.
4 The success of a healthy eating programme in schools.

Answers are at the end of the chapter.

The research question

Once you have identified your research topic you can begin to frame your research question. First, list all of the questions that you'd like answered yourself. The list may be very large or very small. It may have a number of inter-related questions or it may have a number of very different questions. In every case, the questions should be linked to the research approach you have decided to use. That means that the format and phrasing of the research question is related to the specific qualitative approach you intend to take. Qualitative research questions often begin with the words 'what' or 'how', and the question should inform your reader what the study will do. Different approaches to qualitative research also tend to lead to different types of questions. You may well already be familiar with some common approaches to qualitative research (for example, grounded theory, discourse analysis, interpretative phenomenological analysis), and we will outline the basics of several of the most widely used approaches in Chapter 7. For now, however, it is simply worth highlighting that in order to ask a meaningful research question, you need to have an idea of the sort of assumptions you're making about your research, and the analytic approach you're adopting.

For example, phenomenological studies have questions seeking to explore meaning, to elicit the essence of experience. So, a researcher interested in the topic of sibling relationships might frame their research question as follows: 'What is the experience of sibling relationships?' In contrast, discourse analysis focuses on the ways in which language is used to construct 'reality'. A study on the same topic of sibling relationships might therefore ask the question: 'How are sibling relationships constructed in discourse?'

Similarly, since a key feature of an excellent project is coherence between your research question, method and analytic framework, your analytic approach will determine what kinds of methods are appropriate for you to use when collecting and analysing data. For example, the research question, 'How are sibling relationships constructed in discourse?', suggests that you will be using a version of discourse analysis. Which version you use will in turn determine the kinds of data you collect, such as 'naturally occurring' talk between siblings during meal times at home or 'researcher generated' talk from interviews you've conducted with siblings about their relationships.

Given the close relationship between the approach you are adopting and the question(s) you ask, you therefore need to take time to familiarise yourself with the sorts of approaches available to you before settling on a question. If you set your research question before you know which approach or method you're going to use, you may be storing up trouble for yourself further down the line!

> ## Top tip: assumptions and research questions
>
> Make sure that your research question is consistent with the approach you are adopting. It's easy to fall into the trap of deciding what question you want to investigate before you've properly considered how you are going to analyse your data and what assumptions you're going to make about your data.

So, having listed all possible research questions, now revise them so that they reflect the most appropriate approach and method that would be used to address them. Now, consider them carefully so that you can choose the best one. Initially a qualitative research question can be broad, rather than narrowly focused. You can then work to refine and focus it. That is because qualitative research is usually cyclical rather than linear (Reason and Rowan 1981).

To say that qualitative research is cyclical means that it aims to address research questions through a gradual immersion into the topic. The idea is that your ideas about what to focus on develop as you come to know more and more about your topic, either through reading, thinking about what you've read, or early stages of data analysis. So, for qualitative researchers writing a research question is an iterative activity, as there may be various points in the research project in which the researcher re-evaluates their question, considering ways in which it may be more focused or even re-focused. Note, though, when it comes to writing up, the usual format is to write the report focusing on the final research question and not any early or interim questions. Figure 2.1 below illustrates how your research question might develop during the project.

For further information on the changing nature of qualitative research questions, and some examples, see Chapters 3 and 4. Although your research question at the beginning of a project can be broad, it still needs to have some focus. Your research question should not be so broad that it fails to give any direction or guidance to the researcher. So, for example, 'Why do people self-harm?' is relatively broad, and for most research projects this is the kind of question that is likely to be a general aim (that is, the study might aim to make some contribution to answering this kind of question, rather than to answer it in full). The kinds of questions that are posed as research questions need to be much more focused and narrow. For example, something like 'What are the reasons for self-harming behaviour given by adolescents?' is more focused, is easier to research and can be addressed more fully and in more depth by a particular research project. What is also important about this example, though, is that it is not so narrowly focused that it is uni-directional and leading. Some flexibility in your question, but without completely lacking focus, is important for an excellent qualitative study. This flexibility also allows for your research question to develop as your study unfolds. For example, in the early stages of analysis you may notice things that you hadn't previously thought about, and these may lead to new questions arising.

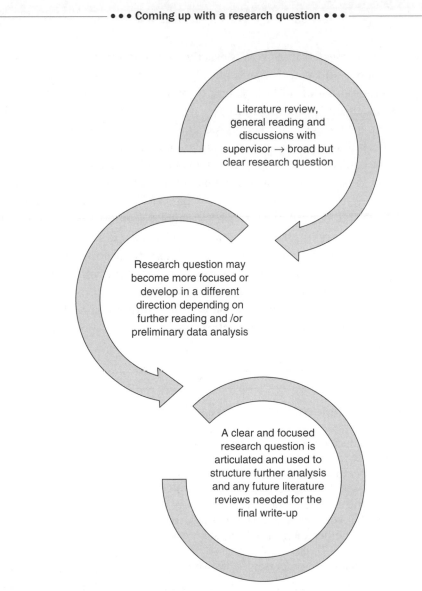

Figure 2.1 Developing and re-developing the research question

---

Activity 3: broad or narrow?

Consider the following questions. Are they too broad, too narrow, or about right?

1 How far do male nurses embody the male hegemonic identity?
2 What is the experience of living with diabetes?
3 Do children sent to day-care have problems?
4 How do football fans using online message boards account for their team's poor performance?

Answers are at the end of the chapter.

Make sure your research topic covers exactly what you want to research – no more and no less – and your research question asks exactly what you want to investigate – no more and no less. 'Eating disorders' is too large a topic if you want to discuss anorexia alone. 'Is anorexia represented as a female adolescent concern in teen magazines in the UK?' is too small a research question if you also want to discuss bulimia, or anorexia in males, or anorexia in middle age. Bite off as much as you can chew thoroughly and then chew it! And of course, if you are in doubt about the chewability of your research question, ask your supervisor.

Finally a strong research question should pass the 'so what?' test. That is, what is the potential benefit of answering the research question? Does it matter? Will it actually say anything? If you cannot make a definitive statement about the purpose of your research, it is unlikely to become an excellent qualitative project. Remember that you are the person who will have to present a clear and strong rationale for why you asked that question and why you tried to answer it in the ways that you did – so if you're not sure that you will be able to answer the 'so what?' question, you need to do some work here before moving on.

In a nutshell: make your research question excellent

- Take time to decide upon your research area.
- Consider your research topic carefully.
- Make sure the topic can be researched qualitatively.
- Ask yourself whether the question is suited to the approach you are taking.
- Check that the question is grounded in relevant research.
- Make sure that your research question is focused.
- Ask yourself whether the research question asks precisely what you want to ask.
- Check that your question passes the 'so what?' test.

Summary

Figure 2.2 summarises the process of developing your research question. Choosing a research question can be a very challenging exercise. However, it is vital that you take time to do it thoroughly. The ultimate success of your project depends upon asking an appropriate and clear question. The question must be suitable for qualitative research, and for the specific approach you are using. It must be grounded in research. It must also be articulate and clear and ask precisely what you want to find out. Knowing this will help you plan your project, the topic of the next chapter.

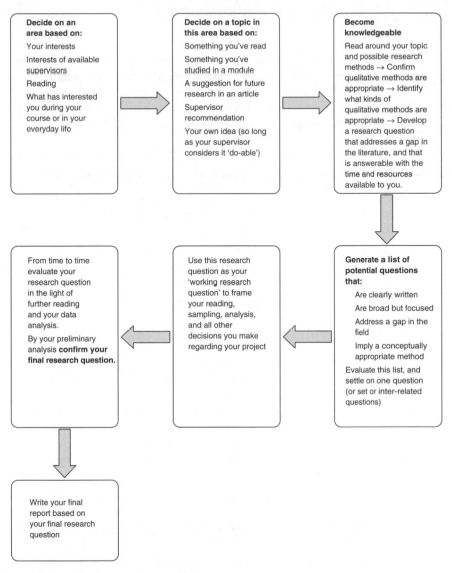

Figure 2.2 Research questions flow-chart

Answers to Activity 2

1 As currently phrased, this would be more suitable to a quantitative project measuring the correlation between hours of playing violent games and subsequent violent behaviour. A qualitative project might explore the experience of playing violent computer games, or the way in which the link between violent computer games and violent behaviour is socially constructed by the media.

(Continued)

(Continued)

2 As with question 1, this could be suitable for either a qualitative or quantitative investigation. The notion of a 'link' between two phenomena implies that one is looking at relationships, which may lend itself more easily to a quantitative study. However, a qualitative project asking questions about the quality of relationships occurring between people living in close proximity to each other would be interesting.

3 This would make for a potentially interesting study using a phenomenological approach (see Chapter 7).

4 This topic would probably be well-suited to a quantitative study which could aim to measure success. However, a qualitative project might explore what healthy eating means to children (which might yield important findings about reasons for – and barriers to – the success of the programme), or how healthy eating programmes perpetuate discourses of expertise and control.

Answers to Activity 3

1 This question offers some room for development. Definition of terms will give it appropriate focus.

2 This question is very broad. It is unclear whether the study will look at people with insulin dependent diabetes or non-insulin dependent diabetes and what exactly it is aiming to investigate. The question needs focus.

3 The question does not make clear what type of 'day-care' is assumed or what 'problems' includes. This question needs focus.

4 This question is specific enough to make for a manageable project. The focus on 'accounts' points to the appropriateness of a qualitative (most likely a discourse analytic) approach.

References

Bakan, D. (1996) 'Some reflections about narrative research and hurt and harm', in R. Josselson (ed.) *Ethics and Process in the Narrative Study of Lives*. Thousand Oaks, CA: Sage. pp. 3–8.

Chatterton, H., Ewan, L., Kinmond, K., Haire, A., Smith, N. and Holmes, P. (2008) 'Observation of meaningful activities: a case study of a personalized intervention on post-stroke functional state', *Journal of Neurologic Physical Therapy*, 32, 52–9.

Ewan, L. M., Kinmond, K. and Holmes, P. S. (2010) 'An observation-based intervention for stroke rehabilitation: experiences of eight individuals affected by stroke', *Disability & Rehabilitation*, 32, 2097–106.

Payne, G. and Payne, J. (2004) *Key Concepts in Social Research*. London: Sage.

Reason, P. and Rowan, J. (1981) *Human Inquiry*. Chichester: John Wiley.

Silverman, D. (2006) *Interpreting Qualitative Data* (3rd edn). London: Sage.

Smith, J. A., Flowers, P. and Larkin, M. (2009) *Interpretive Phenomenological Analysis: Theory, Method and Research*. London. Sage.

Strauss, A. and Corbin, J. (1990) *Basics of Qualitative Research: Grounded Theory Procedures and Techniques*. Newbury Park, CA: Sage.

3

PLANNING AND ETHICS

Cath Sullivan and Sarah Riley

—————————————— Aims and scope ——————————————

This chapter focuses on planning and ethics. Our aim is to help you identify the key stages of doing a successful project, starting from the point of having at least an initial idea of your research question (see Chapter 2). We leave you at the point of having completed a comprehensive plan and submitted an ethics application.

Your dissertation is likely to be the biggest independent piece of work that you will do for your degree. One of the challenges in doing a large piece of work is to identify the many small steps that taken together culminate in a successful project. Identifying these steps requires planning.

Planning your project is vital. Good preparation is the key to a good outcome for all kinds of projects – as you'll know if you've ever done DIY or home improvements (or just watched the television shows).

Planning: why this is important

If you have a plan, then you can implement a well thought-out study. Well thought-out studies are likely to:

- increase the coherence between the different phases of your project (for example data collection and analysis);
- increase the quality of your project (through knowing and applying best practice);
- reduce unpleasant surprises (for example, realising you can't answer your research questions with the data you've collected);
- give you a sense of confidence in your work;
- be completed on time.

To plan your research project you need to develop your research questions into a project plan. A project plan allows you to identify what you are going to do and with whom. This means working through a number of distinct phases that are summarised in the box below and form the structure of this chapter.

In a nutshell: planning phases

Planning should include the following phases.

- Plan your method: data collection and analysis.
- Plan your participants (or other forms of data collection): sampling and recruitment.
- Plan for the resources you need: information, support, materials and equipment.
- Plan permissions such as ethics.
- Having done this you will be able to:

  - create a plan by outlining the key steps you need to take to complete your project;
  - successfully submit an ethics application so that you may start your research.

For the rest of the chapter we outline your objectives and key tasks for writing a comprehensive project plan and a successful ethics application. Learning to assess a situation and make a decision to move a project forward requires a set of skills that develop over a lifetime. Your student research is part of this process so don't expect to know everything; remember that you're learning on the job. Try to find a happy balance between being as prepared as possible, while recognising that you will learn through doing along the way. Planning your project is about being in a position to make the best possible decision you can at the time you make it. Below we give you some tried and tested ways to help you.

How to make it brilliant – know your stuff!

- Give yourself a good understanding of the relevant literature. Read reports of similar research projects and qualitative methods books.
- Weigh up decisions by writing down the pros and cons.
- Imagine carrying out your plans. Are they feasible? Have you forgotten to factor in something important? For example, if you're working with school children, don't schedule your data collection time during their holidays.
- Consider your interests and experiences. Do you need to get more experience or familiarity with your participant groups before you collect data?
- Be realistic in what you can do in your time frame.

- Work out how your study can best meet the criteria in your dissertation marking scheme.
- If you feel unsure of how to proceed, return to your research question and consider how your plan can best help you answer your question.
- Always run key decisions past your supervisor.

From research question to project plan

Planning your method

Your first objective in planning your project is to work out the best method to address your research questions(s) in a way that is practical within the timescale and with the resources you have. It's often useful to ask yourself the following questions.

- What methods have been used in previous similar studies?
- Is it appropriate to reproduce or challenge them?
- What other methods do I know about and what are their potential uses?
- What resources do these different methods require (including time) and do I have access to them?

As we saw in Chapter 2, your research question often suggests what method(s) to choose. For example, if you want to see how people make sense of an issue together then focus groups or some naturally occurring talk between several people is going to be more useful for you than individual interviews. Similarly, particular methodologies (principles of research methods) are often closely linked to the use of specific methods, so your decisions on what methods to use may be already structured by your methodology. For example, if you want to apply discursive psychological analysis to your subject, then you'd need to be thinking about how to record 'naturally occurring' talk that isn't a product of research, such as focus groups. If you're struggling with these questions, or think that there should be a method you don't know about that's more appropriate for your study, try the following.

- Look up previous work in your topic area.
- Go to the library and read through some qualitative research methods books.
- Speak to your supervisor.
- Join/start an online discussion thread on a relevant discussion board (for example, one run for psychology students or for qualitative researchers – ask your supervisor or librarian for recommendations).

If you want to use a method you haven't already been trained in, then you need to consider the implications this will have. For example, will it make things unnecessarily difficult for you and jeopardise your mark? Or, conversely will it help you demonstrate initiative and originality? Also check if you can access training (for example, if you can sit in on a relevant class) and if there is appropriate supervision available for you using this method. Discuss these issues with your supervisor.

The decisions you make in terms of what research questions and method you decide upon will be informed by a range of issues, including your personal perspectives. It's useful therefore to reflect on how your perspectives are informing the choices that you're making regarding your method and analysis, so that you can explore the background that might be structuring your thinking. This kind of self-reflection can allow you to make more self-aware decisions and is an important aspect of qualitative research called 'reflexivity'. Chapter 8 considers reflexivity in more detail and can help you develop ideas on how to build self-reflection into your planning stages.

Want to know more about methods resources?

There are many useful resources for qualitative researchers. These include:

- Most university libraries have qualitative research methods books and you should be able to borrow from other libraries through inter-library loans. Even in a virtual world, it is often beneficial to peruse these books to get a sense of the issues, methods and debates in qualitative research.
- Dig out your research methods lecture notes from courses you've taken – you may be surprised by how much in there is useful now!
- Browse academically credible web resources, such as the online journal *Forum: Qualitative Social Research*: **http://www.qualitative-research.net/index.php/fqs**

Top tip: Wikipedia

It is increasingly common for people to use Wikipedia as a source of information. However, for academic work, we would advise against using Wikipedia (and many other Internet sources) because it is not a peer-reviewed or independently evaluated source, unlike journal articles and academic text books. Sometimes people look at Wikipedia to get a sense of some of the key issues regarding a topic or person, and while it can give a useful overview for some topics you cannot guarantee your topic is one of them. So, if you do get information from Wikipedia make sure you double-check it and use more acceptable sources to reference the information in your written work.

Planning your participants

Your research question should have got you thinking about your sampling and recruitment strategies. Because qualitative research projects are usually in-depth, small-scale projects, the research question often names the participants, either in terms of a general group (for example, young women) or a more specific group (for example, female school leavers in transition to vocational training). At this stage your objective is to plan how to get an appropriate sample to answer your research question and then how to recruit this sample.

If you are unsure about who your participants are, then a useful strategy might be to return to your research question and see if you can make it clearer and more focused (see Chapter 2).

Sampling

Sampling will depend on your research question and what you want to be able to claim from your data analysis. Qualitative research projects rarely aim to generalise to a population in the same way that quantitative projects do. This can lead to students feeling that qualitative research isn't valid. However, one way to think of the usefulness of qualitative research that is not statistically representative is that it gives you an understanding of the subjective experiences, processes or sense making of a group of people in a particular context. This understanding can add to our knowledge about a subject and may be relevant for similar subsequent studies.

For example, Riley et al. (2010a) showed that a sense of belonging was an important outcome for their participants who were part of a 'free party' (illegal 'rave') sound system. While a sense of belonging has often been an important aspect of youth subcultures, their qualitative analysis showed how participants contextualised this belonging as a form of resistance to an increasingly individualist and competitive world. This kind of insight would not have arisen as readily from a quantitative study. And although not generalisable, the findings were able to contribute to future studies by showing that the issue of what 'belonging' means may be a useful topic to explore in relation to young people's identity.

Research that is not statistically representative employs different sampling procedures to research that seeks to produce generalisable findings. The two most common sampling techniques used to recruit people who fit the research criteria are 'opportunity' or 'purposive' sampling.

'Opportunity' (sometimes called 'convenience' sampling) involves a researcher recruiting people who the researcher has relatively easy access to. For most student qualitative research projects this approach is appropriate as long as you are careful about what conclusions you can draw from your findings.

Purposive sampling is a more focused form of opportunity sampling. Researchers opportunistically recruit participants whose characteristics make them likely to be 'information rich cases', defined by Patton (2002: 46), as 'those from which one can learn a great deal about issues of central importance to the purpose of the research'. An example of purposive sampling is deviant case sampling (also known as 'negative case' sampling), in which researchers look for examples that are exceptions to their initial findings. By exploring such exceptions to the rule, researchers can develop their analysis, by either rejecting their ideas because the deviant case analysis shows that their ideas don't match significant sections of their data or because it allows them to understand the sense making they're exploring better. For example, Riley et al. (2010b) explored examples of when their magic mushroom using participants deviated from what they called a discourse of 'controlled consumption'. The researchers identified times when their participants also described themselves as engaging in high levels of magic mushroom use, but noted that these examples were given in the context of stories in which drug use had led to problems. This deviant case analysis therefore enabled the researchers to strengthen their argument that their participants were drawing on a discourse that constructed appropriate drug use as that which is moderate and controlled.

Sometimes researchers combine sampling techniques. For example, one of our students 'Beth' wanted to look at how women of different ages negotiated contemporary beauty ideals. She recruited an older group from her mother's friends and a younger group from her own friends. The sampling strategy Beth used had an 'opportunity sampling' element, because it involved recruiting people the researcher happened to come into contact with. It also had an element of 'purposive sampling' to it, in that the groups that participants were drawn from were selected because they allowed Beth to make a comparison that was specifically related to the project aims. Beth got a good mark for this study, and part of this was because she explored how researching people she knew may have affected her findings and in this way showed how she was careful about what conclusions she could draw (for more on the impact of the researcher on the research, see the discussion of reflexivity in Chapter 8).

On occasion qualitative researchers want to extrapolate their findings to the wider population. There are different quality criteria you can employ to do this. For example, you may aim to reach 'theoretical saturation', in which you keep recruiting until you hear no more new stories from several participants (allowing you to make the claim that you have accessed the most common accounts). Alternatively, you can employ sampling strategies from experimental work that seek to identify representative samples. If you want to employ these techniques, you will need to refer to specialist text books and your supervisor.

Qualitative projects that use existing texts as data also need to develop a sampling procedure. Although a representative sample may not be needed (or even meaningful), researchers still have to have a systematic procedure that can be justified in relation to the research question and the quality criteria of the method being used. For example, a student wanting to perform a discourse analysis of public constructions of obesity might pick a month such as January, when diet talk is fashionable in the press, and look at articles from the 10 most read newspapers that mention 'obesity'. An alternative strategy would be to identify a key story that generated a lot of media attention (such as the launch of a report on childhood obesity) and, using this story as an example of public discourse on obesity, analyse all the articles that discussed this story. Experienced qualitative researchers should be able to identify appropriate, systematic and meaningful sampling procedures for projects analysing existing texts, so see your supervisor for advice. Your librarian may also be able to help you identify ways of searching for publicly available texts. For example, you can access newspaper articles using search engines such as Nexis. (For more discussion on data collection see Chapter 6.)

In a nutshell: sampling

The method of sampling you choose should be the one that will:

- best help you address your research question(s);
- allow you to conduct a systematic and logical sampling procedure;
- work within the time and resources that you have.

Want to know more about sampling?

There are many good sources and we recommend the following for general discussion of sampling:

Denscome, M. (2003) *The Good Research Guide: For Small-scale Social Research Projects* (2nd edn). Buckingham: Open University Press.
Robson, C. (2011) *Real World Research* (3rd edn). Chichester: Wiley.
The following sources give more information about purposive sampling:
Gordon-Finlayson, A. (2010) 'Grounded theory', in M. Forrester (ed.) *Doing Qualitative Research in Psychology: A Practical Guide.* London: Sage. pp. 154–76.
Charmaz, K. (2008) 'Grounded theory', in J.A. Smith (ed.) *Qualitative Psychology: A Practical Guide to Research Methods* (2nd edn). London: Sage. pp. 81–110.

Recruitment

Your sampling strategy helps you plan who you want to recruit. Your next task is to plan how to recruit. Your first step here is to decide if you can recruit your participants directly or if you need to go through people who control access to potential participants. If recruiting directly, plan how you will access people that meet your criteria. For example, will you approach people on campus until you get enough participants or will you recruit a small number of people and then ask these people to recommend you to other people in their social networks?

People who control your access to potential participants are called 'gatekeepers'. They can be extremely helpful, but sometimes they can feel like a barrier to your research. Plan time to work with gatekeepers, and in some instances the participants and their community, so that you can identify their needs and concerns and make sure that your project addresses them. You will also need to plan how to make participating in your project attractive to potential participants, so that it is easier to recruit people. For example, plan a project on a topic that people want to talk about or plan to give your participants a more tangible benefit, such as feeding their responses back into a relevant institutional policy. If you do pursue this latter option, it is advisable to discuss it with your supervisor (and also see the discussion about offering incentives to participants, below) as you might find yourself promising more than you can deliver! As with all your planning activities, work out what is feasible with the resources and time that you have.

Top tips: recruitment

Recruitment tends to go well when you take account of the following:

- Potential participants (and/or gatekeepers) find your study interesting and relevant or see a direct benefit to participating.
- You approach the participants in a positive and pleasant manner.
- Your method is convenient to the participants (for example, busy people might give you an interview, but may be less likely to find a mutually convenient time to participate in a focus group).
- You identify and address any concerns that participants may have (particularly as the general public are often aware that psychologists sometimes design studies, such as those by Stanley Milgram [1974], that are deceptive or demonstrate negative characteristics of the participants).
- You build in time to reflect on your relationships with potential and confirmed participants, so that you can increase your self-awareness in relation to the decisions you make and the way you interact with others.

Recruitment: a successful story and a cautionary tale

Mark wanted to recruit people involved in 'free party' events for his study on social identities in youth cultures. He approached a friend who was involved in a range of music scenes, who gave him the phone number of 'Louise'. Louise agreed to meet Mark at a party, but when Mark arrived, Louise had already left. On the phone, Louise told Mark to look for a guy called 'Steve' driving a blue car. Seeing a group of people standing around some parked cars, Mark asked for Steve and soon found himself explaining the situation to him. Steve walked Mark around the party, introducing him to everyone he knew. Steve also told Mark of subsequent parties and introduced him to people there. Mark ended up joking that Steve wasn't a gatekeeper, but a 'gateopener'.

A very different experience happened to Jessica when doing research in schools on body image. With her supervisor Jessica approached the school head via email, who said the school would support the project and to contact the relevant year leader. This year leader appeared very interested and arranged a meeting with Jessica, herself and three student representatives to discuss the project. At the meeting all parties were enthusiastic about the project and the students agreed to help with recruitment and participate themselves. When Jessica tried to arrange another meeting with the school, all emails and phone messages were ignored.

What do these stories tell us? That you never quite know how a project will go, so:

- be flexible;
- respond to opportunities (safely);
- use the resources you have to hand (such as friendship groups);
- have a plan B, in case participants withdraw; and,
- reflect on your relationships with your participants and potential participants and how these may affect your project or interactions with others.

Planning resources: information, support and equipment

A qualitative research project needs a range of resources, which include information, support, and equipment. Your objective at this planning stage is to have a sense of what these resources are and how to use them.

Planning your information needs

All qualitative researchers need to develop their knowledge of the topic they're studying and the method(s) they're using. While these forms of knowledge should develop throughout your project, there is usually a bigger focus on them at the planning stages of the project when you're working out what to do. There may also be a focus towards the end of the project, when you'll want to check for newly published research or for literature that has come to take on more relevance as your project developed. Reviewing relevant literature is a significant activity for any qualitative research project, and Chapter 5 is dedicated to talking you through this.

Planning for support

Students who do well in their research projects tend to be proactive, independently using the various information resources they have to plan their project. However, the best students also consult with their supervisor, drawing on the experience of their supervisor to help with their decision making. So, plan to schedule regular meetings with your supervisor. Depending on the system operating within your department, you may also want to think about times when your meetings with your supervisor may not be as easy to schedule. For example, your supervisor may not be as readily available during student vacations, when staff might take their holidays; or during particularly busy periods of the academic year. Talk to your supervisor about the frequency and timing of meetings and try and find out if there are any particular periods of time when they will be more or less available. (See Chapter 4 for more on the student–supervisor relationship.)

Other staff who can offer you support include your department technician and librarian (university libraries often have a dedicated member of staff to support students and staff in a faculty, school or department).

Other students can also be a source of support. Try setting up regular study group meetings with other students working on similar topics or with similar methods. At these meetings you could discuss a reading (for example, on a method), talk about the decisions you've made regarding your projects, or look at each other's data or analysis. Many qualitative researchers do this kind of small group work because other people's perspectives can be invaluable in the development of one's thinking, especially when it comes to interpreting data.

Study group meetings tend to work best when everyone involved contributes and there is a theme for each meeting (for example, to read a paper). They do not work if participants compete or create anxiety through comparisons. Look for individuals who you think might work well with you or ask your supervisor for the names of others they are supervising who are doing similar work.

Planning equipment needs

Qualitative researchers often use specialist recording and transcribing equipment. Your library or department may have digital (or cassette) recorders or transcription machines that you can borrow. While some students get by using the technology that they have to hand, such as mobile phones, specialist equipment makes transcription easier and more pleasant, so get advice. Find out as much as you can about what is available and how the system works for borrowing equipment so that you can build this into your planning.

Top tips: planning for equipment needs

- Talk to your supervisor and/or librarian/technicians about which equipment would be best and how to gain access to it.
- Find out how you can reserve equipment and what demand is like.
- Work out how long you might need it for and check that you can borrow it for this amount of time, as sometimes there are time limits on equipment loans.
- Explore online resources that may be helpful. For example Audacity offers free software that can help with the process of transcribing digital recordings (http://audacity.sourceforge.net/).
- Try to plan for equipment failure. For example, bring spare batteries or extra recording equipment.

Planning the development of materials

Qualitative data can include any combination of text or visual images. However, the most common texts tend to be transcribed audio recordings, either from discussions that were recorded for research purposes (for example, interviews and focus groups) or from recording discussions that would have occurred without the researcher being present (for example, weight-loss clinic sessions). If you elicit data through interviews or focus groups, then you can develop a range of materials to facilitate your participants' talk. Materials include interview or focus group schedules, vignettes (hypothetical stories about other people), 'memory work' (participants share a previously prepared story of a memory), television clips and photographs ('photo-elicitation'). You need to plan for identifying materials that will elicit rich and detailed talk.

Alternatively, you may want to look at data that already exists without you having to record it, such as blogs, online discussions, newspaper articles or comic books. If the data is in the public sphere, then usually you do not need to get the authors' permission to use such data for research purposes, but if it is private (such as a members-only discussion board, or a Facebook page), then you must get permission from all the people concerned (ethics is discussed in more detail later in the chapter).

To plan for what materials you want to use or develop try to read a range of published qualitative work, including work that reports studies that use methods you are interested in and articles that focus specifically on discussing methods. While you are reading, consider the advantages and disadvantages of each method in relation to how you could use it to address your research question. You may want to make a list of pros and cons and discuss your ideas with your supervisor. For further advice on equipment, materials, data collection and transcription see Chapter 6.

What now?

The final stage of effective planning is to write down a project plan. A project plan is a succinct outline of your rationale, method and procedure. We recommend that you develop a project plan on one side of A4 paper, so that you can see the structure of your project in a single glance. You can do this as a piece of text, as in the example provided in Chapter 4, or in some schematic form, such as a mind map (see, for example, www.thinkbuzan.com). However you decide to present your project plan, you need to include information on the background to the study, your research question(s), your method and form of analysis. In this way you can articulate why your study is important; what you're going to do; when, how and with whom you're going to do it; and what equipment you'll need.

To write your plan you need to be able to answer the following questions:

- Why is my study important?
- What has been done before?
- What are the gaps in the literature that my project will address?
- What are my research question(s)?
- What research method will best let me answer my research question(s)?
- Who are my participants and what is my recruitment strategy? Or in the case of already existing data, what is the corpus of my data?
- What is my sampling strategy and rationale?
- What equipment, materials and skills do I need? And how will I gain access to or develop them?
- Where will I go for support in doing my project and how can I plan for this?
- Will my data need recording and transcribing or other forms of work before I can analyse it?
- How am I going to analyse the data in a way that lets me answer my research question(s)?
- Now that I understand my project better do I need to modify my research question to make a better/more coherent project?

If you can't answer these questions, then you need to go through another cycle of planning. Qualitative research is often cyclical (see Chapter 4 for discussion of cyclical designs), so don't think of this as a waste of time, but part of the sharpening up processes that go into making an excellent research project. Speak to your supervisor as necessary in order to formulate answers to these questions and complete your design.

Figure 3.1 'The planning process', summarises the processes we've discussed in this chapter, and introduces the next topic of the chapter: your ethics application. Remember that as you write your project plan, start marking down a time frame for when to do these activities. Chapter 4 contains an example of a project plan, which you can use to help you do yours, and also discusses timetables in more detail. For now, we note that an important deadline to plan for will be your ethics application, and if the ethics submission dates are infrequent at your institution, it may be useful to find this out first and work

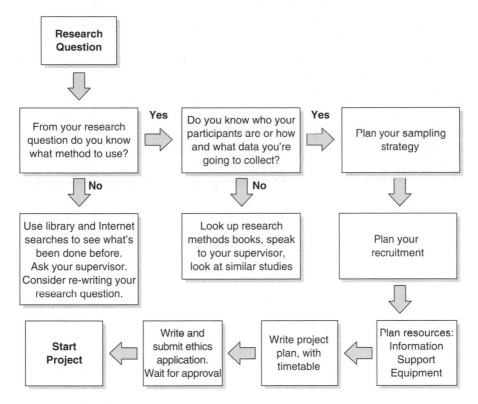

Figure 3.1 The planning process

out your project plan around this date. Submitting a successful ethics application is a significant part of conducting a research project, and all research, including that done by students must be subject to ethical review and approval. We focus the rest of the chapter on this subject.

Planning for ethical research

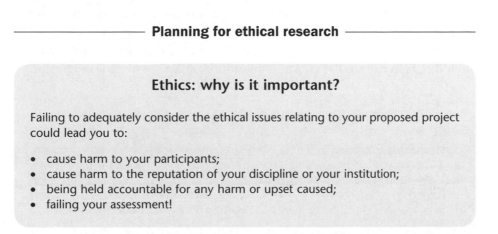

Ethics: why is it important?

Failing to adequately consider the ethical issues relating to your proposed project could lead you to:

- cause harm to your participants;
- cause harm to the reputation of your discipline or your institution;
- being held accountable for any harm or upset caused;
- failing your assessment!

All researchers must gain permission from their institution to conduct their planned research, and if you are working within another organisation, you need to fulfil any ethical requirements of that organisation too. The UK National Health Service (NHS), for example, has its own ethics application process that often requires specialist knowledge and a significant amount of time. See your supervisor for advice on NHS ethics applications if this is relevant to you. For university applications you should find out what your application procedure is early on in your planning, so that you can submit an application in good time to conduct your research. Getting permission to conduct your research involves you making an assessment of the ethical issues that are involved in your research and outlining how you might address these issues. Your objectives for planning ethical research should be as follows:

- Understand what research ethics are and how these apply to your study.
- Make sure your research project will be conducted in an ethical way and meets any relevant guidelines (for example, psychological research in the UK should adhere to the British Psychological Society ethical guidelines).
- Find out what the ethics procedure is at your institution (and any other relevant institution that you or your participants may belong to), including deadlines for applications.
- Write and submit an ethics form that is accepted by your institution and any other appropriate governing body, making sure that your application is submitted in good time for you to do your study.

Understanding research ethics

Research ethics are about designing and executing research in ways that are regarded as morally acceptable. Making moral decisions is a subjective process and ethical standards tend to be derived through agreement by groups of people. This means that ethical standards change over time and are always subject to some discussion and debate. Ethics applications are often evaluated by a committee, which may pass an application, reject it or ask for changes to the study so that it meets the committee's judgment of ethical standards. Ethics is also an ongoing concern as issues may arise throughout the project and researchers should remain alert to the ethical implications of their work as it progresses.

Cautionary tale: unexpected revelations

Sameeha was interested in the relationships between identity and consumption, and interviewed five people about their music collections. Two of the participants described traumatic life experiences at the time of buying particular songs, such as having an eating disorder and a miscarriage. Sameeha hadn't expected to hear such personal and painful accounts and didn't know what she should say.

What can we learn? Plan for the unexpected. Have some set phrases ready for difficult situations, however unlikely you think they'll be. For example, if a participant is upset, offer them the chance to stop the interview or take a break. When we ask people to share aspects of their lives with us, it is our duty to make this experience a safe one. It's also important to have relevant sources of help to hand (such as contact details for organisations that offer support and advice in those areas, or resources for counselling or medical advice) so that you can provide these for your participants in case they need help or support afterwards.

Some qualitative researchers argue that qualitative research tends to be more ethical than other forms of research. This is based on the idea that qualitative work is less likely to deceive its participants, and has a more egalitarian conceptualisation of research as 'with participants' rather than 'on subjects'. However, not all researchers would agree with this (see, for example, Condor, 1997), and it is important to remember that qualitative work will only be ethical if we focus carefully on the ethical implications of our work. Consideration is needed in particular because the way we tend to collect data means that we often ask participants to disclose personal information and to do this we form a relationship, or at least a rapport, with our participants. This combination of creating a relationship and asking for personal information may make participants vulnerable to disclosing more than they had wanted to, feeling exposed or even used. So, even projects that seem to have few ethical issues need to be carefully considered.

In a nutshell: ethics

Ethics is about:

- 'making ... decisions about what would be morally right and wrong to do' (Chamberlain, 2004: 129);
- making sure your project follows any relevant guidelines for good ethical conduct – such as those written by your institution or by a relevant professional body (for example, British Psychological Society ethical guidelines which can be downloaded from their website: http://www.bps.org.uk).

There are a number of key ethical issues that you will need to consider when designing ethical research. These are listed below and then discussed in detail in the rest of the chapter. Note though, that there may be other issues that are specific to your project.

- doing genuine and competent research;
- informed consent;
- confidentiality;
- anonymity;
- harm and distress;
- deception and debriefing;
- right to withdraw;
- effects beyond the participants themselves.

Genuine and competent research

Research needs to be conducted honestly. This means being truthful about how you conduct your research and what you found. Practices such as inventing data, deliberately reporting data in a way that is knowingly misleading or lying about what you found are clearly unethical and are also treated as breaches of student discipline.

Research also needs to be conducted competently. Without the necessary skills to do research properly, researchers may make crucial mistakes that lead to untrustworthy findings, wasting the time of their participants or even causing them harm. When judgments are made about this criterion, the level of training held by a researcher is taken into account. This is one reason why you have a supervisor and why, in many cases, you will be steered towards methods that are appropriate for somebody with your degree of training. So don't worry unduly if things don't go quite according to plan all the time. For example, all qualitative researchers will have experienced interviews that haven't gone as well as they might have hoped (see Nairn et al., 2005). The process of reflecting on such experiences, and discussing with your supervisor what you might have done differently, will help to develop your research skills.

Informed consent

This is the basic principle that participants should, wherever possible, be given sufficient information about what is involved in the research so that they can make a fully informed choice whether to participate. Participants must know what will be required from them, who is doing the study, and what will be done with the information they give.

Participants must also be clearly communicated with in language that they can understand. Do this by avoiding jargon and considering how the type of participants you're working with are likely to understand the concepts and words you're using to describe the study. For example, instead of saying this study is about 'the role of body art in self identity', you could say 'this study is about what your body art means to you'. Communicating clearly can be difficult sometimes and involves making a judgment about how much technical information somebody needs in order to give informed consent.

Procedures for gaining informed consent involve speaking to your participants and you would also usually give them written information. In cases where written consent is needed, you will need a consent form that explains the study and that your participants can sign to indicate their agreement to participate and to confirm that you have informed them fully about what this involves. Many research methods books, including Robson (2011) offer templates to develop materials such as consent forms. You can also find similar information at: http://www.esds.ac.uk/qualidata/. Below we offer you one example from a study on friendships and body image. You should note that this study also developed an information sheet detailing the study for participants and parents/guardians to read and a consent form for the parents/guardians.

Top tip: sample consent form

You are invited to participate in a research project, which is being conducted by Lucy Smith who is a student at Global University. The study explores how young women feel about their bodies, their concerns and how we might reduce them. Participation involves meeting with Lucy and approximately four other young women from your school to discuss body image. This sheet is for you to keep and tells you more about the study and what it involves.

- Group meetings with girls from Year 10 will be run by Lucy Smith, who is being supervised by Dr Alison Jones (a psychologist at Global University). There will be three weekly meetings, which will last about 60 minutes. The meetings will be audio-recorded, and then written out as a record of what people have said.
- All names of people and places (including schools) will be removed from the written notes of the interviews, so nobody outside the group will know who was in the group.
- If you agree to come to a group discussion, but feel at any stage that you would like to leave, you are free to do so at any time and do not have to give a reason.
- Once the group discussion has taken place and has been recorded, it will not be possible for you to get back the information that you have given.
- Lucy will write a written report in which she will include, word-for-word, some of what has been said in the group discussions. She will make sure that this is done in a way that makes it difficult for people to know who said what and will never give your name.

(Continued)

(Continued)

- The researchers will not tell anyone else in the school what you have said. When they tell people what was said in the group discussions, they will not tell them which member of the group said what. The only situation where they will break this promise is if you tell them about a situation where you or somebody else is in danger. If this happens, Lucy will speak to you about it and explain that she needs to speak to the school nurse.

If you (or your parents) have any questions about this study, then feel free to contact Lucy Smith (lsmith7@global.ac.uk) or her supervisor:

Dr Alison Jones, Senior Lecturer in Psychology, Department of Psychology, Hampton Building, Global University, New Town CW54 8JH, Tel: 01875 369426, email: ajones1@global.ac.uk

The researcher will detach and keep this section

Body Image and friendship group study

I agree to take part in the project meetings under the conditions described above:

Signed: .... Date: ....

Except under very special circumstances, we need to ensure that our participants are deemed to be competent to give their own consent. If your research involves working with anyone who has learning difficulties or some kind of cognitive impairment that might inhibit their ability to consent, or anyone who is under the age of 16, you will normally be expected to gain consent from somebody else on their behalf. In the case of children, this means gaining parental consent, or gaining equivalent consent from somebody who is legally responsible for that child in place of their parents (*in loco parentis*). You should remember that if you are dealing with populations who are incarcerated, permission may be required for you to approach these people to invite them to participate in your study, but they should ordinarily still be seen as capable of giving their own consent. The fact that they are incarcerated does not in itself mean that anybody else can consent on their behalf. It is important to be sensitive, in fact, to the potential coercive effects of requests for participation coming through third parties with a high level of power over potential participants (for example, teachers, prison staff, clinicians, doctors).

If you obtain consent from some other individual, it is also important to remember that this does not mean that the participant themselves has to participate. In the case of children, for example, parental consent does not mean they must participate – we still need to get some form of agreement from the participant themselves – and this is known as gaining 'assent'. For example, if you were videoing a child for an observational study, and the child cried and refused to engage with you, you should 'read' this body language as a sign that they are withdrawing their agreement to participate.

The flowchart in Figure 3.2 'Consent flowchart', will guide you through making the decision about who you need to obtain consent from. Note that gaining assent and consent on behalf of a participant requires specialist knowledge, so ask your supervisor for help.

One way of attempting to increase the chances of gaining consent from potential participants is to use rewards or incentives. Examples of rewards that are sometimes given in return for participation in research include:

- paying participants for their time;
- reimbursing travel expenses;
- providing gifts or vouchers;
- entering participants into a prize draw;
- offering students course credit or similar rewards.

The use of rewards and incentives has ethical dimensions and it must be considered carefully in the context of the specific project in which their use is planned. In general it is important to balance the size of any incentive against the potential risks that might be involved in participating in research. Obviously, it is vital to prevent harm wherever possible and minimise risk (this is discussed in more detail below) but there may be occasions where participation in research involves a small risk for participants (risk of becoming distressed if discussing sensitive topics, for example). In such situations we must be extremely careful to ensure that we use rewards that while providing an incentive to participate are not so great that people are likely to give consent even in situations where they are concerned that participating in the project could be distressing, harmful or unpleasant for them. In essence, it's appropriate to give a small incentive but we must be careful that this is not so great that it overrides a participants' urge to say no for some non-trivial reason.

If you are considering using any kind of incentive then you will need to talk this over with your supervisor and you will also need to provide details of this in your ethics submission and show that you have considered any ethical ramifications. You should also bear in mind that some universities may have specific rules that ban or limit the use of incentives and rewards in student research projects (in order to prevent wealthy students from gaining unfair advantage, for example).

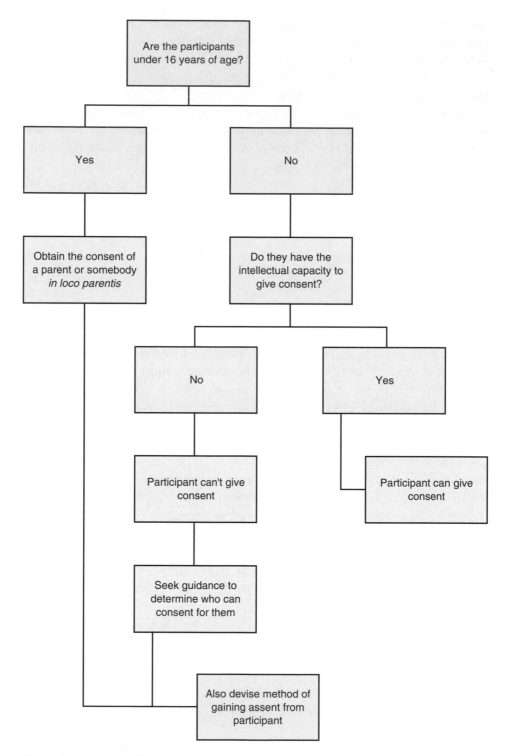

Figure 3.2 Consent flowchart

Confidentiality

The issue of confidentiality in research is not as straightforward as it may at first seem. Since our aim as researchers is to communicate our findings, what we mean by 'confidentiality' – that we will not tell others what participants said in a way that will allow them to be identified – is somewhat different to the common sense understanding of 'confidential' as meaning 'I tell you and you tell nobody else'. As researchers, we therefore need to tell potential participants what we mean by 'confidentiality' and explain clearly what will be done with the information we plan to collect, who it might be shared with (and who it won't be, in some cases) and in what format it might be passed on or presented.

One issue that must be considered in relation to confidentiality is that of whether there may need to be limits to the promise of confidentiality. There may, very exceptionally, be circumstances where researchers will pass on information gleaned from a research participant to a third party. Such circumstances generally only occur when there is a significant likelihood of serious harm to an identifiable individual, whether that is the participant themselves or somebody else. For example, participants might tell a researcher that they, or somebody else, intends to harm themselves or another person, or is planning to commit a serious criminal offence.

The principal way to try and tackle this is to identify in advance any obvious limits to confidentiality and communicate these to participants when they consent. Earlier, we met Lucy Smith and her supervisor when discussing consent forms. Lucy's study was about issues to do with body image and she and her supervisor were aware that this could be sensitive or troubling for some participants. One issue that they identified was that participants might reveal the intention to harm themselves (for example, this could arise in the context of distress or in relation to eating disorders) or might reveal knowledge that somebody else was likely to harm themselves. If this happened, it would present Lucy with a conflict between her responsibility to treat the participant's account as confidential and her wider responsibility to protect people from serious harm. In order to pre-empt this in a way that balanced these two demands, Lucy made it clear to her participants on the consent form that she would break confidentiality if she was made aware that somebody was in danger. It is not always possible to identify all limits to confidentiality before the research commences, although clearly all reasonable attempts should be made to do this beforehand. If a situation like this arose that was unanticipated, it would be important to talk the dilemma over with your supervisor, possibly in conjunction with your departments or university's ethics committee in order to identify the best course of action. This issue is also interesting because it highlights that ethics is not just a static thing that is established before your research begins but is a dynamic process that is ongoing throughout the project.

When considering issues of confidentiality, make sure you can answer the following questions about your study.

- How will I store the data so that confidentiality is protected?
- How will I use the data, to whom will I reveal it and in what format?
- How do I make it clear to my participants how I will store their data and what I will do with it?

It is fairly common to get confused about the distinction between confidentiality (which is about what we plan to do with the information we collect) and anonymity (which is about whether information that we use or reveal can be identified as relating to a particular individual). Next, we consider anonymity in detail and we would advise that you pay careful attention to the distinction between this and confidentiality.

Anonymity

Except in exceptional circumstance, participants' anonymity must be protected, so that other than the researcher(s) nobody will know the participants' name or be able to identify them from other descriptions of them in the data. Qualitative researchers protect anonymity by:

- giving participants pseudonyms (false names);
- changing or removing identifying information (for example, place names, job titles);
- checking that all these procedures have been carefully done for all data that might be shared, published or otherwise introduced into the public domain (for example, interview transcripts included as appendices in a report).

Occasionally we may ask participants' permission to reveal such information. You must have a strong reason for this and make sure your participants understand the implications. For example, in a study on identity and social networking, your participants might not mind their Facebook page being publicly discussed in academic circles now, but they may not be so keen if your write-up got uploaded onto the web and prospective employers found their photographs of drunken nights out.

Protecting anonymity in your data usually involves changing your transcripts. To illustrate, in an interview a participant might describe themselves in a way that could enable someone else to identify them, for example, by saying:

well ... it all started when I was Headteacher of Middlewood Primary School in Birmingham ...

If we were to transcribe this talk or present it in any publications or presentations, we would need to change the identifying markers, which in this case, is the name of the school and the city. We could do this by cutting out this information or by using pseudonyms, as in the examples below:

well, it all started when I was Headteacher of [name of primary school] in [name of City] ...

or

well, it all started when I was Headteacher of 'Eastville' Primary School in 'MidCity' ...

If you are using images, note that there are various debates about how to manage anonymity with visual data – for example, using photographs that do not include people's faces or using software (for example, Photoshop) to blur faces. If this is relevant to you, read visual research methods texts for ideas and discuss your options with your supervisor.

Want to know more about the ethics of visual research?

The ESRC (Economic and Social Research Council) is the biggest funder of social science research in the UK. It offers various documents about research methods produced by its National Centre for Research Methods. A useful document, entitled 'Visual Ethics: Ethical Issues in Visual Research', can be found at: http://eprints.ncrm.ac.uk/421/

Harm and distress

Potential for harm must be considered and areas where harm could occur must be identified. You should also talk this through with your supervisor and any other people who might help you to identify sources of harm (sometimes non-psychologists can give us a better idea of how participants might respond to certain materials or issues). You also need to consider if your participants are particularly vulnerable, for example if you are working with people who have experienced some kind of trauma that relates to the research question.

Activity: where's the harm?

Below are two examples of research proposals that were submitted for approval. Measures were put in place to deal with the potential sources of harm before approval was granted and these studies were conducted. For each example, note down the potential sources of harm to the participants and ways that you might deal with these issues so that participants would not experience harm.

Example 1: A student wanted to find out about people's attitudes towards illegal downloading of music and piracy. He planned to run focus groups asking people about their experiences and attitudes.

Example 2: On placement for a police force, a student wanted to investigate rape victims' experiences of the police investigation processes. She sought permission to interview eight women in their homes, recruiting through posters placed in a rape crisis centre.

As these examples illustrate, 'harm' can be conceptualised quite broadly and you need to think hard about any possible sources of harm while you design your research. You should also consider the issue of harm in relation to whether you need to place limits around your assurances of confidentiality (see above).

In a nutshell: potential sources of harm

Harm can include many things such as
- physical harm;
- embarrassment or personal offence;
- trauma;
- the reduction or erosion of one's rights;
- loss of property or reputation;
- psychological distress or strong negative emotions such as anger.

Once potential sources of harm have been identified, steps must be taken to prevent them from causing harm. You might handle this by warning participants at the recruitment stage so that those who think they might be harmed can choose not to take part (although we must be careful with this as people might not always anticipate the effects of studies on themselves).

Your focus should be on the prevention of harm. But it might also be appropriate to have some measures in place in case the prevention doesn't work. For example, researchers might offer to guide participants towards sources of professional help for issues that the research may have raised (for example their doctor, a professional counselling service, or organisations such as Childline or Victim Support in the UK). While it is important to identify external sources of support for your participants, this should never be a substitute for making all reasonable attempts to prevent harm from occurring.

Deception and debriefing

Deception (either by deliberately misleading or by omission of important information) has often taken place in psychological research. We can probably all describe Milgram's (1974) famous obedience experiments where he convinced participants that they were giving real electric shocks to other participants. Studies that employ deception often conflict with the principle of obtaining informed consent. Most studies will not pass an ethics committee if they employ significant forms of deception. There are no set rules about when deception is allowed, but if you answer 'yes' to the following questions then your research is likely to involve unacceptable levels of deception.

- Does the deception hide something about the procedure that is particularly likely to be crucial for consent (for example, does the researcher plan not to tell them that the interview is likely to take four hours? Or is the researcher interacting online without saying they're going to use these interactions as data for a research project)?
- Is the thing that is not revealed to them particularly likely to lead to harm or distress (for example, are they not told that they are going to be asked about their experiences of exam stress and how they cope)?

At the end of the data collection researchers often 'debrief' participants about the study. Debrief sessions can involve:

- explaining the study in more detail;
- fully explaining any deception if it has been used (this is essential);
- providing a written debrief for participants to take away;
- thanking the participant for their time;
- reiteration of contact details for researchers if they have questions afterwards;
- providing sources of help and support in case the measures taken to prevent distress don't work or if the experience of participating in the study triggers the participant to seek other support;
- explanations of aspects of the design that the researcher didn't explain beforehand;
- offers to send transcripts or the report (although your final project report that you hand in to your institution is not always the best thing to send to participants as it is written for an academic audience);
- an opportunity for participants to talk without being recorded about the topic or their experience of participating in the research.

Right to withdraw

Participants should always have the right to withdraw from any data collection sessions or research procedures (such as an interview). This right should be communicated to them before they give their consent. You also need to consider the issue of withdrawal after data collection. Usually, there will logically be a point when participants can no longer withdraw. For example, a participant can no longer withdraw their data if you have quoted them in a write-up that has been submitted and may be in the public domain. At the consent stage, therefore, explain to your participants their right to withdraw, what this means and the limits to this withdrawal (for example, that they can stop at any time during the interview and withdraw their data immediately or, if they decide after the interview to withdraw, they can withdraw their data but only up until a certain date, such as one month before you have to hand in your work).

Effects beyond the participants themselves

Ethics is not just about the effect on the participants, but the potential impact the study has on other people. For example, research materials that might inadvertently reinforce racist stereotypes will be problematic not just because they might cause offence to individuals who read them, but because they reinforce such stereotypes in society more widely. Thinking through these broader consequences often involves considering what the media, policymakers, or political groups might do with your research findings.

Want to know more about the wider impact of research?

For a discussion on how homophobic comments from straight men influenced the discussion of risk in relation to HIV/AIDS see:

Kitzinger, J. (1994) 'The methodology of focus groups: the Importance of interaction between research participants', *Sociology of Health and Illness*, 16(1), 103–21.
Or for an example of a reflection on the potential harm to participants of a study on illegal drug use see:
Measham, F., Aldridge, J. and Parker, H. (2001) *Dancing on Drugs: Risk, Health and Hedonism in the British Club Scene.* London: Free Association Books.

Your research may also affect you emotionally, such as feeling distressed when a participant shares a story of a traumatic experience. If this is relevant for you, make sure you've got support arranged and speak to your supervisor. You and your supervisor will also need to consider any other implications for your safety as you plan your research and a risk assessment might need to be completed. Talk to your supervisor about any potential safety issues (for example, collecting data in potentially risky situations, contact with strangers or certain kinds of equipment or substances) and remember that your project should not put you in harm's way without protection.

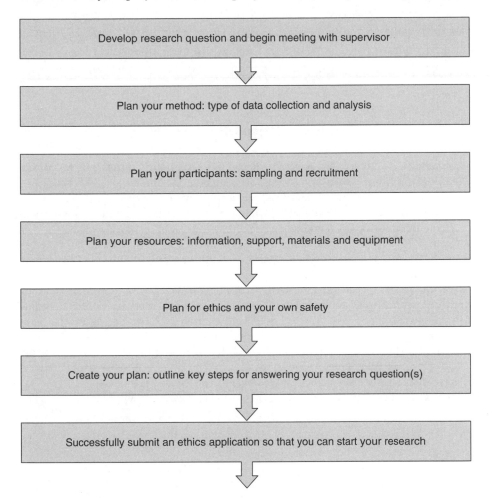

Figure 3.3 Summing up the planning process

Want to know more about ethics?

King, N. (2010) 'Research ethics in qualitative research', in M. Forrester (ed.) *Doing Qualitative Research in Psychology: A Practical Guide*. London: Sage. pp. 98–118.

The British Psychological Society's code of conduct can be downloaded from their website, and this covers research ethics for psychologists (http://www.bps.org.uk/).

Conclusion

You should now be in a position to create a comprehensive plan for your project, with clear ideas for what methods and resources you will use and why. The process of planning as we have described is summarised in Figure 3.3 'Summing up the planning process'.

Now its time to implement your plan. To do so, you will need to focus on managing your project in terms of timetabling and supervision (discussed in Chapter 5); collecting your data (Chapter 6) and data analysis (Chapter 7).

References

Chamberlain, K. (2004) 'Qualitative research, reflexivity and context', in M. Murray. (ed.) *Critical Health Psychology.* Basingstoke: Palgrave Macmillan. pp. 121–136.

Condor, S. (1997) 'And so say all of us? Some thoughts on "experiential democratization" as an aim for critical social psychologists', in T. Ibanez and L. Iniguez (eds) *Critical Social Psychology.* London: Sage. pp. 111–46.

Milgram, S. (1974) *Obedience to Authority: An Experimental View.* New York: Harper & Row.

Nairn, K., Munro, J. and Smith, A.B. (2005) 'A counter-narrative of a "failed" interview', *Qualitative Research*, 5, 221–44.

Patton, M.Q. (2002) *Qualitative Research and Evaluation Methods* (3rd edn). Sage: London.

Riley, S.C.E., Griffin, C. and Morey Y. (2010a) 'The case for "everyday politics": evaluating neo-tribal theory as a way to understand alternative forms of political participation, using electronic dance music culture as an example', *Sociology*, 44(2), 345–63.

Riley, S.C.E., Thompson, J. and Griffin, C. (2010b) 'Turn on, tune in, but don't drop out: The impact of neo-liberalism on magic mushroom users (in)ability to imagine collectivist social worlds', *International Journal of Drug Policy*, 21, 445–51

Robson, C. (2011) *Real World Research* (3rd edn). Chichester: Wiley.

4

MANAGING THE PROJECT

Sarah Riley and Nigel King

Having developed a clear plan for your research and got it ethically approved, you're ready to start doing your research. This can be an exciting time – you can feel like you're finally doing research and being a 'proper' psychologist. But, it can also be a very stressful period.

Stress can occur when you're not clear on what you're doing, when you're doing it or why you're doing it. Another source of stress can be your supervisor – if they seem unavailable for example, or that experience of impending doom when they want to see you and you haven't done any work. And because qualitative projects often involve in-depth interactions with other people, a third potential stressor is the emotional work that comes with such interactions.

A little bit of stress might be good for focusing your mind on your project, but too much stress is never helpful. So in this chapter we outline some of the ways that you can manage your qualitative research project to maximise pleasure and minimise pain. To do so we consider: time management and planning; the student–supervisor relationship; and the dynamics between you and your research participants.

In a nutshell: managing the project

This chapter is structured around the following key issues:

1   Time management:
    creating a feasible project;
    using sub-goals;
    planning for the cyclical nature of qualitative analysis.

(Continued)

(Continued)

2 The student–supervisor relationship:
   a unique relationship that develops over time;
   the need to harmonise your working styles;
   how to be proactive.

3 The impact of the researcher on the research:
   considering the power dynamics between you and your participants;
   how class, gender, ethnicity, and embodiment may impact on your research.

4 The impact of the research on the researcher:
   learning to negotiate the emotional aspects of research, including upset and frustration;
   how research can change our perspectives and relationships.

In order to illustrate some of the key issues in this chapter, we will use an example of 'Suzy's' final year project, described in the box below. Like all successful projects, Suzy faces some challenges along the way. It's how she deals with these – in discussion with her supervisor – that ultimately make her project a success.

Success story: strangers in a strange land?

Suzy Lee came to Britain from Singapore to study psychology at Goldborough University. Having been attracted to qualitative methods in her second year, she has chosen to carry out a qualitative project, examining overseas students' experiences of coming to study in the UK. She wants to use a phenomenological approach to explore this topic, because her interest is in what 'being an overseas student' is like for her participants, and she plans to use semi-structured interviews to collect her data. She completes an ethics approval form, which is passed following some minor amendments.

Following her first meeting with her supervisor, Dr Hilton, Suzy agrees to develop an interview schedule and carry out and transcribe one preliminary interview, so she and her supervisor can look at it together. She interviews a close friend and is quite pleased with the data she obtains, though feels at times she rushed through certain topics and didn't probe enough beyond a fairly superficial level. She discusses her concerns with her supervisor, having provided him with the transcript to read, and they together conclude that part of the problem may be that the topic is too broad. Suzy therefore changes her aims to narrow the focus down from the experience of being an overseas student as a whole to that of the initial arrival, course induction and the first few weeks of study.

Suzy carries out three more interviews with the revised aims and some related modifications to questions. Another four participants are identified through snowball sampling and both she and Dr Hilton are happy with the outcomes in terms of the depth of the accounts provided. Next she carries out some preliminary analysis on all four interviews to present to her supervisor. Through doing this, she notes that the final participant describes some very different experiences from the first three. Reflecting on this with her supervisor, she suspects that the national/cultural background of the students may be important: the last participant came from Ghana, while the three previous ones all came from South East Asia (Singapore, Hong Kong and Indonesia). She therefore recruits two more participants from different parts of the world – one from Libya and one from Greece. In between carrying out interviews, Suzy makes a start on drafts of her literature review and methodology sections.

Following the lengthy and painstaking process of transcribing all the interviews, Suzy embarks on analysing the data. She is worried that she is several weeks behind her original timetable, and may find it difficult to carry out the analysis properly and write up her project as well as possible. She reviews her plans with Dr Hilton and decides to exclude the first interview from the full analysis; the fact that it was wider in scope than the following ones reassures her that she can present this as a methodologically based decision. Suzy completes the analysis, and is happy to find she is able to highlight some really interesting detail in the lived experience of her participants. Having already made a good start on the first sections of her project, and with ongoing advice from her supervisor, Suzy is able to submit the finished work two days before the deadline.

Time management and planning

Part of Suzy's story involves focusing on time management and planning at different stages in her project. In Chapter 3 we discussed planning a timetable and ethical issues at the beginning of your project. It's also good practice to revisit your timetable once your project has been granted ethical approval.

Timetables are useful because they help you identify the stages that you need to go through to do an excellent project. Often we think that we know these stages, but it's only when we write them down that we realise there were gaps in our knowledge or problems with what we planned to do (for example, forgetting to factor in school holidays in a school-based project). Timetables are also useful in helping you keep track of your project, so you can spot if you are beginning to slip behind your schedule, and can do something about it before it's too late. Finally, a good timetable helps you focus on doing the work in hand, rather than using important brain power just to remember all the things you need to do!

In a nutshell: writing timetables

To write a timetable that will help you manage your project and not sit on a pinboard being studiously ignored or making you feel guilty, we recommend that you do the following:

- Outline the activities you need to do ('sub-goaling'). The more specific you make these the better.
- Consider how these activities will flow from one to the other.
- Consider the resources you need for each of these activities.
- Ask yourself if these activities are feasible and feasible in the time you've allocated to them.
- Recognise that qualitative projects often have cyclical not linear designs.

Don't just take our word for it – these principles follow from Locke's goal setting theory (see, for example, Locke and Latham, 2002), which is 'probably the most consistently supported theory in work and organisational psychology' (Arnold et al. 2005: 327).

Step 1: outlining your activities

Think through all the steps you need to go through to complete your project. These steps are likely to include the range of activities we list below, which we will discuss in more detail in the following section.

- Identifying a research question, conducting a literature review and developing a conceptual framework for your study.
- Considering the ethical implications of your study and submitting an ethics application.
- Deciding appropriate participants (numbers, sampling and recruitment strategy).
- Identifying equipment needed and where to source this (such as interview guides/schedules, recording equipment, transcription equipment).
- Recruiting participants (if relevant).
- Collecting data (for example, interviewing participants).
- Transcribing and anonymising data.
- Cycles of data analysis, which may also involve reviewing your research questions.
- Reviewing the literature (for new work and in the light of your analysis).
- Writing up (which in itself is likely to create another cycle of analysis).

For more details on planning for these activities see Chapter 3.

Step 2: considering the resources, feasibility and flow of activities

Your activities will either flow from one to another or run in parallel. For example, you could recruit all your participants first, or aim to be recruiting and collecting data simultaneously by interviewing participants as you recruit them. It is useful to imagine yourself doing each activity and seeing how these activities fit together. Write down these activities and against each activity write down the dates when you plan to do them. Ask yourself if what you plan is feasible. For example, can you recruit 10 participants in a week? And if so, what exactly do you need to do to achieve that? Remember also, to plan your activities around other activities that either you or your participants have to do (for example, when you need to focus on exams or other assignments or when participants will be away on school holidays).

Step 3: outline a cyclical design

Traditional scientific research takes a linear design, in the sense that research-ers aim to follow a set of processes in this order: identify a theory → create a hypothesis to test the theory → collect data → analyse data → conclude if hypothesis is supported. This model is called 'linear' because one thing follows another in a set order and these activities do not cross over. It is often consid-ered the hallmark of quality in quantitative research. However, for qualitative researchers, data collection, analysis and theory development can all fold into each other and do not need to be kept separate. This produces a 'cyclical' research design, as can be seen in the example of Suzy's project (Figure 4.1).

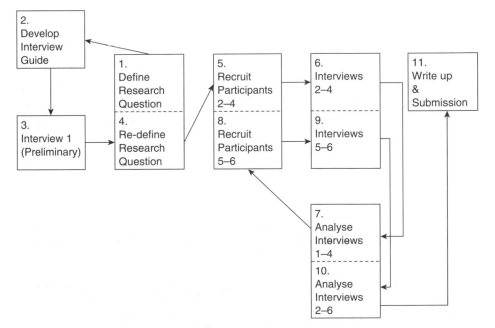

Figure 4.1 Example of a cyclical design, from Suzy's project

It may be that your project is much simpler than that shown in Figure 4.1, but even the most straightforward qualitative projects require you to undertake several cycles of analysis (see Chapter 7 for more on analysing your data).

During data analysis qualitative researchers often revise their research questions. For example, Kathy Charmaz (1995) talked about her work with chronically ill people. Such work might start with a broad question, such as, 'How do chronically ill people experience their illness?' However, as the data is analysed, key themes that come out might suggest a more focused question. For example, if a key theme to emerge from participants' talk is 'disclosure' in that chronically ill people have to decide whether to disclose their illness when they meet people, then the researcher might reframe the research question to something that more specifically addresses this theme. For example, 'How do chronically ill people manage disclosure?' The researcher would then have to decide if this question can be answered using the current data set or if it required the collection of new and more focused data. If you feel you need to redefine your research questions in the light of preliminary data analysis, make sure you discuss this with your supervisor first (see Chapter 2 for more on research questions).

Cyclical designs mean that you must leave a significant amount of time to do the analysis – we recommend planning to leave between one-third and one-quarter of your project time for analysis and write-up. Even experienced researchers tend to underestimate how long particular stages of a research project will take, so it is not a bad rule of thumb to work out how long you need for each activity on your timetable – and then double it. The box below shows the timetable produced by Suzy for her project on overseas students' experiences, which was based on the suggestions we outlined in Chapter 3. As we noted in our summary of Suzy's project above, in reality there was some slippage at the data collection and analysis stage, but she was able to retrieve this because she and her supervisor monitored her progress against the timetable regularly. It's also worth noting that your timetable will of course vary depending on the way in which the project is organised at your institution.

Suzy's original project timetable

OCTOBER

Define research question; start literature review/background reading (topic and method); develop interview schedule; complete ethics form; organise equipment

NOVEMBER

First wave of participant recruitment; complete equipment booking and material development (interview schedule); carry out and transcribe preliminary interview; revise interview schedule as necessary; work on literature review

---

DECEMBER/JANUARY

Recruit rest of participants; interview participants; transcribe interviews; complete drafts of literature review and methodology sections

FEBRUARY/MARCH/APRIL

Complete transcription of interviews; analysis; review literature for recent work, or work that is now relevant to the analysis

APRIL/MAY

Write-up and submission

Timetables: the last word

You can use your timetable to facilitate good communication with your supervisor. Bring your timetable with you to meetings and discuss your plans. Once your project is up and running, keep your timetable somewhere you can see it and refer to it. If you find yourself getting behind you may need to revise it – in which case it's always advisable to consult your supervisor.

Top tip: keeping track

If you are going to leave your project for any length of time write yourself a note that outlines what you were doing or thinking at the time. Include, for example, any decisions you had recently made, the rationale behind these decisions, and any plans you had to action these decisions. This note will act as an *aide-mémoire* – bringing you back into the moment when you left your project. If you don't write such a note you may find that when you come back to your project you've forgotten much of what you'd been thinking and you'll have to spend precious time trying to make sense of your own paperwork!

The student–supervisor relationship

Each relationship between student and supervisor is unique and develops over time as both parties learn about each other's preferred styles of working and approach to undertaking qualitative research projects. It might be the first time that you've worked with your supervisor and this can make it intimidating or leave you unsure of what's expected. Here we will start by examining the key issue of communication between student and supervisor, and then look at some of the main causes of problems in this relationship and what you might do about them. We will then pay particular attention to how you can make the supervisory relationship work at its best at the crucial stage of data analysis. Finally we will discuss some of the issues that can arise when supervision is provided to groups of students rather than on a one-to-one basis.

Good communication between you and your supervisor means that you are likely to develop a sense of shared ownership of your project. This will let you feel positive about and interested in your work and thus more likely to work harder on it and enjoy working on it. And in turn, it means that your supervisor is more likely to give you the focus and in-depth advice you need to develop the project into an excellent qualitative study. If that wasn't motivation enough, remember that learning to manage your supervisor at university will help you develop a set of skills you can transfer into your future (or current) employment. Below we outline some of the ways to facilitate good student–supervisor relationships.

In a nutshell: how to have a positive student–supervisor relationship

- Develop mutual respect and shared interest in the subject (for example by reading up on the subject before your first supervision meeting).
- Have regular and meaningful contact (for some people this may be monthly meetings, for others you may want more contact towards the beginning and end of the project – discuss this with your supervisor as your institution may have particular guidelines on the timing and number of meetings).
- Use your timetable to set clear goals and deadlines.
- Have early in-depth discussions to enable clear and shared understanding of the project, and to find out what your supervisor's expectations are for both of you (such as when you should meet or who initiates meetings).
- Try to recognise your own and your supervisor's preferred communication styles and reflect on how to harmonise these.
- Make notes during your meeting so that you can follow up what you've agreed
- Keep your supervisor informed if you are having difficulties or if you want to significantly change your plan.
- Use other relevant resources (for example, if you're having literature review problems make an appointment to see your librarian in the first instance).
- If your supervisor has published in the area of your study – read their work.

Troubleshooting: if the relationship sours

The supervisory relationship is often enjoyable and valuable for both parties. But, as with any kind of relationship, things sometimes go wrong. In this section we will consider some of the main causes of problems in this relationship, and how you might try to prevent or alleviate them.

Lack of work by the student

Supervisors know when you haven't done any work and get frustrated if they're having meetings they think are a waste of time. So if you haven't done any work and have a meeting set up, then do one of the following.

- Postpone the meeting, but only for a few days so that you can do some work and get on top of the project. If you leave it for longer, you're likely to be avoiding a problem that will only get worse with delay.
- Quickly review what you've done so far on the project before your meeting, so at least you can start from where you left off last time you saw them.
- Be open about your lack of work and explain why. Often students haven't done work because there's a problem. For example, time management, not really understanding what to do, not having the confidence to do what's been agreed, personal problems interfering with work or participants apparently stalling the project. Your supervisor is there to help make your project run as smoothly as possible, so bring these issues to their attention. Most times they'll have solutions for you; after all, they've probably had to deal with similar problems before with other students or in their own work.

Lack of engagement by the supervisor

You should feel a sense of ownership of your project, and there will be times when your supervisor will encourage this by taking a more 'hands off' approach. Indeed, some students can expect too much input from the supervisor – it is not the supervisor's job to tell you how to conduct your research, or to analyse your data for you. Most supervisors will be good at managing this process, knowing when to give more direction, and when to stand back a little. Occasionally, however, you might encounter a supervisor who perhaps isn't as engaged with your project as they might be.

Managing a supervisor who doesn't seem engaged is a difficult task, particularly because of the power imbalance in the relationship. If you think you have this problem it's probably useful to deal with it in stages. First, reframe your thinking and consider that your supervisor has your best interests at heart, but for some reason is not able to apparently act in that way. This might help you identify ways of improving your supervisor's engagement with you. For example, is it a time management problem? Your supervisor may receive up to 100 emails a day and sometimes they overlook one. So if you've sent an important email and haven't had a reply after a couple of days, it's ok to send a polite reminder. Similarly, if you think your supervisor only skim reads emails, then make your emails short and clear, and schedule meetings to discuss issues in depth.

If, after trying to see the problem from the supervisor's point of view you are still left with the conclusion that they are not interested in your project, then you need to develop a different strategy. We would always suggest you try to discuss your concerns with your supervisor first, as politely and calmly as possible. Avoid accusations, as these may tend to provoke a hostile response by backing the supervisor into a corner. Focus instead on how you have experienced the supervision process and what you feel about it. It may be helpful to acknowledge that you might have misread the situation, allowing the supervisor to take your feelings seriously without having to become defensive to save face. If such an approach still fails to resolve the situation, you will probably have to involve an outside party (or parties). You may approach another member of staff who you have a relationship with (for example, a personal tutor) to see if they can liaise with your supervisor on your behalf or help you with a strategy for dealing with your supervisor. Alternatively, there may be a lecturer who has overall responsibility for running the project module who is in the best position to help you.

Should all such efforts prove unsuccessful, you may decide that the only option is to change supervisors. It is important to find out on what criteria your institution would consider such requests. For example, claiming a clash of personalities will probably not get you very far, but if you feel that your study has now developed into an area more appropriate for another member of staff then you may be able to argue more successfully for a change.

Sometimes these problems are easily resolved and it's a transferable skill to learn to behave in a professional and diplomatic way in the face of difficulties. However, if you are upset or feel you need support, then use the resources you have at your institution to help support you – such as personal tutors, year leaders, programme directors, student representatives or the student union.

The over-controlling supervisor

Occasionally, students may feel that far from being disengaged, their supervisor is assuming too much control over their project. They are telling the student exactly what to do and when to do it, and may seem dismissive of suggestions that counter the direction in which they are leading the project. If you feel this is happening to you, again we suggest you try to think about how the situation may appear to your supervisor. If you have fallen behind your original schedule, and/or have repeatedly failed to complete work agreed in the previous meeting, they may feel that they need to impose more direction on you to recover your situation. Once you are back on course, your supervisor will probably be happy to allow you to assume more control. Another possibility is that what you perceive as excessive control is just a sign of your supervisor's enthusiasm for your project – this is particularly likely where you are working in an area that is very closely aligned to their own interests. In most respects such enthusiasm is greatly to your advantage: you will certainly get your supervisor's full attention, they will be able to direct you to cutting-edge literature and you will be able to learn directly from their own research experience. So long as you also show excitement about the topic, negotiating for more control over the direction of your project should not be difficult.

The most serious problems relating to supervisor control occur in the very rare instances where a student feels that the supervisor is attempting to use their project purely for their own ends: for example to collect additional data that they are then going to use in their own research. There is actually nothing wrong in principle with a student's project being incorporated into the supervisor's programme of research, so long as this is done openly and the focus on the project as a major piece of assessed academic work is not lost. Indeed, you may have a great deal to gain from such an arrangement, in terms of support, access to resources and perhaps the possibility of publishing your work (see below). However, if the supervisor appears to be only interested in what your project can do for them, you need to address this just as you would for the case of the seriously disengaged supervisor discussed above. The bottom line here is that your project is *your* work – in all likelihood the single most important piece of work you produce in your degree. It is never right for your supervisor to take over ownership of it.

Sometimes when your project has gone very well, and produced really interesting findings, your supervisor may suggest that you try to write it up for publication in an academic journal, with their help. This can be an extremely valuable opportunity for you if you are planning to go on to postgraduate study, perhaps with a view to an academic or practitioner career. Should you decide to attempt this, it is important that you are committed. You will also need the skills to do this or have a supervisor who is happy to apply their writing skills.

Discuss authorship at the outset. It is entirely appropriate that your supervisor should be included as an author on any resulting journal article, but equally they should have an active involvement in the writing process – commenting on drafts, perhaps writing certain sections, and so on. Writing a journal article is a very different task from writing a student research project, and involves a good deal of hard work. So although some professional bodies suggest that students should be first authors on their work, in many instances it is entirely appropriate for a supervisor to be first author. (For further discussion of writing up for publication see Chapter 10.)

Supervisor's lack of qualitative research experience

While most institutions try to match student projects to supervisor expertise, sometimes this is just not possible – perhaps your department only has a few members of staff with qualitative expertise, or your supervisor has been allocated on the basis of topic area rather than methodology. You may then find yourself in the uncomfortable position of knowing more about the methods you want to use than your supervisor does, and feel anxious that they are unable to advise you as to whether you are going about your research in the right way. Some strategies for dealing with this situation include the following:

- Share with your supervisor some of the methodological literature you have found most useful.
- Ask whether it is possible to see examples of qualitative projects from previous years.
- Talk about your research with friends from your course who are also doing qualitative projects (though be very careful not to plagiarise their work).
- Ask your supervisor whether you could approach another member of staff for specific expert advice. They may prefer to do this for you on your behalf.

Remember that good supervision is more about helping you manage the process of your research rather than the fine detail; methodological expertise on the part of your supervisor is certainly an advantage, but not the most critical aspect of project supervision.

Supervision and data analysis

One of the great things about qualitative projects is the data. You'll probably have loads of it and it will all be interesting. But trying to find patterns in your data or move your analysis from descriptive to conceptual analyses are significant challenges. The best way to meet these challenges successfully is to be able to talk to your supervisor about your data, and to do this you need to be familiar with it. This may sound obvious, but often students aren't as familiar with their data as they think they are.

To be familiar with your data you need to read through your transcripts (or other forms of data that you're using) several times. Make sure you can talk confidently about what's in them and try to outline some codes or patterns in the data that you can take to your supervisor. If you're struggling with the analysis in some way, try to reflect on what it is that you're finding difficult. For example, does it all seem relevant, none of it relevant, or can you not find a way to 'break into' the data. Talking to your supervisor about the exact nature of your difficulty will help them find solutions that work for you. (Also see Chapter 7 for advice on troubleshooting common problems with your analysis.)

Supervisory relationships in group supervision

Some universities now organise project supervision on a group basis, rather than one-to-one. There are two main models of this. It may involve a true group project in which each student collects data on the same topic and then all the data are shared among the group. Data are then analysed and the research project written up on an individual basis. Alternatively, students may be conducting separate individual projects, but with a common broad topic and/or methodology. Usually where group supervision is used there is some one-to-one contact with the supervisor in the latter stages of the project, but most sessions are held with the whole group. There are a number of important points to reflect upon if you are to get the most from group supervision.

- Make an effort to contribute to sessions. If you just sit quietly in the corner you will not gain all you could from supervision. In particular, don't worry that your question or comment may seem foolish – in all likelihood if something has occurred as an issue for you it will have done so for other members of the group. They will probably be grateful to you for raising it.
- Learn from your fellow students. Meet outside of the supervision sessions to share your thoughts, ideas or concerns. The opportunity to gain from peer interaction is a real bonus of group supervision. Students can benefit from group work in terms of sharing the work load – such as identifying relevant readings or reducing the amount of transcription you need to do. Group projects can also create the kinds of benefits students get from study groups, such as being able to develop, explore and share ideas. But be careful if sharing the details of your analysis and write-up. Although fruitful synergies can occur doing this, it can also lead to intentional or inadvertent plagiarism, so in general we would recommend that when it comes to writing up you do this individually.
- Do not put up with free-riding from other members of the group. By this we mean cases where one person makes little or no contribution to the group, but then expects other members to help them out. If you feel this is happening, talk to your fellow supervisees and together explain to the person involved why you are not happy with their behaviour. Should the problem persist, talk to your supervisor about it.

Dynamics between you and your participants

The other relationship you have to think about in your research is the one you have with your participants. And, as with your supervisor, this relationship is a two way process – who you are will affect how your participants engage with you. And in turn, your participants – and perhaps the project topic itself – may affect you, sometimes in unexpected ways.

In a nutshell: researcher–participant relationships

All relationships – however positive – contain power relationships, and it is important for researchers to reflect on how power may manifest itself in their projects. Researchers are usually considered to hold more power (reversing your situation with your supervisor).

(Continued)

(Continued)

As researchers we are powerful because we are in charge of the project (we ask the interview questions, for example) and because we represent institutions (such as a university or an academic discipline such as psychology or sociology). These institutions are loaded with social power, so although you may see yourself as 'just a student', you need to be sensitive to participants who may see you as representing something much more powerful.

Characteristics such as your age, gender, ethnicity and other aspects of what you look like will also affect how participants engage with you. For example, one of Sarah's students ran a series of focus groups with women significantly older than herself about their experiences of contemporary beauty ideals. Tensions emerged in the process because it was apparent that the participants were comparing themselves to her and finding themselves wanting (in their eyes she was young and beautiful, and they were older and less beautiful). The student had not considered herself beautiful and so hadn't prepared for how her appearance was viewed by her participants.

It's useful to consider, as thoughtfully as possible, how you differ from your participants and how that might impact on their responses to you (this is part of a wider issue called 'reflexivity', which is discussed in more detail in Chapter 8). How you as a person may affect the way that participants respond to you is an issue to discuss with your supervisor before you start collecting data. To make the most of your discussion we recommend that you read up on the subject (see for example, King and Horrocks, 2010).

Sometimes it may feel that the participants have more power than you. After all, you usually need them more than they need you. You may experience participants who were apparently very supportive of the project now acting in ways that seem to be sabotaging it. And you'll almost certainly be 'stood up' on occasion, which is frustrating. Alternatively, there may be cross-overs with other power structures, such as gender, that make you feel vulnerable or wrong footed – see for example, Riley et al. (2003) for an analysis of such examples. It's important to talk to your supervisor if you have any of these feelings or if these experiences are troubling you.

Cautionary tale: the researcher–participant relationship

While Suzy enjoyed interviewing her participants, her fourth interview raised some difficult issues for her. The participant was Lastri, a first-year, female student from Indonesia. Lastri is 19 years old and had only had one brief trip to England before coming to study here. While there are many Indonesian students at the university, Lastri is the only one on her course and in the student accommodation block where she lives. She told Suzy that she felt very isolated and lonely, and was too shy to try and get to know British students, whose interests and lifestyles often felt very different from hers. After the interview, she emailed Suzy several times, saying how nice it was to talk to someone who was interested in her story, and asking whether Suzy could call round and see her some time. Suzy was worried about Lastri's well-being, and also felt uncomfortable that she was trying to develop their relationship into a friendship that Suzy didn't want.

Suzy took her concerns to her supervisor, Dr Hilton, who reassured her they were legitimate. He talked about how researchers' perspectives on relationships with participants differed, but that sometimes researchers feel that more is being asked of them than they can give. He also noted that it was important that Lastri wasn't negatively affected by her participation in the project. So together they worked out a plan for finding support for Lastri that didn't rely on an unwanted emotional relationship with Suzy.

They decided that Suzy should identify appropriate sources of support for Lastri and make contact with them to help facilitate the development of Lastri's social network. After some email communication with the overseas students support officer, Suzy met with Lastri and introduced her to two students who had volunteered for a student buddy system where older students provide social support for new students. Suzy also sent Lastri an email with links to some clubs and societies that matched interests she had mentioned in the interview. At this point she carefully explained that her research perspective meant that she needed to keep a bit of distance between herself and her participants and so wouldn't be able to meet up with Lastri, but would love to hear from her with an occasional email. From her response, Lastri seemed happy with this. At the end of the term Lastri sent Suzy an email saying she now felt she was settling in much better to university life.

The nature of qualitative work means that you may emotionally connect with your participants, particularly if your project involves repeated meetings or sensitive questions. Even apparently 'safe' questions such as the example of asking about a music collection can illicit powerful emotions and stories from participants (see Chapter 3's cautionary tale 'unexpected revelations'). You need to plan strategies for dealing with these situations and for how your research may 'spill over' into other aspects of your life. For example, is there a chance that in your social life you could bump into a participant? Do participants have a right to think of you as a friend if you've met them several times and they've told you intimate details about their life? Alternatively, if you recruit friends or family members as participants, how might the research process impact on your subsequent relationships with them? It is useful to reflect on these issues as you plan your study, so that you can best protect and support yourself and your participants.

An important way that research can spill over into researchers' lives is when you respond emotionally to what participants have told you or what you have found out about vulnerable people's lives (this can happen even if you are working with secondary data or data produced without interacting with participants, such as Internet archives). If you are dealing with sensitive issues or feel upset by your data make sure you speak with your supervisor, and if necessary, organise other forms of support such as those offered by your university counselling service.

Our last comment on how research can affect the researcher is to note that knowledge is a powerful thing. It can change you. And with any change there is a loss of the old self. Sarah, for example, has been delighted watching some of her students gain a feminist political consciousness through their thesis only to realise that this process was double-edged: the students had gained and celebrated a new way of thinking but in doing so they became alienated from some of their previous relationships.

Conclusion

A well-run project is one that is thoughtfully conceived, and where the researcher regularly refers to and updates their plan if necessary. We hope we have given you some useful guidance as to how you might achieve this. All projects have their ups and downs, but if you can plan ahead so that you have a sense of the activities you need to do to successfully bring together this significant piece of work, then you are in a good position to ride through any difficult patches. While we have focused on potential problems in this chapter, remember that completing your own research project, and developing a good working relationship with your supervisor, can be among the most satisfying aspects of your student career.

Want to know more about supervisor relationships?

http://www.vitae.ac.uk/

This is a website for postgraduate students, but with information on the supervisor–supervised relationship that is relevant for both undergraduate and postgraduates.

References

Arnold, J., Silvester, J., Patterson, F., Robertson, I., Cooper, C. and Burnes, B. (2005) *Work Psychology: Understanding Human Behaviour in the Workplace.* Harlow: Pearson.

Charmaz, K. (1995) 'Grounded theory', in J.A. Smith, R. Harré and L. Van Langerhowe (eds) *Rethinking Methods in Psychology*. London: Sage. pp. 27–49

King, N. and Horrocks, C. (2010) *Interviews in Qualitative Research*. London: Sage.

Locke, E.A. and Latham, G.P. (2002) 'Building a practically useful theory of goal setting and task motivation: a 35-year odyssey', *American Psychologist*, 57, 705–17.

Riley, S., Schouten, W. and Cahill, S. (2003) 'Exploring the dynamics of subjectivity and power between researcher and researched', *Forum for Qualitative Social Research*, 4(2). Online journal available at: http://www.qualitative-research.net/fqs-texte/2–03/2rileyetal-e.htm (accessed 3 September 2010).

5

DOING A LITERATURE REVIEW

Michael Forrester

Introduction

An excellent research project hinges on a good research question, and a good research question requires you to be familiar with previous research and theories. This is why one of the initial tasks associated with a dissertation, a final-year project and other similar research-focused activities is conducting a literature review of previously published work. Typically this would follow on from you having already gained some familiarity with an area from an appropriate textbook where they are available.

Literature reviews usually happen at three key points in a project:

- during the development of your research question;
- during the planning stages, as you work out the rationale of the steps you need to take to complete your project; and
- towards the end of the project, either because:

  - preliminary analysis points you towards literature you had not previously considered, or
  - to check for relevant studies published since your previous literature searches.

In this chapter my aim is to provide guidance on how to carry out a literature review during the development of your research question. Please note, however, that if you plan to use grounded theory, then your review would be delayed and carried out after some initial data collection (see Chapter 7). You need to carry out a thorough literature review at this stage to:

- find out what has already been done;
- understand the kinds of questions people interested in your general topic area have already been asking; and
- get to grips with the issues that are relevant to your area of interest.

To help you with this task, this chapter is divided into four main sections representing key components of a literature review. Although the focus of this chapter is on doing a literature review in order to develop your research question, these components are relevant for any other time in your project when you need to do a literature review.

In a nutshell: key literature review components

- Searching and locating relevant research, journals, books and related information sources.
- Identifying and categorising literature in a given area (including establishing what constitutes 'relevant' material).
- Constructing an account (telling a story) about the research, which can be chronological, thematic and/or discipline focused.
- Understanding the relationship between your literature review and research question(s).

In order to illustrate how these four components relate to each other, throughout the chapter I will use an example based on a literature review I recently carried out on conversation analysis (CA) research on pre-school children's conversational skills. The selected example is deliberate because the topic is of interest to a range of researchers, but the method I'm interested in is a specialist area. This meant that I had to find ways of identifying relevant studies from a large pool of research, much of which was not relevant to my needs. I then had to find ways of synthesising the relevant studies, so that I could write a review. The problems I encountered are similar to those that students face when conducting a literature review at the beginning of their project, and so my example helps demonstrate some solutions to these challenges.

Finding relevant material

There are a number of key bibliographic information systems that you can call upon when first searching (for example, ISI's Web of Knowledge; PsycINFO; EBSCOHost; PEP-Web Search). These facilities hold vast databases of published research, but may not contain all the studies relevant to your project. This is because these databases are associated with particular institutions or disciplines. For example, PsycINFO holds information on psychological publications, and so psychology students studying the topic of 'motherhood' might miss relevant sociological studies if they only used PsycINFO for their literature search. It's important therefore to think about the topic that you're studying and the available bibliographic information systems your institution offers, so that you can identify which combination of databases you could use to best suit your needs.

By this stage it is likely you will have gained some familiarity with the various bibliographic information systems available to you and have some knowledge of the practicalities of accessing them. But, if you're unsure, speak to your librarian.

One of the difficulties in doing a literature review to develop your research question is knowing what to search for when you don't yet know what might be relevant. So to conduct your review you need to be able to:

- search effectively; and
- determine relevance.

To search effectively you need to develop a strategy to search bibliographic databases that is consistent, realisable and methodical. This involves:

- doing a series of searches that strategically use key words, 'wildcards' and 'Boolean operators' (discussed below) to identify studies that are relevant to your project;
- organising your search findings so that you can conceptually map out the thinking of previous researchers on your subject.

Bibliographic information systems work by identifying articles (and other academic outputs such as book chapters or conference proceedings) that have the key words you've entered somewhere in the article (usually the title, author or abstract).

You can combine key words together in various ways to structure these searches. For example, you can ask for articles in specific journals by specific authors with a specific key word in the title. Alternatively you could give a combination of key words to be found in the title or abstract. This is where 'wildcards' and 'Boolean operators' (for example, AND, OR, NOT, WITH) can be used. These are codes that you can use to specify your searches. For example an asterisk (*) is a wildcard that allows you to search for different variants of the same term, and can be useful if you're looking for all the work by a particular author.

For example, a search for Forrester M* would identify publications by me where I've used my initial and also where I've called myself Michael (or Mike). It would also identify work by all the other Forresters whose first initial is M. So, if you only wanted to focus on my work because you were interested in CA, you might use the Boolean operator AND; to ask for 'Forrester M* and conversation analysis'. Asterisks are also useful if you've got a topic term that can be shortened, for example, if you were interested in research on children's talk you could type in 'children and talk*' which would pick up research with children that use either the term 'talk' or 'talking'.

There are many wildcards and Boolean operators, and not all are used across all the bibliographic information systems. So check the online help of the system you're using.

Want to know more about searching databases?

For an accessible and detailed discussion of how to use key words, wildcards and Boolean operators see:

Shaw, R. (2010) 'Conducting literature reviews', in M.A. Forrester (ed.) *Doing Qualitative Research in Psychology: A Practical Guide.* London: Sage. pp. 39–56.

Top tip: strategies for identifying relevant publications

- Start with everyday common sense terms.
- As your search progresses start to recognise the common terms used by authors doing research relevant to your study.
- Search by author for researchers active in your area (ask your supervisor for suggestions).
- Combine your key word searches with wildcards and Boolean operators.
- Use citation searches: if there is a key study in your area, you can use 'citation search' to identify all the papers that reference this key study. This gives you a way of identifying publications that might not use the key words you're searching with but are relevant to your work because you share the need to cite this key study.

However, knowing how to combine key words is not enough if you don't know what key words to use. If you are new to an area, initially only trial and error will reveal whether words closely associated with your key terms turn out to be relevant. At the beginning of a research project, one strategy is to use the most common everyday uses of words that seem relevant to your interests. Putting in these general terms and combining them with other related words will allow you to retrieve many items which may be relevant.

To identify which of these returns are relevant to your study you need a way of systematically analysing the kinds of studies being identified by these key words. Adopting a consistent and careful procedure to searching allows you to:

- create searches that pick up relevant studies;
- 'sift' though the output so you can ignore irrelevant articles;
- summarily describe the studies you find.

By developing a systematic way to search the literature and keep a record of your findings you can quickly gain a good idea of how many relevant studies there are in a field. And before long you will have a good sense of what previous researchers have found out or established, and some of the gaps in their knowledge that you might be able to address with your study.

Top tip: systematically analysing search results

Shaw (2010) provides a set of accessible conceptual tools for systematic searching. Her procedure is to create a mind map of all relevant search terms and use these terms with the 'CHIP' tool (below) to help structure your search terms and to create a summary description of the literature in the field. The CHIP tool requires you to consider the articles you've identified in terms of:

1 the Context of the particular study;
2 How the study was conducted;
3 the Issues examined; and
4 the People involved in the study.

In the literature review I carried out, the relevant terms were 'child', 'conversation' and 'analysis'. Notice immediately the numerous other possibilities associated with each of these terms given in the box below.

Possible search terms associated with three words

Child: infant, school-child, youngster, kid, development, (and more).
Conversation: talk, talking, dialogue, discourse, communication, converse, chat, speaking, speech, rhetoric, communicative (and more).
Analysis: examine, scrutiny, inquiry, break-down, examination, interpretation.

Searching using all these terms would help me identify relevant studies with children that didn't use my specific term of 'child' (for example, those that used 'infant' or 'development'). But using all these terms would also create an overwhelming number of studies, which I wouldn't be able to sift through, and which, for many different reasons would not be relevant to my search. I therefore needed to refine my search strategy.

When refining your search strategy you need to strike a balance between finding 'everything' ever published about a topic and not having such a specific focus that you miss important work within your topic of interest. In a final-year undergraduate project or dissertation at postgraduate level you are not expected to include and review all possible material. Rather, you should review a selected set of work that is relevant to your research topic area.

Top tip: refining the search procedure

My aim was to find studies of children that have involved research using the methodology of CA (which is influenced by a theory known as 'ethnomethodology'). Consider the results of the following searches.

1 Child* = > 100,000 items found
2 Child* and conversation = 1015 items found
3 Child and conversation analysis = 289 items found
4 Child and ethnomethodology = 16 items found

Notice the gradual 'funnelling' of the search and the corresponding reduction of found items. The relatively large number returned for the first three searches is misleadingly high and is likely to include a lot of irrelevant material. Reasons for this include that in search 3, for example, the database will search for anything that includes either 'child and conversation' or 'child and analysis'. I could have chosen to search 'child and conversation with analysis', which may have narrowed my search in the right direction, but instead I relied on my knowledge of the area: 'Conversation analysis' is often described as a form of ethnomethodology and introducing this term immediately constrained the number of returns. I was therefore able to develop my search with my knowledge as a researcher in this area. Novice researchers may have had to more greatly rely on Boolean operators or sift through the titles or abstracts of the 289 articles until they got a sense of the key words being used for articles relevant to their research.

The actual number of articles you need to review will depend on the specific topic area you are working in and the question you are asking. If you find you have either many more, or significantly fewer, items than you would expect from looking at other review articles, then it is likely that your focus is too general or has not become fine-grained enough. In the latter instance it may be that that your searching procedures are possibly missing potentially relevant material. When in doubt ask your supervisor for guidance on this point.

Top tip: read your supervisor

If your supervisor is actively researching in the area of your project, look up their work and include it in your review!

Establish relevance

Alongside the practicalities of actually searching for material, doing your literature review also develops other important skills. In particular, you need to begin evaluating whether a piece of work is relevant or not, and, related to this, whether the research is likely to be of greater or lesser value to your research question (if you have one at this stage). Both dimensions (relevance and value) depend on a variety of factors.

In a nutshell: relevance and value

Ask yourself:

1 Is the focus of my research within or across discipline boundaries (for example, psychology, sociology, social anthropology)?
2 Within a topic area, how is the work evaluated by other researchers?
3 What kinds of methodology are deemed appropriate for the questions asked in this area?
4 What are the main theoretical ideas in the area and does the study I'm looking at explicitly or implicitly orient towards these ideas?
5 What is realisable research in the area in question? Identifying what is typically done, and what might be possible, will help you evaluate any new work you come across. (Also see Chapter 2 for developing your research question.)
6 How relevant does the study I'm looking at seem to my research supervisor or other researchers? When in doubt, advice and guidance from these sources can be invaluable.
7 Don't forget to build up a set of detailed notes that categorise your studies with reference to these questions!

As you begin your search it will quickly become apparent what kinds of questions researchers in any given area have been asking; the kinds of methods they tend to use in their investigations; and, either implicitly or explicitly, the theoretical orientations that are prevalent in a particular area.

One of the most important sources of information to you during your initial searching are the abstracts (or summaries) of papers or research studies, which are often provided through commonly used information systems (sometimes referred to as 'abstracting' systems). Let us turn to some examples from the search stage of my recent review and consider two different studies. I want to highlight aspects of the rationale as to why one paper is included in my review, while the other is not and through doing so highlight the strategies you might use (see Table 5.1).

There are a number of strategies that can be used in combination to help decide about the relevance and value of an article for your review. Below I will outline two of them using my literature review as an example.

In a nutshell: identifying relevance

Strategy 1: Consider (a) the words used, (b) the source of the publication and (c) the authors.

Strategy 2: Being clear about what you are looking for when analysing abstracts.

Table 5.1 Example abstracts examined during review

Paper 1: Ensor, R. & Hughes, C. (2008). Content or connectedness? Mother-child talk and early social understanding. *Child Development, 79*(1), 201–16.	Paper 2: de Leon, L. (2007). Parallelism, metalinguistic play, and the interactive emergence of Zinacantec Mayan siblings' culture. *Research on Language and Social Interaction, 40*(4), 405–36.
Abstract 1: 'Despite much research into individual differences in social understanding among preschoolers, little is known about corresponding individual differences within younger children. Likewise, although studies of preschoolers highlight the importance of mental-state references, other aspects of talk have received less attention. The current study involved 120 families with 2-year-olds; video-based transcripts of observations of family interaction were coded for quantity, connectedness, and content of mothers' and children's talk. At 2, 3, and 4 years of age, children completed social understanding and verbal ability tests. Mothers' connected turns and mental-state reference within connected turns showed independent associations with children's social understanding (as did children's mental-state references, both overall and within connected turns). Connected conversations provide a fertile context for children's developing social understanding.'	Abstract 2: 'In this article, I investigate how two young Tzotzil Mayan siblings playfully manipulate the sequential structure of adjacency pairs to align, to confront each other, and to challenge family roles and hierarchies. The young learners' intentional disruption reveals the early control of dialogic repetition typical of Mayan languages. More important, it illustrates the children's development of communicative competence as they reorganize greeting structures or reauthorize messages through frame shifts. In the case of a greeting game, the siblings disrupt its inherent sequential structure using semantic counterpointing with different address terms. When conveying a question sent by an adult, the 4-year old playfully repeats it and recycles it across several turns in alignment with his younger brother and his grandfather. The subversion of the social organization of talk shows how the children interactively construct an emergent sibling culture that contests the social organization of the age-graded structure of the extended family.'

Strategy 1: Consider (a) the words used, (b) the source of the publication and (c) the authors

Being methodical is key to completing a literature review. So try to be consistent in your approach to each item you examine. As you begin to identify possible papers and chapters, you will quickly start to develop an expertise on the key words, relevant journals and names of the authors who are publishing in your area.

With Paper 1, we find 'mother–child talk' and 'early social understanding' as two typical examples of terms generally related to child conversation. With Paper 2, we find a somewhat different set of phrases or terms, including, 'metalinguistic play', 'interactive emergence' and 'siblings'. As a researcher in CA, I know that the terms in paper 2 are more usually associated with the topic area of my review. For a less experienced researcher, you can make these judgements by relating these terms to what you already know about the subject from your lectures, other reading or discussions with your supervisor.

It is important to remember that you are learning on the job. So, neither you nor your supervisor should expect you to be an expert in the area. It is inevitable that with your first searches a number of publications that could be relevant might escape your attention. Similarly, you might include publications that are not very relevant. Don't worry – your skills and expertise will improve with practice.

As you develop your literature searching abilities, you will be able to tell how likely it is that a paper will be relevant by looking at the journal a paper is published in. For example, although on the face of it, *Child Development* would seem to be a more directly appropriate publication for research on language in children, I know that it is actually the journal that paper 2 is published in (*Research on Language and Social Interaction*) that has a history of publishing CA papers.

As for the authors of papers and chapters, the more you search the more likely it is that you will discover researchers who have published a lot in one specific area and this will give you a clue to the potential relevance of the publication. Again, it can help a great deal if you have already discussed with your supervisor what journals and authors are more likely to publish relevant material for your study.

Strategy 2: Being clear about what you are looking for when analysing abstracts

When it comes to reading and assessing abstracts we can go through a process similar to CHIP (see top tips box above) in order to establish whether an article is worth obtaining and reading. There are a number of specific questions you can ask which will help guide your assessment.

1 Who are the people being researched in this study and are they likely to be relevant to my specific review?

2 What kind of methodology was used? If there is a tendency to use a specific qualitative method for the kind of project you're interested in this question may be relevant. But note that many topics are studied using different methods, so studies that use a range of methods may be relevant for you.
3 What is this research about?
4 What are the main findings? And what does this contribute to the topic?
5 How likely is it that this research will be relevant to my review?

Below, I have addressed these questions by comparing the two abstracts I'd given you earlier. For my review, I was interested in conversation analytic work on children's conversational skills during the pre-school years. This meant that I was looking for papers that used a specific method (CA) to investigate a specific topic (young children's conversational skills).

The processes I went through to assess the relevance of these papers are similar to those that you need to go through for your study. But, your study may require a less focused review. For example, you may not want to limit yourself to research that only used one method. Typically, a review of an area includes research that has used a range of different methodologies. Table 5.2 compares the two abstracts.

The example in Table 5.2 shows you the benefit of developing expertise in recognising technical terms or terms more associated with particular kinds of research. You can see that care should be taken during the early phase

Table 5.2 Key questions for summarising and evaluating the relevance of research papers to your review

	Paper 1	Paper 2
Q1: Who?	120 children in 3 age groups Irrelevant. CA studies rarely use such large samples	2 pre-school siblings Relevant. The intensive work done in CA means CA studies often focus on only a small number of participants
Q2: Methodology?	Quantitative (Coding and correlations) Irrelevant. CA does not usually employ a coding procedure or statistical analysis	Qualitative – CA Relevant. Although CA not mentioned explicitly, CA terms are (e.g. 'adjacency pairs')
Q3: Research Question?	Individual differences in social understanding across ages Unclear. Terms used are ambiguous and could be relevant (e.g. social understanding)	What constitutes sibling culture and its emergence? Relevant. Technical terms used in CA are evident in the abstract
Q4: Findings?	Association between mother's words and children's social understanding	Demonstration of children's conversational skills in use of turn-taking structures
Q5: Relevance?	Irrelevant. No terms evident that a CA researcher would use Unlikely to be relevant	Relevant. Technical terms used in CA are evident (e.g. 'turn-taking') Likely to be highly relevant

when you are becoming familiar with an area, and it may be that at first you want to be over-inclusive to compensate for a lack of expertise. Over time, you will start to recognise certain phrases and terms that serve as important clues to relevance. Reading about your subject and speaking to your supervisor about the most relevant key words, journals, authors and technical terms, will also help.

Telling the Story of Your Review

Once you have found the various journal articles, chapters, books, conference reports or any other relevant publication important for your review (for example government reports) you will then begin the process of writing the actual review. Given that your review might summarise anywhere between 10 and 100 studies, it really helps if, from the outset, you have decided what kind of review you will carry out. The number of studies you review will depend very much on the question you are asking and whether other researchers have addressed similar issues or questions to yours.

It is important for you to recognise that a literature review is not simply some kind of list of every relevant study carried out to date. Once you've got a big pile of relevant studies it can be hard to resist the temptation to describe one study after another, but this creates an overly descriptive list with few element of evaluation, critique or narrative structure.

Students who use overly descriptive styles of writing tend not to:

- explain why these studies might be of interest;
- clearly highlight the focus of the studies;
- show how the studies they are reviewing fit into a more general picture of the emerging or existent literature;
- critically evaluate the literature they are reviewing;
- offer a coherent narrative.

Top tip: two key ingredients

To write an excellent review you should:

- critically evaluate the literature you are reviewing; and
- offer a coherent narrative.

For more information on critical thinking see Chapter 1, and for writing styles see Chapter 9.

Top tip: avoid writing your review as a list

The following paragraph illustrates the descriptive and list-like style of reviewing literature that you should avoid:

Anderson, Smith and Jones (1998) did x, y and z in 19xx found out A, B and C. Brightlight, et al. (1999) then tested adults on the x, y, and z test and found out A, B and C. Tolstoy and Bekaerman (2001) investigated children age 3 and 5 and replicated the results of Jones and Solder (1993). Another study that looked at X was Zentner (1994) who found Y. [And so on, and so on, and so on].

Rather than being descriptive, you need to develop your own narrative. This does not mean writing a fictional creative story, but it is a creative act to bring together the research relevant to your study in a way that shows your reader the patterns in what you've found in an evaluative and coherent way. In this way you should tell a good story that highlights the issues, findings and debates in the field and which leads to you being able to ask a relevant and interesting research question, or set of research questions.

Reviews that have their own narrative:

- offer a coherent, logical story that is written in your own words;
- include relevant studies and interpret them;
- set out a framework so that the reader can gain a good idea of how one study is related to another;
- use these studies to develop a conceptual understanding of the topic;
- draw out the significance of these studies for our understanding of the topic.

For more ideas on how to narrate your literature review see Chapter 9.

In a nutshell: telling a good story

A good literature review should include the following key components:

1 Provide a good overview of previous research work that is understandable and coherent to the reader. Paying attention to how you set out the introductory paragraphs can really help here.
2 Provide a framework that will enhance your ability to write a critical review. (See Chapter 1 for a discussion on how to develop your critical thinking.)
3 Towards the end of your review, as well as at key points throughout, it is very important to draw out the rationale behind the question you are going to ask for your project. This will be related to the review in specific ways and the reader will recognise why it might make sense to ask the questions you pose given the background literature.

Top tip: writing a review with interpretation

The following paragraph shows the interpretive style that you should try and strive for:

> In charting key aspects of the child's conversational skills and understandings, Wootton (1997) comments that intersubjective 'understandings' have three important properties: they are local, public and moral. For example, these understandings are public in that the child's conduct is systematically sensitive to agreements and preferences which have been overtly established within earlier talk. Detailing and examining intersubjective understandings is central to the work of Tarplee (2010), who addresses the inherent difficulties of using concepts such as 'feedback' to explain language development. Looking at displays of understanding, on a turn-by-turn basis, Tarplee (2010) highlights the child's orientation to sequential implicativeness, and makes the point that the particular kind of parent-child interaction where linguistic pedagogy is relevant is constituted by the structure of the talk itself.

This paragraph introduces three studies, explains how they relate to one another, and provides some evaluative commentary. By writing in this way, you are able to highlight the important questions you want to address, and identify key issues in the field.

Review frameworks

It can be useful to recognise that there are various frameworks for writing a review. These can help you structure your review. Below I examine four: chronological; thematic; cross-disciplinary; and theoretical framework.

Chronological reviews

With this approach your aim is to provide an overview, history or chronology of the literature that you have selected for inclusion in your review. Here you have to be careful that your overview doesn't just simply fall into the trap of being a rather boring descriptive list as discussed above. Instead, try to tell a story about the literature from your notes collated from the articles that you selected as being relevant to your project (see above).

So, for example, after your introduction, which will tell the reader how your review is structured and why it is structured the way it is, you might begin by highlighting the manner in which one of the early studies in the area turned out to be one of the most influential. Alternatively, it might be the case that the early studies in an area quickly changed focus and researchers began to pick up on ideas that did not at first seem related directly to what had gone before.

From here you would then go through each study or even group of studies making sure that you remain focused on communicating (1) what the main findings of the article might be, (2) why this finding might be of interest to the area, and (3) what implications this finding or set of findings has for the literature. It is also very important to link each main paragraph of your review together. You need to keep the reader interested and in touch with the emerging story. So, at the end of one section or subsection, you might conclude by saying:

> It is therefore apparent that the main findings established by the 1990s were (x, y and z) and these ideas continued to have some influence into the 2000s, particularly through the work of Jones et al. (2001).

Then you would move on to discuss Jones et al.'s work. For example, your next paragraph might then go something like this:

> The most significant element that began to emerge around the turn of the century was related to the work of Jones et al. (2001), who alongside Brown's work (2002) established that x, and z were only indicative of a, b and c ...

Reminding your reader what you've said and what you may be about to say is called 'signposting' because it allows you to tell your reader the structure of your review and how your arguments fit together. This allows your reader to more easily follow the flow of your review. (For further discussion on 'signposting' see Chapter 9 on writing up.)

At the end of your chronological review you need to create a summary that leads into the formulation of the research question you are going to ask. We will consider this in more detail in the final section of this chapter below.

Thematic reviews

In any specific area of study it is possible to identify patterns of research and to group the studies according to these patterns or themes. These can be discussed under different headings to give an overview of the relevant research for your project. In my review I identified approximately 40 studies as relevant, which I could classify under five themes or headings: pre-linguistic communication; repair; competencies and understandings; grammar; and childhood.

Using this thematic approach I could then formulate my review by saying, after an introductory paragraph:

> As a guide to the emerging literature, child conversation analysis (CA) research can be classified into five general areas (a) pre-linguistic communication (b) repair (c) competencies and understandings (d) grammar, and (e) childhood. Such a

differentiation is to some extent arbitrary and employed solely for overview purposes. While there may be some link between these sub-themes and disciplinary
agendas there is not always a correspondence between discipline and topic areas.
Furthermore, although there may be an implicit trans-disciplinary orientation to
describing and explaining the *development* of children's conversational skills and
abilities, this is not necessarily a shared aspect of child CA work. This overview does
not cover CA based studies with older aged children or child language impairment.
(Forrester, forthcoming: xxx)

From there it is relatively straightforward to go on and set out each theme.
At the beginning of a theme, remember to use signposting to remind the
reader what it is about. Similarly, at the end of a theme, summarise the key
points and include a linking sentence to the next paragraph.

Advantages of doing a thematic review include:

- You have less concern with who did what and when and in what particular order. This is
especially useful if research developments in your area of interest occurred in parallel
rather than linearly, which often happens in areas that employ qualitative methods such
as in health psychology, clinical psychology and critical/discursive psychology.
- This structure encourages analysis and interpretation of the material, since identifying
your themes requires you to think analytically about the topic.
- Identifying and drawing out themes facilitates the production of a coherent account of a
body of literature and critical discussion of the material from a particular theoretical or
methodological perspective. This is often a hallmark of an excellent project.

Cross-disciplinary review

Areas where we find a significant number of qualitative studies tend not to be
located solely within a single discipline. My example review is a good instance
of this, since a number of different disciplines employ this qualitative method
when looking at children's early conversational competencies. When carrying
out my review I could find at least five, including: linguistics; sociology; psychology; social anthropology; and education.

Rather than a thematic organisation one could provide a cross-disciplinary
framework where studies within a particular discipline can be described and discussed with reference to the theoretical focus that a specific discipline might
orient towards. For example, within my research area there are a number of CA
studies that look in detail at particular linguistic elements of the child's early talk –
such as phonetics (Tarplee, 1996). In contrast, in the sociology of childhood
researchers have considered how children's conversational participation might
be subject to specific discursive formulations provided by adults (Hutchby, 2010).

When going through the various studies relevant to your project you could
firstly locate where each work sits and then, when summarising the work,

provide some background to the distinct disciplinary orientation these studies tend to have. This will also help you identify issues yet to be addressed from the perspective that you are coming from.

Cross-disciplinary reviews are usually written with a bias towards your own discipline. For example, you might highlight the work carried out by researchers in your own discipline, or evaluate work in other disciplines in the light of what it can offer to your own. If you are unsure about whether material from a discipline other than your own is appropriate for inclusion you should check this with your supervisor.

Theoretical framework reviews

Sometimes students take a specific theoretical viewpoint from which to review the relevant literature for their study. This theoretical framework acts as a lens so that now the studies are not only described and evaluated in general terms, but are evaluated specifically in relation to how they relate to the assumptions of a particular approach. Students who are drawing on a standpoint that contrasts with the more dominant perspectives in the discipline often use this kind of review, for example, if they're taking a critical psychology, social constructionist or psychodynamic approach. Alternatively students might use this type of review when they are using a very specific approach, and they want to focus their project (and hence literature review) on engaging in detail with the debates and issues within this particular approach. My review would be such an example, as it was exploring pre-school conversation skills from within an ethnomethodological theoretical framework.

Taking up of a particular viewpoint, and then providing a review that offers a critical account, is a skill that is acquired through the process of doing literature reviews and gradually gaining a deeper understanding of an area. As you develop your skills you will also begin to develop your own particular theoretical allegiances and orientations, which may influence how you want to write your review.

From literature review to research questions

The final and key element of a literature review is the relationship between the review and the research question you are going to pose for your study. I said earlier that towards the end of your literature review it is important to draw out the rationale behind the question you are going to ask for your project. Whatever framework you use for organising your review, the final section should be written especially carefully. Here, ensure that what you write makes your review and critical commentary lead logically onto your own specific question or questions.

Often a review is described as a process of gradually funnelling down from the 'bigger more general' issues down to sub-themes, and then onto the specific issues or area you want to address. In experimental studies, it is at this point that specific hypotheses are outlined (again, ones that make sense given prior studies and the issues identified). However, in qualitative methodological approaches, specific hypotheses are not typically set out. So, the production of a literature review which highlights the main issues and themes serves as the background for the reasons why the particular question you are going to ask makes sense. You haven't simply dreamt up a question on the spur of the moment – instead you have provided a reasoned and defensible background to the question(s) you are now going to address in your project. The reader should be able to guess the kind of research question you are likely to ask from the commentary and rationale that the review has provided. See Figure 5.1 as an example from my review.

CA research on children, adult-child talk, and topics germane to understanding how children learn to talk are gathering momentum. There are number of identifiable themes in the Literature that linguists and child language researchers might subsume under the term 'developmental pragmatics'. We have seen for example, the problems and issues which have arisen with the analysis of prelinguistic communication, the questions surroundings identifying repair skills, and the perplexing question of what exactly constitutes a participant skill during the child's early years.	Shows the topic is relevant and interesting Reminds reader what they've been told Reminds reader there's more to know and where the 'big' questions are
However, what is distinct about child-CA is the careful focus on how, why and under what conditions younger members of any culture gradually attain the skills necessary for producing those reflexively accountable sense-making practices that constitute talk-in-interaction. Ethnomethodologically informed child-CA extends the boundaries of traditional language acquisition research and reminds us that this is first and foremost, a social-discursive practice, and it is for this reason that this project is going to focus on the question of how children gradually learn to close a conversation, an issue which has yet to be addressed in the literature. This answer to this main question will be gained through asking a number of related subsidiary question: under what conditions and at what age do children first recognise the end of conversation? What particular structures are utilised in their own first attempts at endings?	Reminds reader of the approach being used, what its aims are and why it's useful Introduces main area for research question States main research question and that it addresses a gap in the literature Explains how this research question will be answered through specific, interrelated sub-questions

Figure 5.1 Example how to conclude a review and articulate your research questions

Conclusion

When you first set out to think through what you might examine in your project it might seem a straightforward task to review what has been done before in whatever area you are interested in. Hopefully by now you can see that it is important to be methodical in your search procedures and your analysis of prior work. Similarly, it should be apparent that when you report your literature review you should write a coherent, critical and engaging account of the field, which logically leads to your research question(s). The following list of summary points should help keep you focused on the most important elements of the task:

1 Make sure you spend sufficient time developing suitable search strategies and becoming familiar with the various information systems available to you (for example, Web of Knowledge; PsycINFO).
2 Employ a consistent and methodical procedure when reading and evaluating abstracts and other summaries of relevant work: this will really help you with deciding whether a piece of research is worth following up or not.
3 Don't be put off by obscure words, phrases and associated terminology when you begin. Familiarity with technical terms in a specific area will grow as you become immersed in the research literature.
4 When writing your review avoid descriptively listing studies. Instead, critically engage with your literature and focus on developing a narrative of the research for your reader.
5 For the organisation of your literature review, make sure you have a useful framework, and flag up what you are doing in your introductory section. The reader will value being guided through an unfamiliar area of research with a clear and interesting account.
6 When writing your review, make sure different sections and paragraphs link well with each other. It is also very useful to remind the reader where they have got to by using mini-summary sentences.
7 Focus on providing an engaging critical account of the research literature. This is particularly important towards the end of the review where it is much better to articulate a critically informed summary or conclusion rather than a simple summary set of statements.
8 The most essential linking paragraph or section of your review is between the summary conclusion and the setting out of the question or questions you aim to address with your research project. This provides the rationale for what you are going to do and provides a coherent background context for all that will follow.

Want to know more about writing reviews?

See Chapter 9 in this volume. Also:

Fink, A. (1998) *Conducting Research Literature Reviews: From Paper to the Internet.* Thousand Oaks, CA: Sage.
Cooper, H.M. (1998) *Synthesizing Research: A Guide for Literature Reviews.* Thousand Oaks, CA: Sage.

(Continued)

(Continued)

Shaw, R. (2010) 'Conducting literature reviews', in M.A. Forrester (ed.) *Doing Qualitative Research in Psychology: A Practical Guide.* London: Sage. pp. 39–56.

Some good examples of literature reviews include Azar (2007), Brocki and Wearden (2006), Brosch et al. (2010), Freeman and Gosling (2010), Heinrich and Gullone (2006), Hennessey and Amabile (2010), Pincus and Lukowitsky (2010), Raylu et al. (2008), Sullivan and Cottone (2010), Woodard (2003) and Young (2004).

References

Azar, O.H. (2007) 'The social norm of tipping: a review', *Journal of Applied Social Psychology*, 37(2), 380–402.

Brocki, J.M. and Wearden, A.J. (2006) 'A critical evaluation of the use of interpretative phenomenological analysis (IPA) in health psychology', *Psychology & Health*, 21(1), 87–108.

Brosch, T., Pourtois, G. and Sander, D. (2010) 'The perception and categorisation of emotional stimuli: a review', *Cognition & Emotion*, 24(3), 377–400.

Forrester, M.A. (forthcoming) 'Conversation analysis and child language acquisition', in J. Wagner and K. Mortensenthe (eds) *Encyclopedia of Applied Linguistics*. New York: Wiley-Blackwell.

Freeman, H.D. and Gosling, S.D. (2010) 'Personality in nonhuman primates: a review and evaluation of past research', *American Journal of Primatology*, 72(8): 653–71.

Heinrich, L.A. and Gullone, E. (2006) 'The clinical significance of loneliness: a literature review', *Clinical Psychology Review*, 26(6), 695–718.

Hennessey, B.A. and Amabile, T.M. (2010) 'Creativity', *Annual Review of Psychology*, 61, 569–98.

Hutchby, I. (2010) 'Feelings-talk and therapeutic vision in child-counsellor interaction', in H. Gardner and M.A. Forrester (eds) *Analysing Interactions in Childhood: Insights from Conversation Analysis*. Chichester: Wiley-Blackwell. pp. 146–62.

Pincus, A.L. and Lukowitsky, M.R. (2010) 'Pathological narcissism and narcissistic personality disorder', in *Annual Review of Clinical Psychology, Vol 6*, pp. 421–46.

Raylu, N., Oei, T.P.S. and Loo, J. (2008) 'The current status and future direction of self-help treatments for problem gamblers', *Clinical Psychology Review*, 28(8), 1372–85.

Shaw, R. (2010) 'Conducting literature reviews', in M.A. Forrester (ed.) *Doing Qualitative Research in Psychology: A Practical Guide*. London: Sage.

Sullivan, C. and Cottone, R.R. (2010) 'Emergent characteristics of effective cross-cultural research: a review of the literature', *Journal of Counselling and Development*, 88(3), 357–62.

Tarplee, C. (1996) 'Working on young children's utterances: prosodic aspects of repetition during picture labelling', in E. Couper-Kuhlen and M. Selting (eds) *Prosody in Conversation: Interactional studies*. Cambridge: Cambridge University Press. pp. 406–435.

Woodard, F. (2003) Phenomenological contributions to understanding hypnosis: review of the literature. *Psychological Reports*, 93(3), 829–47.

Young, J.T. (2004) 'Illness behaviour: a selective review and synthesis', *Sociology of Health & Illness*, 26(1), 1–31.

6

COLLECTING YOUR DATA

Siobhan Hugh-Jones and Stephen Gibson

One of the most exciting and attractive aspects of doing qualitative research is the availability of diverse and intriguing sources of data, and ways of collecting it. Yet this open-endedness can also be a hazard, particularly when researchers do not give enough attention to the relationships between what they want to know (the research question), the best way(s) of getting data to help answer that question (data collection), how they will go about making sense of that data (data analysis) and the conclusions that can be drawn from their analysis. So, in this chapter, we help you to ask the right questions about data collection so that your research has a considered and appropriate method of data collection – one of the hallmarks of quality in any project.

In a nutshell: collecting your data

This chapter is structured around the following key issues:

1 Understanding the importance of epistemology and ontology: we begin by briefly reminding you of the importance of these issues which were introduced in Chapter 1. We return to them throughout this chapter in order to emphasise that remaining aware of the assumptions you make about your data will help you to produce research of the highest quality.
2 Deciding what data to collect and how to collect it: we take you through some key decisions you'll need to make.
3 Approaches to data collection: the bulk of the chapter provides snapshots of some of the methods of data collection you might want to use, and we provide references to key sources for exploring these in more detail.
4 Practical issues: we finish off by dealing with a series of practical issues that you need to consider, such as recording and data storage.

Epistemological and ontological assumptions

Over the course of this chapter and the next, we will be outlining various ways of collecting and analysing your data. However, as we have indicated in earlier chapters, it is important to recognise at the outset that it is not always possible to simply 'mix-and-match' approaches to data collection and analysis. Instead, your method of data collection and your analytic approach should be consistent with each other, with the research question(s) you are addressing, and – ultimately – with the epistemological and ontological assumptions you are making about your data. Are you treating your data as a route – however partial and imperfect – to underlying 'thoughts', 'beliefs' or 'experiences'? Or are you treating your data as action-oriented accounts constructed to perform a particular function in a particular context? The various approaches to qualitative research (see Chapter 7) involve sometimes quite different assumptions about the nature of the world (ontology) and the nature of knowledge (epistemology) and these have important implications for how you view your data and its relationship with 'reality'. In this respect, there can be as much – if not more – of a divergence between different qualitative approaches as there is between qualitative and quantitative approaches.

How do I decide what data to collect?

Often when we start a piece of research, we already have in mind where, or from whom, we might collect data. However, it is worth pausing at this stage to really think through whether you have thought of all possible sources of data, and have decided upon the optimal data source(s). Think about the potential of various types of data to answer your research question(s), the practical access you have to either participants, or to existing data, and the time you have available (see Chapter 3 for more on these planning issues). You should also think about how you will deal with tricky issues like generalisability (see Chapter 3) when you discuss your results and whether this might impact on your data collection.

In qualitative psychology, there are relatively few dictates about what method of data collection must be used for a particular research agenda. Rather, the quality and rigour of the research is judged on the appropriateness of the data for answering the research question, which will in turn be informed by the analytic approach you intend to adopt. The best way of getting to grips with this is to read around so you can see how data collection is typically done in your chosen methodological approach. This raises the issue of the relationship between method and methodology (see Chapter 1) with the former simply referring to the way in which you collect your data (for example, interviews, focus groups, diaries), and the latter involving a broader range of decisions regarding the assumptions you will be making about your data, what sort of questions you will be asking of it, and how you will analyse it. Methodology thus links your epistemological and ontological assumptions, your research question(s), and your methods of data collection and analysis (see the 'methodological kite' in Chapter 1). These need to be consistent with one another for your work to make sense and 'hang together'. In this chapter we focus on questions of method, and in the next chapter turn to questions of analysis. However, both method and analysis should be viewed within the overall framework of your methodology.

Data collection: key decisions

- What do I want to know? (Or, what is my research question?)
- Who or what could help me answer/understand that?
- Is one source of data enough or do I need to look at others also?
- How much data should I collect?
- What equipment/resources do I need?
- How am I going to analyse my data?

The question of how you are going to analyse your data is particularly important – as with any form of research, whether qualitative or quantitative, you must have a clear idea of how you are going to analyse your data before you collect it. Chapter 7 deals in more detail with analysis and Chapter 3 with planning.

Top tip: flexible research questions

Don't worry too much if you find yourself tweaking your research question as data collection progresses – as long as the relationship between them remains consistent, you're okay (see Chapter 2 for more on research questions).

Critical issue: collection or generation?

Although we've followed convention and called this chapter 'Collecting your data', we might instead have called it 'Generating your data'. This is because many qualitative researchers emphasise that the idea of data existing independently of our research is problematic (see for example, Speer, 2002). Rather than being something already in existence that we collect, we might therefore think of data as being created or generated by our research activity. You might want to consider what this means in relation to your choice of language when writing up your research.

Approaches to data collection

In this section, we present overviews of eight of the most widely used approaches to data collection for qualitative research in psychology: semi-structured interviews, narrative interviews, focus groups, diaries, naturalistic data, archival data, Internet data and visual data. We provide snapshots of these approaches, highlighting their key features and indicating useful resources where you can find fresh ideas and more details on how to use these methods. We also outline some key points about mixing methods.

Semi-structured interviews

Semi-structured interviews (SSIs) are a particularly popular form of data collection in qualitative research for many reasons. SSIs are popular because interviews are:

- a culturally familiar form of interaction for most people (Atkinson and Silverman, 1997);
- relatively inexpensive and easy to arrange;
- flexible, and can be used to address almost any subject matter;
- able to generate rich data that is suitable for different forms of analysis.

SSIs involve direct questions but with freedom for either the interviewer or interviewee to raise issues not previously anticipated or to dismiss questions deemed less relevant to particular participants. This allows a balance in the process between researcher-led questions (based on topics relevant to theory) and participant-led issues (that may help the researcher identify important issues that they would not otherwise have considered).

Interviewers and interviewees draw upon everyday conversational skills during interviewing (Hester and Francis, 1994), but the SSI is a particular type of conversation that is driven by a research agenda and that involves the assumption that the interviewee will disclose things while the interviewer does not (see Madill, 2011). Interviews are usually recorded and transcribed for analysis (see below and Chapter 7 for more on transcription).

Importantly, there are some conceptual differences in the ways that SSIs can be understood. These relate to debates on ontology, epistemology, context, co-construction and autobiographical memory (for example, Potter and Hepburn, 2005; Thomsen and Brinkmann, 2009). For example, the SSI can be viewed as a means to access and explore subjective experience, as a co-constructed version of reality or as a discursive performance (Hugh-Jones, 2010). To be able to use SSIs competently you will need to have an understanding of where your research fits into these debates. If you're not sure turn to Chapter 1, and also speak to your supervisor.

Interview research begins with a set of questions and probes (called an interview schedule or guide) that relate to your research question in a way that bears your intended method of analysis in mind. Interview questions can be difficult to produce, particularly as the use of leading and directive questions, for example, should be avoided (see Madill, forthcoming, for interview techniques and useful examples). Conducting the interview is always harder than novice researchers anticipate, and the importance of piloting, practice and reflecting on completed interviews should not be underestimated.

Top tip: transcribe your pilot

Enhance your interviewing skills – and your analysis – by taking time to conduct and transcribe a pilot interview before embarking on your main round of interviewing. Examine the transcript to see how your role as the interviewer has shaped and constrained the sorts of responses provided by the participant, as well as to get a sense of which questions and prompts seemed to work and which didn't. This can form a crucial part of your approach to reflexivity (see Chapter 8 for more on reflexivity and Chapter 4 for an example of how a pilot interview allowed a student, 'Suzy', to develop her research).

Want to know more about semi-structured interviews?

Hugh-Jones, S. (2010) 'The interview in qualitative research', in M.A. Forrester (ed.) *Doing Qualitative Research in Psychology: A Practical Guide*. London: Sage. pp. 77–97.

King, N. and Horrocks, C. (2010) *Interviews in Qualitative Research*. London: Sage.

Kvale, S. (1996) *InterViews: An Introduction to Qualitative Research Interviewing*. London: Sage.

Madill, A. (in press) 'Interviews and interviewing techniques', in A.T. Panter (ed.) *APA Handbook of Research Methods in Psychology*. Washington, DC: APA.

Narrative interviews

Narrative psychology is a relative newcomer to qualitative methods, having emerged following a 'turn to narrative' in the mid-1980s. Narrative psychologists have argued that psychology should explore the 'story' as a metaphor for human experience (instead of, for example, humans as information processors [Sarbin, 1986]). Although there are divergent forms of narrative psychology, they share an understanding that stories play a crucial role in almost every human activity because as we tell stories about ourselves we make sense of our experiences and our lives. Narratives therefore:

- function to organise and structure action and experience;
- are central in the formation, maintenance, development and renegotiation of identity.

Although narratives can be found within many types of data collection (such as interviews, focus groups and diaries), narrative psychology has been developed to study narrative form and function in its own right (Hiles and Čermák, 2008). Narrative approaches can be used to examine specific events or life histories, and the construction of meaning-making, self and identity within them (see the dedicated journal *Narrative Inquiry* for examples).

Although there are many ways to explore narratives (such as in diaries or autobiographies), the life-history narrative interview is particularly prominent, aiming to elicit a detailed narrative from the participant (McAdams, 1993). It explores seven areas: (1) life chapters (assigned and described by the participant); (2) key events/nuclear episodes (for example, peak experiences, earliest memories and turning points, and their meaning); (3) significant people and their impact; (4) future script (goals, dreams, plans); (5) stresses and problems; (6) personal ideology (fundamental beliefs and values); and (7) life theme(s).

Want to know more about narrative interviews?

McAdams, D.P., Josselson, R. and Lieblich, A. (eds) (2006) *Identity and Story: Creating Self in Narrative. Washington*, DC: APA.

Hollway, W. and Jefferson, T. (2000) *Doing Qualitative Research Differently: Free Association, Narrative and the Interview Method*. London: Sage.

Mishler, E.G. (1986) *Research Interviewing: Context and Narrative*. Cambridge, MA: Harvard University Press.

Focus groups

Focus groups typically involve 6–10 participants talking about a particular phenomenon (for example, neighbourhood crime) or shared experience (for example, marriage in later life). Due to the semi-public nature of focus groups, overtly sensitive and private subject matter are not always appropriate for focus group research.

Focus groups are not one-to-one interviews with many people, but function to promote and encourage collaborative responses. Often, hearing other people's accounts, experiences or opinions can prompt and help others to reflect on, and articulate, their own perspective. Focus groups can therefore offer something more than what we glean in individual interviews (see, for example, Flowers et al., 2000). Focus groups are therefore often used to examine group interaction itself (Puchta and Potter, 2004), and can also be used to explore participants' perspectives, or their responses to an intervention or to your research findings (see Chapter 8 for more on asking research participants to subsequently reflect on your findings). As well as being a sole method to explore an issue, focus groups can also be used to identify a range of prominent issues that can then be further examined with different methods.

As the group dynamic is fundamental in focus groups, they need to be planned (in relation to the selection of participants and questions, for example) so that the potential for dialogue and debate is enhanced. For this reason, focus groups typically feature participants deemed to be similar on some key variable(s) (for example, status, gender or ethnicity), but who are not so homogenous that they have no difference of opinion or experience. Focus group participants are not usually known to each other, and ideally will not be likely to meet again in the future. In focus groups the interviewer is known as the moderator and their role is to facilitate the group's discussion, and to optimise each participant's potential for contribution; this also means there is less researcher control than there may be in other methods.

Top tip: encouraging interaction

One of the main advantages of focus groups over one-on-one interviews is that they allow for interaction between participants. You therefore need to ensure that the way in which you run your focus group encourages your participants to talk to each other, rather than simply taking it in turns to talk to you. To facilitate this, it can be useful to explicitly state in your introduction to the focus group that you value participants discussing issues with each other. Running one or two pilot focus groups will also help you get a feel for how best to facilitate this process.

Thematic, discourse analysis (DA) or conversation analysis (CA) can easily be applied to focus group data, although interpretative phenomenological analysis (IPA) of focus group data is also emerging (see Palmer et al., 2010). Methods of analysis are discussed in Chapter 7.

Want to know more about focus groups?

Barbour, R.S. and Kitzinger, J. (eds) (1999) *Developing Focus Group Research: Politics, Theory and Practice*. London: Sage.
Kitzinger, J. (1994) 'The methodology of focus groups: the importance of interaction between research participants', *Sociology of Health and Illness*, 16, 103–21.
Krueger, R.A. and Casey, M.A. (2009) *Focus Groups: A Practical Guide for Applied Research* (4th edn). London: Sage.

Diary methods

Diary methods have been prominent in recording patient experiences in health research since the 1930s and are now popular in social, personality, developmental and clinical psychology. Diary methods are particularly attractive to those interested in daily experience because they allow sensations, thoughts and emotions to be recorded with little retrospection, and are relatively unobtrusive in individuals' natural settings (Bolger et al., 2003). Furthermore, participants can ascribe their own meaning-making to their recordings (Alaszewski, 2006) or can comment on the importance of events to them (see Jacelon and Imperio, 2005). Diaries also have the potential to be unique spaces for 'identity narratives' (see, for example, Monrouxe, 2009). In line with these different possible objectives of diary-based studies, diary data can be subjected to a range of analytic methods, including DA, IPA and narrative analysis.

Diary records can either be interval-contingent (at specified times) or event-contingent (following certain events, which can be conceptualised as objective and/or subjective, such as having anxious thoughts or feelings). Diary studies can also be used as a preliminary stage of data collection to inform subsequent stages, for example, in the development of interview schedules (see Carter, 2002). Reporting periods typically last between one day and four weeks (Keleher and Verrinder, 2003).

Limitations of (solicited) diary methods include high rates of attrition (Kaun, 2010) and the reliance on participants to complete entries; there is thus a need to balance immediacy of recordings with the need to avoid being overly intrusive. In addition, participants may not complete entries in the level of detail anticipated by researchers (although see Green et al., 2006), and the extent of entries can vary considerably from participant to participant (Bolger et al., 2003).

Completing diary entries may also impact upon the thoughts and feelings being reported (Day and Thatcher, 2009) or upon future behaviour or diary entries (Finley, 2010; Merrilees et al., 2008). This is not necessarily problematic (diary keeping can be therapeutic to participants [Peel et al., 2006]), but you should show awareness of these complexities in your use of diary data and the claims you make about it in your analysis.

Alongside paper-and-pencil and audio diaries, the use of both solicited and unsolicited online diary data (for example, weblogs) is increasingly popular, particularly as it can prompt participants to record entries and can time-stamp their recordings. Ethical issues related to online diaries do exist and include identifying what are public and private domains, data storage, and the fact that participants may disclose more online than they might do in other contexts (Kaun, 2010) – see Chapter 3 for more discussion of ethical issues.

Top tip: think about the audience

Whether you use solicited or unsolicited diary data, remember that it is always written to someone (even if only to the self). Consider carefully how this may shape the resulting diary entries, bearing in mind your methodological approach.

Want to know more about diaries?

Alaszewski, A. (2006) *Using Diaries for Social Research*. London: Sage.
Bolger, N., Davis, A. and Rafaeli, E. (2003) 'Diary methods: capturing life as it is lived', *Annual Review of Psychology*, 54, 579–616.
Kaun, A. (2010) 'Open-ended online diaries: capturing life as it is narrated', *International Journal of Qualitative Methods*, 9, 133–48. http://ejournals.library. ualberta.ca/index.php/IJQM/article/view/7165/7022
Monrouxe, L.V. (2009) 'Solicited audio diaries in longitudinal research: a view from inside', *Qualitative Research*, 9, 81–103.

Naturalistic data

Naturalistic, or naturally occurring, data can be defined as that which exists independently of the researcher. As used in CA and DA, it typically refers to talk-in-interaction, although other types of data can be naturalistic in form (for example, diaries, media, Internet data). Potter suggested the 'dead social scientist test' to discern whether data is naturalistic; the test involves asking 'if the researcher got run over on the way to the university that morning, would the interaction nevertheless have taken place, and in the way that it did?' (2004: 612). This contrasts with data that has come into being only because of the active involvement of the researcher (as in interviews and focus groups).

There has been lively debate around the nature and importance of naturalistic data, and it is sometimes viewed as a much-needed antidote to limitations that are inherent in interview research, such as lack of attention to context and the impact of the interviewer. In contrast, Potter and Hepburn (2005) argue that naturalistic data has several commendable features.

- It can represent live interaction and experience, reducing the reliance on retrospective accounts.
- It reflects the participants' priorities more than the researcher's and avoids 'flooding' the participant accounts with the concerns of the researcher.
- It avoids positioning participants as disinterested experts on their own and others' practices and thoughts.
- Problematic inferences about the data are avoided as the topic itself is studied directly.
- It may bring up novel insights that were beyond the boundaries set by the researcher.

In response to calls for more (or exclusive) reliance on naturally occurring data, it has been argued that interviews are important instances of interaction in their own right and can be used in ways that acknowledge that they are not simplistic reflections of 'reality' (Speer, 2002: 512). Furthermore, it is important to remember that even naturalistic talk always has to be selected, recorded, transcribed and processed by the researcher. Indeed, some authors have questioned whether the researcher can ever be removed from any data (Ashmore and Reed, 2000). At the very least, dealing with naturalistic talk must involve a sensitivity to who is talking and why, and to what might be at stake in the interaction.

Conversation and discourse analytic work with naturalistic data has drawn extensively upon telephone conversations (for example, Kitzinger and Kitzinger, 2007; Patterson and Potter, 2009; Potter and Hepburn, 2003). However, other interesting work has used family meal time talk (Wiggins and Potter, 2003), beauty salon interactions (Toerien and Kitzinger, 2007), police interrogations (Stokoe, 2009, 2010), talk in parapsychology experiments (Wooffitt et al., 2010), and discussions between counsellors and children whose parents are divorcing (Hutchby, 2007). Internet data is also increasingly common (see section below), as are mobile phone conversations (Hutchby and Barnett, 2005) and text messaging (Spagnoli and Gamberini, 2007).

As with all methods of data collection, there are ethical considerations specific to the collection of naturalistic data, particularly around informed consent. This may apply even if the data are publicly available, given that the originator of the data may not have had an opportunity to consent. You should consider this issue – the British Psychological Society's (2009) Code of Ethics and Conduct (section 1.3) is a good starting point.

Want to know more about naturalistic data?

Rapley, T. (2007) *Doing Conversation, Discourse and Document Analysis*. London: Sage.

Potter, J. and Hepburn, A. (2005) 'Qualitative interviews in psychology: problems and possibilities', *Qualitative Research in Psychology*, 2, 281–307. (Also see the commentaries published in response to this.)

Speer, S.A. (2002) '"Natural" and "contrived" data: a sustainable distinction?', *Discourse Studies*, 4, 511–25.

Archival data

Increasingly, when academics carry out a research study, there is an expectation that the data will be deposited in an archive on completion of the study. In the

UK, the Economic and Social Data Service (ESDS) maintain several data archives, one of which – Qualidata – is devoted entirely to qualitative research data (see: http://www.esds.ac.uk/qualidata). Despite this, it is still relatively rare for student projects to make use of archived data. In the UK, this is largely because it is typically a requirement of undergraduate degrees accredited by the British Psychological Society (BPS) that the research component involves the collection of original empirical data. However, there are signs that such considerations may be in the process of being relaxed, and in any case it is perfectly possible to use archived data as a supplementary to data that you have collected yourself.

One of the key advantages of archival data is that it enables your investigation to take on a historical perspective. Indeed, Collins (2010) has recently argued that historical research represents an important but under-used qualitative approach in psychology. As an example, there have recently been studies exploring various aspects of Stanley Milgram's (1974) obedience experiments which have drawn on archived material held at Yale University Manuscripts and Archives Service, which houses the Stanley Milgram Papers collection. Russell (2011) has drawn on Milgram's notes and other materials to build up a picture of how Milgram developed his experimental set-up so that his first 'official' experiment yielded a shockingly high level of obedience. In a slightly different vein, Gibson (2011) has used recordings and transcripts of the obedience experiments to develop an approach to obedience and disobedience informed by qualitative approaches which had not been developed when Milgram originally analysed his data.

Indeed, thinking of archival data as novel historical data points to a grey area surrounding what counts as 'original' data – there is as much skill and care needed in collecting archival data as in any other data collection method.

Top tips: archival data

- Make sure you're aware of the permissions required – the researcher who collected the data may need to give their approval, or the participants may need to be contacted to give additional consent. The data may also be protected by copyright. The archive holding the data will be able to tell you this information, and assist you in securing relevant permissions.
- Be aware of the limitations of the data – for example, you may have access to interview transcripts but not to the audio recordings. More generally, make sure you remain aware that you don't have access to the 'insider' knowledge about a dataset that one has when analysing one's own data.
- Make sure you consider the purpose for which the data was originally collected – this forms a key part of a reflexive approach to archival data (see Chapter 8 for more on reflexivity).
- Make sure you're familiar with your department's regulations on the use of archival data in student projects. Your supervisor will be able to advise on this.

Want to know more about archival data?

Parry, O. and Mauthner, N. (2004) 'Whose data are they anyway? Practical, legal and ethical issues in archiving qualitative research data', *Sociology*, 38, 139–52.

Fielding, N. (2004) 'Getting the most from archived qualitative data: epistemological, practical and professional obstacles', *International Journal of Social Research Methodology*, 7, 97–104.

Corti, L. and Thompson, P. (2004) 'Secondary analysis of archived data', in C. Seale, G. Gobo, J.F. Gubrium and D. Silverman (eds) *Qualitative Research Practice*. London: Sage. pp. 327–43.

Internet data

The Internet is an important focus for psychological inquiry because it:

- shows us 'psychology' in action (e.g. how people manage online identities and communities);
- gives us access to large numbers of people, who may otherwise be hard to reach;
- is a pervasive technology, allowing us to explore a range of local, national and global issues of interest to psychologists.

In a nutshell: Internet data

Internet data suitable for qualitative analysis is generally collected by two methods:

- online interviewing (solicited data)
- the collection of pre-existing material (unsolicited data)

Online interviewing can be synchronous (such as via instant messaging) or asynchronous (such as via email), and may also involve the use of webcams (see for example, Matthews and Cramer, 2008). Online interviewing can be used:

- for accessing participants unable to attend a face-to-face interview;
- where people may feel uncomfortable sharing their perspectives on sensitive matters in a face-to-face setting (see, for example, Hugh-Jones et al., 2005);
- when Internet activity is itself the focus of your inquiry (for example, in understanding cyber subculture [Williams, 2006]).

In addition, online interviewing saves on transcription time. Considerable thought must be given, though, to the many ethical and practical issues surrounding online interviewing (see British Psychological Society, 2007; Evans et al., 2008) and critical insight into the pros and cons of online interviewing (compared to face-to-face interviewing) should be apparent in your work (see Hussain and Griffiths, 2009; Jones, 1999; Kazmer and Xie, 2008; van Eeden-Moorefield et al., 2008).

Pre-existing Internet data sources suitable for qualitative analysis are extensive, and include web pages themselves (from news reports to health information), bulletin boards, blogs, chatrooms and other social networking spaces. Analysis of unsolicited Internet data has become particularly prominent in health and identity research (for example, O'Brien and Clark, 2010; Riley et al., 2009; Sneijder and te Molder, 2009).

Use of pre-existing Internet data requires considerable thought around methods of sampling. For instance, will you select data at random from a defined set or do you have specific criteria for selecting data? Similarly, it is important to consider what type of – and how much – data you will include and exclude (see Robinson, 2001, for a useful discussion). Ethical issues are also prominent with the use of pre-existing Internet data, particularly around what constitutes public or private domains (see British Psychological Society, 2009; Brownlow and O'Dell, 2002).

Internet data can be subjected to a variety of analytical methods and a combination of these data collection approaches is also workable (see, for example, Murray, 2005).

Want to know more about Internet data?

Evans, A., Elford, J. and Wiggins, D. (2008) 'Using the internet for qualitative research', in C. Willig and W. Stainton-Rogers (eds) *The Sage Handbook of Qualitative Research in Psychology*. London: Sage. pp. 315–33.

Hine, C. (2000) *Virtual Ethnography*. London: Sage.

Kazmer, M.M. and Xie, B. (2008) 'Qualitative interviewing in Internet studies: playing with media, playing with the method', *Information, Communication and Society*, 11, 257–78.

Mann, C. and Stewart, F. (2000) *Internet Communication and Qualitative Research: A Handbook for Researching Online*. London: Sage.

Visual data

Since the 'turn to language' in the 1970s and 1980s (Reavey and Johnson, 2008), qualitative researchers in psychology have largely been concerned with talk or text as the primary means of conveying or constructing meaning. Yet communication is multi-modal – not only do people speak, but they experience and view their world in material (or cyber) space.

When adopting the definition of 'discourse' as being 'wherever there is meaning' (Parker, 1999: 1), it is apparent that analysis of data in other modalities (most commonly visual and auditory data) can constitute a valuable contribution to our understanding of psychological and social phenomena (Lynn and Lea, 2005). Moving beyond the spoken or written word may involve a particularly ethical and inclusive form of data collection, especially where articulation on the topic may be difficult for participants or researchers (see, for example, Liebenberg, 2009; Wright et al., 2010).

To date, where qualitative researchers in psychology have considered non-textual forms of data, they have focused mostly on visual data. Visual data can be collected in a range of ways; researchers can:

- solicit visual data from participants (using drawings, performance, video diaries, photo elicitation or photovoice [Catalini and Minkler, 2010]);
- examine unsolicited/pre-existing data (such as photographs, books, paintings, film, graffiti, advertisements);
- combine data from varying modalities (such as Anderson's [2004] 'walking interview' and Guijarro and Sanz's [2008] study of text and imagery in children's books).

Top tips: visual data

If you are considering using visual data, ask yourself these important questions.

- What role will it play in your research; for example, will it be used to facilitate discussion and/or will it be analysed in its own right?
- Will you carry out analysis alone or will it be a collaborative venture with your participants?

Murray's (2009) synopsis of critical debates around visual methods and Reavey and Johnson's (2008) introduction to this area are useful starting points if you are considering using visual methods. In addition, it is worth bearing in mind that there are some ethical issues which are particularly relevant to visual data. Ethical guidance on the use of visual data is likely to be harder to find than guidance on other methods. For example, in the UK, the British Psychological Socitey (2009) Code of Ethics and Conduct does not offer extensive guidance on the collection or use of visual data, other than stating that audio, video or photographic recordings of participants can only be done with their permission. However, you will need to consider issues around privacy, unintended identification of others, re-presentation and ownership of the images (see Temple and McVittie, 2005).

Want to know more about visual data?

Reavey, P. (ed.) (2011) *Visual Psychologies: Using and Interpreting Images in Qualitative Research*. London: Routledge.

Reavey, P. and Johnson, K. (2008) 'Visual approaches: using and interpreting images', in C. Willig and W. Stainton-Rogers (eds) *The Sage Handbook of Qualitative Research In Psychology*. London: Sage. pp 296–314.

Temple, M. and McVittie, C. (2005) 'Ethical and practical issues in using visual methodologies: the legacy of research-originating visual products', *Qualitative Research in Psychology*, 2, 227–39.

Mixing methods

Having introduced a range of methods of data collection, it is important to highlight that these need not necessarily be thought of as mutually exclusive alternatives but can be combined to form a mixed methods approach. Often when researchers talk about mixed methods they mean the use of qualitative and quantitative methods in the same project, although it is just as possible to use different qualitative methods together. One of the key advantages of mixing methods is to enable you to gather data from a range of different sources and to consider how it does, or does not, converge – something known as *triangulation*.

In a nutshell: triangulation

Triangulation refers to the combined use of different datasets collected by more than one method or from different participant groups. Triangulation can be thought of as a form of quality check on your data; for example, does data from different methods point to similar findings? However, how you think about triangulation does depend on the epistemological and ontological features of your research (see Madill et al., 2000).

Activity: the challenges of triangulation

Consider the following research scenario. How might you respond to these challenges?

A researcher is interested in the ways that primary school classroom teaching assistants promote the social and emotional development of children with particular needs. Schools, and individual assistants, have agreed to

(Continued)

(Continued)

take part on the basis that multiple data sources will be examined, including interview data from parents, pupils and other staff. However, some classroom assistants are concerned that the study might not adequately capture the depth of their engagement with pupils as this develops over long periods of time. They are also concerned that the study might not identify what value they bring to pupils, particularly as no objective measures of academic development are being used.

How might a researcher manage potentially competing interests of different participants in a way that does not diminish the benefits of triangulation? Some suggested solutions to this problem are identified at the end of the chapter.

Regardless of whether you mix different methods of qualitative data collection, or qualitative and quantitative methods, the crucial point is to be consistent in the sorts of assumptions you make about your data. So, although you can relatively easily mix *methods* of data collection, mixing methodologies is much more problematic (see Frost et al., 2010). If you are planning to mix methods, the recommendation is to have a clear understanding of the ontological and epistemological frameworks that underlie the methods you're using and aim for consistency throughout the project. Remember that epistemological and ontological coherence is one of the hallmarks of an excellent qualitative study. If you're not sure what we mean by this, see Chapter 1 for further discussion on ontology and epistemology, and Chapter 8 on quality criteria.

Cautionary tale: methodological mix-ups

Karen was interested in finding out about people's attitudes to the prison system. She initially planned to use a questionnaire with standard Likert response scales in order to determine people's attitudes on a number of relevant issues. She then intended to conduct follow-up interviews with a small number of participants and analyse them using discourse analysis in order to see if people with different types of attitudes constructed the prison system in different ways. However, after reading around discourse analysis (see Chapter 7) and discussing her ideas with her supervisor, she realised that her ideas were problematic insofar as discourse analysis challenges the whole idea of people having identifiable 'attitudes' as conventionally understood. Once she grasped this, she adapted the study to use discourse analysis to show how even people with apparently strong attitudes towards the prison system may display the sorts of variability in their discourse that analysts such as Potter and Wetherell (1987) and Billig (1989) have identified.

The key lessons from this tale: read up on your chosen approaches in advance, and always discuss your ideas with your supervisor.

Want to know more about mixed methods?

Todd, Z., Nerlich, B., McKeown, S. and Clarke, D.D. (2004) *Mixing Methods in Psychology: The Integration of Qualitative and Quantitative Methods in Theory and Practice.* Hove: Psychology Press.

Yardley, L. and Bishop, F. (2008) 'Mixing qualitative and quantitative methods: a pragmatic approach', in C. Willig and W. Stainton-Rogers (eds) *The Sage Handbook of Qualitative Research in Psychology.* London: Sage. pp. 352–69.

Practical issues in data collection

How much data do I need?

Students frequently ask this question, but it is a tricky one to answer. There are no hard-and-fast rules, and it is crucial that you are guided by your supervisor who will be able to tailor advice to your specific project far better than we're able to. As a general rule, fewer participants are involved in qualitative projects than would be in experimental or survey studies. This is because qualitative studies typically collect more data from individual participants. The amount of data you collect will also depend on the particular approach you take. Finally, you need to consider what is feasible to do in the time allocated to your project. All of these issues need to be fully discussed with your supervisor. As a guide, however, we offer the general guidelines below for final year undergraduate projects, based on the recommendations of Gough et al. (2003).

In a nutshell: how much data do I need?

Method of analysis	Recommended (minimum) hours of data
Thematic analysis	5 hours (inc. pilot work)
IPA	5 hours (inc. pilot work)
Grounded theory	5 hours (inc. pilot work)
Conversation analysis	1–2 hours
Discourse analysis	3–4 hours
Narrative analysis	3–4 hours

Adapted from Gough et al. (2003: 12).

It is worth noting that, although the difference between undergraduate and postgraduate research is more about the conceptual level of the work than the size of the data set, it is also likely that postgraduate research would require more data than the minimum figures given here.

If your data consist of written documents (such as media reports, diary methods or Internet discussion forums) then you will need to adapt these guidelines somewhat. In terms of the extent of printed material, five hours' worth of interview transcript could run to something like 100–125 pages of A4 paper (single line spacing, 12-point font size). This should give you a rough idea of how much data from written documents would be roughly equivalent. However, if you are using unsolicited data on the Internet (for example, discussion forums), then given that you don't need to recruit participants, conduct interviews and then transcribe them, it is reasonable to assume that you should be analysing a more extensive dataset. Again, your supervisor should be in a position to advise you on what is likely to work best in your specific project.

Recording

If you are using interviews or focus groups, or want to analyse 'naturalistic' conversational data, then you will need to make recordings using either audio or video technology. Audio recording is easy and relatively cheap, with most researchers using digital recording devices of some sort. Most such devices are the size of an MP3 player, and work in a fairly similar fashion, with the obvious exception that they record sound. The quality, even from relatively inexpensive devices, is typically very good, and they usually record sound into files that can be used on any standard computer. Most come with a USB connector so that you can simply transfer your files to your computer when you are done.

Top tip: batteries not included!

Always take spare batteries with you. This sounds obvious, but it is easy to forget and you will kick yourself if you lose data simply because you can't record it. Technical problems do happen, but you can prepare for them – if possible, you could even take a spare recording device with you in case one stops working.

If you are using Internet data, you should make sure that you save copies of the web pages you want to analyse. Because of the rapidly changing nature of online material, it can be useful to set a particular date and time on which to sample your materials and save them to your computer. Make sure that you then use the stored data rather than returning to the website, as the material on it might have changed.

Cautionary tale: the disappearing webpage

Umit was interested in the way in which fans of a television science fiction programme, Farscape, displayed their identity as fans of the show, and how they defined what counted as committed or 'genuine' fan behaviour. He planned to use data from an Internet discussion forum devoted to discussion among Farscape fans, and he spent quite a bit of time reading around topics such as identity, as well as methodological literature on discourse analysis – the approach he was planning to use. However, he didn't print out or save copies of the actual discussions themselves when he first decided to pursue the project, assuming that they would be available online when he came to do his analysis. When he returned to the website several weeks later he found that the site was no longer online. The lesson here is to be aware that data on the Internet can disappear as quickly as it can appear, so make sure you save a copy of any webpages you think might be useful as data.

Transcription

If you are using audio or video data then you will need to transcribe your data. Although at first glance it might seem that transcription is a routine technical matter, it is actually better thought of as a preliminary part of the analysis. Transcription is theory-laden and the way in which you transcribe your data reflects a range of ontological and epistemological assumptions. For this reason we deal with it more extensively in Chapter 7 (where you will also find some useful references on transcription), but note here that there are some concrete practical tips that can simplify the process of transcription.

Top tips: transcription practicalities

- The better the sound quality of your data the easier it will be to transcribe. Try to bear this in mind when selecting recording equipment and arranging locations for interviews or focus groups.
- Use a transcription machine – these allow you to control the playback of your recording using a foot pedal, and you can get ones with USB connections, which allow you to transcribe digital sound files using a word processing programme. Ask your departmental technician if you have access to one.
- Allow plenty of time for transcription. For a relatively basic transcription you will probably need around five or six hours to transcribe every hour of recorded data. For a more detailed transcription (as used in conversation analysis and some forms of discourse analysis) it might be closer to 20 hours!

Storing

An issue that is sometimes neglected is how you store your data. It is vitally important that participants' data is stored securely and in accordance with relevant legal frameworks. In the UK, the Data Protection Act applies, and data that might be used to identify participants should not be stored in a way that contravenes this Act.

Top tips: data storage and data protection

- Securely store data that might be used to identify participants – at the very least this means password protecting computer files and keeping any hard copies under lock-and-key.
- Don't retain data that might be used to identify participants for longer than is strictly necessary for your project. Indicate on your consent form how long information will be retained, and after this date, destroy it.
- Anonymised data can (and should) be retained.
- Check the relevant legal framework in your country. You should have someone at your university who can advise you – in the UK, institutions should have data protection officers. If in doubt, ask your supervisor.

Want to know more about data storage?

Howitt, D. (2010) *Introduction to Qualitative Methods in Psychology.* Harlow: Pearson. [pp. 399–402 discusses these issues in the context of research ethics.]
Lancaster University's Social Science Research Ethics website has a useful guide to the key issues of data protection for social researchers in the UK: http://www.lancs.ac.uk/researchethics/1–7-dataproact.html

Note also that the issue of how you store your data is more than simply a matter of data protection. Organising and managing your data effectively will help you to conduct your analysis much more effectively, and make it far simpler when it comes to selecting material to include in your write-up.

Conclusion

In this chapter we have introduced some of the major considerations concerning data collection. To conclude, let us return to the key questions we posed at the beginning of the chapter to show you how we have addressed them.

- What do I want to know? (Or, what is my research question?)
  We have seen how your method of data collection should enable you to answer your research question, as well as being consistent with the other key elements of your methodology – your epistemological and ontological position, and your analytic approach.
- Who or what could help me answer/understand that?
  You should now appreciate that the range of potential data sources in qualitative research are multiple. Interviews are still the most common method of data collection, but more and more researchers are turning to the Internet and other novel forms of data (such as multi-modal data) to help them understand various phenomena.
- Is one source of data enough or do I need to look at others also?
  For many projects, one is likely to be ideal, however we have seen that it is perfectly possible for student projects to combine data from different sources (and to combine qualitative and quantitative data), provided that they don't lead you into epistemological confusions!
- How much data should I collect?
  We have seen how different amounts of data may be appropriate for different qualitative approaches, and emphasised the importance of discussing this issue in detail with your supervisor.
- What equipment/resources do I need?
  Audio recording and transcription equipment are the two most common pieces of kit needed by students doing qualitative projects. The best advice is to think about this early and plan ahead – competition for resources in your department may be fierce! For more on planning see Chapter 3.
- How am I going to analyse my data?
  You'll by now appreciate that how you collect your data depends in large part upon how you plan to analyse it, and in the next chapter we'll take you through a range of approaches to analysis.

Activity: the challenges of triangulation – suggested solutions

This is a complex problem, and not one an undergraduate student is likely to encounter. However, it shows how tricky it can be to triangulate in qualitative research, especially when participants are feeling anxious about what the study might mean for them. In this scenario, it might work to interview classroom assistants first, and have them involved in the design of other data collection methods to be used in the study. This would capitalise on their insider knowledge of classrooms and pupils, and might generate some new ways of capturing the impact that they have with particular children.

References

Anderson, J. (2004) 'Talking whilst walking: a geographical archaeology of knowledge', *Area*, 36, 254–61.

Alaszewski, A. (2006) *Using Diaries for Social Research*. London: Sage.

Ashmore, M. and Reed, D. (2000) 'Innocence and nostalgia in conversation analysis: The dynamic relations of tape and transcript', *Forum: Qualitative Social Research*, 1, Art. 3, http://nbn-resolving.de/urn:nbn:de:0114-fqs000335.

Atkinson, P. and Silverman, D. (1997) 'Kundera's immortality: the interview society and the invention of the self', *Qualitative Inquiry*, 3, 304–25.

Billig, M. (1989) 'The argumentative nature of holding strong views: a case study', *European Journal of Social Psychology*, 19, 203–33.

Bolger, N., Davis, A. and Rafaeli, E. (2003) 'Diary methods: capturing life as it is lived', *Annual Review of Psychology*, 54, 579–616.

British Psychological Society (2007) *Report of the Working Party on Conducing Research on the Internet: Guidelines for Ethical Practice in Psychological Research Online.* Leicester: British Psychological Society.

British Psychological Society (2009) *Code of Ethics and Conduct.* Leicester: British Psychological Society.

Brownlow, C. and O'Dell, L. (2002) 'Ethical issues for qualitative research in online communities', *Disability and Society*, 17, 685–94.

Carter, B. (2002) 'Chronic pain in childhood and the medical encounter: professional ventriloquism and hidden voices', *Qualitative Health Research*, 12, 28–41.

Catalini, C. and Minkler, M. (2010) 'Photovoice: a review of the literature in health and public health', *Public Health Education and Behaviour*, 37, 424–51.

Collins, A. (2010) 'On events and facts: the role of historical accounts in making psychology', keynote address given to BPS Qualitative Methods in Psychology Section Conference, Nottingham.

Day, M. and Thatcher, J. (2009) '"I'm really embarrassed that you're going to read this ... ": reflections on using diaries in qualitative research', *Qualitative Research in Psychology*, 6, 249–59.

Evans, A., Elford, J. and Wiggins, D. (2008) 'Using the internet for qualitative research', in C.Willig and W. Stainton-Rogers (eds) *The Sage Handbook of Qualitative Research in Psychology.* London: Sage. pp. 315–333.

Fielding, N. (2004) 'Getting the most from archived qualitative data: epistemological, practical and professional obstacles', *International Journal of Social Research Methodology*, 7, 97–104.

Finley, N. (2010) 'Skating femininity: gender manoeuvreing in women's roller derby', *Journal of Contemporary Ethnography*, 39, 359–87.

Flowers, P., Knussen C. and Duncan, B. (2000) 'Community, responsibility and culpability: HIV risk-management amongst Scottish gay men', *Journal of Community and Applied Social Psychology*, 10, 285–300.

Frost, N., Nolas, S.M., Brooks-Gordon, B., Esin, C., Holt, A., Mehdizadeh, L. and Shinebourne, P. (2010) 'Pluralism in qualitative research: the impact of different researchers and qualitative approaches on the analysis of qualitative data', *Qualitative Research*, 10, 441–60.

Gibson, S. (2011) 'Milgram's obedience experiments: a rhetorical analysis', *British Journal of Social Psychology*. Advance online publication.

Gough, B., Lawton, R., Madill, A. and Stratton, P. (2003) *Guidelines for the Supervision of Undergraduate Qualitative Research in Psychology.* York: LTSN Psychology.

Guijarro, J.M. and Sanz, M.J.P. (2008) 'Compositional, interpersonal and representational meanings in a children's narrative: a multimodal discourse analysis', *Journal of Pragmatics*, 40, 1601–19.

Green, A.S., Rafaeli, E., Bolger, N., Shrout, P.E. and Reis, H.T. (2006) 'Paper or plastic? Data equivalence in paper and electronic diaries', *Psychological Methods*, 11, 87–105.

Hester, S. and Francis, D. (1994) 'Doing data: the local organization of a sociological interview', *British Journal of Sociology*, 45, 675–95.

Hiles, D. and Čermák, I. (2008) 'Narrative psychology', in C.Willig and W. Stainton-Rogers (eds) *The Sage Handbook of Qualitative Research in Psychology*. London: Sage. pp. 147–64.

Hine, C. (2000) *Virtual Ethnography*. London: Sage.

Howitt, D. (2010) *Introduction to Qualitative Methods in Psychology*. Harlow: Pearson.

Hugh-Jones, S. (2010) 'The interview in qualitative research', in M. Forrester (ed.) *Doing Qualitative Research in Psychology: A Practical Guide*. London: Sage. pp. 77–97.

Hugh-Jones, S., Gough, B. and Littlewood, A. (2005) 'Sexual exhibitionism as 'sexuality and individuality': a critique of psycho-medical discourse from the perspectives of women who exhibit', *Sexualities*, 8, 259–81.

Hussain, Z. and Griffiths, M.D. (2009) 'The attitudes, feelings and experiences of online gamers: a qualitative analysis', *CyberPsychology and Behavior*, 12, 747–53.

Hutchby, I. (2007) *The Discourse of Child Counselling*. Amsterdam: John Benjamins.

Hutchby, I. and Barnett, S. (2005) 'Aspects of the sequential organization of mobile phone conversation', *Discourse Studies*, 7, 147–71.

Jacelon, C.S. and Imperio, K. (2005) 'Participant diaries as a source of data in research with older adults', *Qualitative Health Research*, 15, 991–7.

Jones, S. (ed.) (1999) *Doing Internet Research: Critical Issues and Methods for Examining the Net*. London: Sage.

Kaun, A. (2010) 'Open-ended online diaries: capturing life as it is narrated', *International Journal of Qualitative Methods*, 9, 133–48.

Kazmer, M.M. and Xie, B. (2008) 'Qualitative interviewing in Internet studies: playing with media, playing with the method', *Information, Communication and Society*, 11, 257–78.

Keleher, H.M. and Verrinder, G.K. (2003) 'Health diaries in a rural Australian study', *Qualitative Health Research*, 13, 435–43.

Kitzinger, C. and Kitzinger, S. (2007) 'Birth trauma: talking with women and the value of conversation analysis', *British Journal of Midwifery*, 15, 256–64.

Kitzinger, J. (1994) 'The methodology of focus groups: the importance of interaction between research participants', *Sociology of Health and Illness*, 16, 103–21.

Kvale, S. (1996) *InterViews: An Introduction to Qualitative Research Interviewing*. London: Sage.

Liebenberg, L. (2009) 'The visual image as discussion point: increasing validity in boundary crossing research', Qualitative Research, 9, 441–67.

Lynn, N. and Lea, S.J. (2005) 'Through the looking glass: considering the challenges visual methodologies raise for qualitative research', *Qualitative Research in Psychology*, 2, 213–25.

Madill, A. (2011) 'Interaction in the semi-structured interview: comparative analysis of the use of and response to indirect complaints', *Qualitative Research in Psychology*, 8(4), 333–53.

Madill, A. (forthcoming) 'Interviews and interviewing techniques', in A.T. Panter (ed.) *APA Handbook of Research Methods in Psychology*. Washington, DC: APA.

Madill, A., Jordan, A. and Shirley, C. (2000) 'Objectivity and reliability in qualitative analysis: realist, contextualist and radical constructionist epistemologies', *British Journal of Psychology*, 91, 1–20.

Matthews, J. and Cramer, E.P. (2008) 'Using technology to enhance qualitative research with hidden populations', *The Qualitative Report*, 13, 301–15.

McAdams, D.P. (1993) *The Stories We Live By: Personal Myths and the Making of the Self.* New York: Guilford.

Merrilees, C.E., Goeke-Morey, M. and Cummings, E.M. (2008) 'Do event-contingent diaries about marital conflict change marital interactions?', *Behaviour Research and Therapy*, 46, 253–62.

Milgram, S. (1974) *Obedience to Authority: An Experimental View.* New York: Harper and Row.

Mishler, E.G. (1986) *Research Interviewing: Context and Narrative.* Cambridge, MA: Harvard University Press.

Monrouxe, L.V. (2009) 'Solicited audio diaries in longitudinal research: a view from inside', *Qualitative Research*, 9, 81–103.

Murray, C.D. (2005) 'The social meanings of prosthesis use', *Journal of Health Psychology*, 10, 425–41.

Murray, L. (2009) 'Looking at and looking back: visualization in mobile research', *Qualitative Research*, 9, 469–88.

O'Brien, M.R. and Clark, D. (2010) 'Use of unsolicited first-person written illness narratives in research: systematic review', *Journal of Advanced Nursing*, 66, 1671–82.

Palmer, M., Larkin, M., de Visser, R. and Fadden, G. (2010) 'Developing an interpretative phenomenological approach to focus group data', *Qualitative Research in Psychology*, 7, 99–121.

Parry, O. and Mauthner, N. (2004) 'Whose data are they anyway? Practical, legal and ethical issues in archiving qualitative research data', *Sociology*, 38, 139–52.

Parker, I. (1999) 'Introduction: varieties of discourse and analysis', in I. Parker and the Bolton Discourse Network (eds) *Critical Textwork: An Introduction to Varieties of Discourse and Analysis.* Buckingham: Open University Press. pp. 1–12.

Patterson, A. and Potter, J. (2009) 'Caring: building a psychological disposition in pre-closing sequences in phone calls with a young adult with a learning disability', *British Journal of Social Psychology*, 48, 447–65.

Peel, E., Parry, O., Douglas, M. and Lawton, J. (2006) '"It's no skin off my nose": why people take part in qualitative research', *Qualitative Health Research*, 16, 1335–49.

Potter, J. (2004) 'Discourse analysis', in M. Hardy and A. Bryman (eds) *Handbook of Data Analysis.* London: Sage. pp. 607–624.

Potter, J. and Hepburn, A. (2003) '"I'm a bit concerned" – early actions and psychological constructions in a child protection helpline', *Research on Language and Social Interaction*, 36, 197–240.

Potter, J. and Hepburn, A. (2005) 'Qualitative interview in psychology: problems and possibilities', *Qualitative Research in Psychology*, 2, 281–307.

Potter, J. and Wetherell, M. (1987) *Discourse and Social Psychology: Beyond Attitudes and Behaviour.* London: Sage.

Puchta, C. and Potter, J. (2004) *Focus Group Practice.* London: Sage.

Rapley, T. (2007) *Doing Conversation, Discourse and Document Analysis.* London: Sage.

Reavey, P. (ed.) (2011) *Visual Psychologies: Using and Interpreting Images in Qualitative Research*. London: Routledge.

Reavey, P. and Johnson, K. (2008) 'Visual approaches: using and interpreting images', in C. Willig and W. Stainton-Rogers (eds) *The Sage Handbook of Qualitative Research In Psychology*. London: Sage. pp. 296–314.

Robinson, K.M. (2001) 'Unsolicited narratives from the internet: a rich source of qualitative data', *Qualitative Health Research*, 11, 706–14.

Riley, S., Rodham, K. and Gavin, J. (2009) 'Doing weight: pro-ana and recovery identities in cyberspace', *Journal of Community and Applied Social Psychology*, 19, 348–59.

Russell, N.J.C. (2011) 'Milgram's obedience to authority experiments: origins and early evolution', *British Journal of Social Psychology*, 50, 140–62.

Sarbin, T.R. (1986) *Narrative Psychology: The Storied Nature of Human Conduct*. New York: Praeger.

Sneijder, P. and te Molder, H. (2009) 'Normalising ideological food choice and eating practices. Identity work in online discussions on veganism', *Appetite*, 52, 621–30.

Spagnoli, A. and Gamberini, L. (2007) 'Interacting via SMS: practices of social closeness and reciprocation', *British Journal of Social Psychology*, 46, 343–64.

Speer, S.A. (2002) '"Natural" and "contrived" data: a sustainable distinction?', *Discourse Studies*, 4, 511–25.

Stokoe, E. (2009) '"For the benefit of the tape": formulating embodied conduct in designedly uni-modal recorded police-suspect interrogations', *Journal of Pragmatics*, 41, 1887–1904.

Stokoe, E. (2010) '"I'm not gonna hit a lady": conversation analysis, membership categorisation and men's denials of violence towards women', *Discourse and Society*, 21, 59–82.

Temple, M. and McVittie, C. (2005) 'Ethical and practical issues in using visual methodologies: the legacy of research-originating visual products', *Qualitative Research in Psychology*, 2, 227–39.

Thomsen, D.K. and Brinkmann, S. (2009) 'An interviewer's guide to autobiographical memory: ways to elicit concrete experiences and to avoid pitfalls in interpreting them', *Qualitative Research in Psychology*, 6, 294–312.

Todd, Z., Nerlich, B., McKeown, S. and Clarke, D.D. (2004) *Mixing Methods in Psychology: The Integration of Qualitative and Quantitative Methods in Theory and Practice*. Hove: Psychology Press.

Toerien, M. and Kitzinger, C. (2007) 'Emotional labour in action: navigating multiple involvements in the beauty salon', *Sociology*, 41, 645–62.

van Eeden-Moorefield, B., Proulx, C.M. and Pasley, K. (2008) 'A comparison of Internet and face-to-face (FTF) qualitative methods in studying the relationships of gay men', *Journal of GLBT Family Studies*, 4, 181–204.

Wiggins, S. and Potter, J. (2003) 'Attitudes and evaluative practices: category vs. item and subjective vs. objective constructions in everyday food assessments', *British Journal of Social Psychology*, 42, 513–31.

Williams, J.P. (2006) 'Authentic identities: straightedge subculture, music and the Internet', *Journal of Contemporary Ethnography*, 35, 173–200.

Willig, C. (2008) *Introducing Qualitative Research in Psychology: Adventures in Theory and Method* (2nd edn). Maidenhead: Open University Press.

Wooffitt, R. Holt, N. and Allistone, S. (2010) 'Introspection as institutional practice: reflections on the attempt to capture conscious experience in a parapsychology experiment', *Qualitative Research in Psychology*, 7, 5–20.

Wright, C.Y., Darko, N., Standen, P.J. and Patel, T.G. (2010) 'Visual research methods: using cameras to empower socially excluded black youth', *Sociology*, 44, 541–58.

Yardley, L. and Bishop, F. (2008) 'Mixing qualitative and quantitative methods: a pragmatic approach', in C.Willig and W. Stainton-Rogers (eds) *The Sage Handbook of Qualitative Research in Psychology*. London: Sage. pp. 352–369.

7

ANALYSING YOUR DATA

Stephen Gibson and Siobhan Hugh-Jones

Introduction

Deciding which analytic approach is most appropriate for your project is a central task of doing qualitative research. In this chapter, we help you with your decision making about your data analysis by giving you an overview of:

- what is available to you in terms of the most prominent qualitative analytic approaches used; and
- the principles and practices of data analysis that are shared by qualitative approaches.

We expect this to be especially useful to you at two stages of your project: when you are planning your project and when you start to analyse your data.

In the planning stage, this chapter should be useful for you as you develop your research question (see also Chapter 2). One of the hallmarks of an excellent qualitative project is ensuring coherence between your research question, method of data collection and analytic approach. As you are developing your research question you will need to know several things about data analysis that are considered in this chapter, namely:

- What approaches are available that you could use to answer your question.
- Whether these approaches come with any conceptual 'baggage' that need to be coherent with other aspects of your project (for example, their epistemological assumptions, preference for a specific kind of data collection method, or the way that they would phrase a research question).
- Where you might turn for a deeper understanding of the method that you think you're going to use.
- General principles of qualitative analysis that you should know about before embarking on your study.

You may also find this chapter useful when you start your analysis. Doing an excellent project will mean that you've read more widely on your chosen method of analysis, but the focus in this chapter on the common principles and practices of data analysis that are shared by qualitative approaches will help locate your specific reading within a wider understanding of how to do high-quality analysis. Our 'top tips' sections should also help you with this.

In a nutshell: analysing your data

The chapter is structured around three key questions.

1 What different approaches to data analysis are there?
There are many approaches to choose from. We discuss six of the most popular: thematic analysis; interpretative phenomenological analysis; grounded theory; narrative analysis; discourse analysis; and conversation analysis.
2 How do I decide which approach to take?
Different approaches are better suited to different sorts of questions, and which you choose will depend on your interests and what you want to find out. This chapter includes a decision-making flowchart to help you decide which approach might be most appropriate for your study.
3 How do I do qualitative analysis?
How you do your analysis will vary depending on the approach you select. However, there are some principles and practices that are common to all approaches: remaining 'anchored' to your research question; ensuring an appropriate form of transcription; the importance of careful reading; and conducting a systematic analysis.

Approaches to data analysis

Although qualitative methods have had a place in psychology since the discipline's origins, the last 30 years has seen an upsurge of interest in qualitative methods in the discipline. This has generated an array of exciting, useful and practical approaches to qualitative analysis (Willig and Stainton-Rogers, 2008a). The field is constantly progressing and evolving, with researchers using methods in fresh, flexible ways, applying them to novel areas and to different types of data. For the novice researcher (and even for those more experienced) the considerable number of options available for qualitative analysis can be confusing, if not overwhelming, and the reluctance to specify 'how to do' analysis that occurs with some approaches can create anxieties about whether or not one's analysis is legitimate.

To try to overcome some of these anxieties, we provide overviews of six of the most widely used approaches below. These are thematic analysis, interpretative phenomenological analysis (IPA), grounded theory, narrative analysis, discourse analysis and conversation analysis. As we go through these approaches, we will refer to a number of concepts introduced in Chapter 1 (for example phenomenology, constructionism, critical realism). The intention is to highlight key points and to direct you to resources to help with the 'nuts and bolts' of analysis. In addition to the texts listed after each approach, there are several excellent introductory textbooks on qualitative approaches in psychology. The analytic approaches covered in the most popular introductory texts published in the last five years are listed in Table 7.1. These are excellent places to begin finding out about approaches in more detail, but to do well in your project you will need to use additional publications that specialise in your chosen method of analysis.

Table 7.1 Coverage of introductory qualitative methods texts in psychology

Text	TA	IPA	GT	NA	DA	CA
Forrester (2010a)		✓	✓		✓	✓
Howitt (2010)	✓	✓	✓	✓	✓	✓
Lyons and Coyle (2007)		✓	✓	✓	✓	
Smith (2008)		✓	✓	✓	✓	✓
Willig (2008)		✓	✓		✓	

Note: TA = thematic analysis; IPA = interpretative phenomenological analysis; GT = grounded theory; NA = narrative analysis; DA = discourse analysis; CA = conversation analysis.

Top tip: read widely around your chosen approach

The best projects will display evidence of wider reading beyond standard introductory texts on your chosen approach. Consult some of the more in-depth sources listed in the further reading boxes below and use databases such as PsycINFO to look for the latest research that has used your method of analysis. (See also Chapter 5 on carrying out a literature review.)

As Table 7.1 suggests, thematic analysis tends not to be covered as often as other approaches, yet if you are new to qualitative research, there are good reasons for exploring this approach first.

Thematic analysis

Braun and Clarke (2006) argue that thematic analysis should be seen as a foundational approach for qualitative analysis. By this they mean that it provides the foundations upon which many other approaches are built. In particular, the process of thematic *coding* underpins IPA, grounded theory and narrative analysis. However, Braun and Clarke also suggest that thematic analysis should be seen as an approach in its own right, which may be particularly suited to research questions concerned primarily with the *content* of what people say. Central to thematic analysis is the identification of *themes* in data.

Thematic analysis can be divided into two broad varieties: data-driven and theory-driven analyses. Data-driven thematic analysis involves trying to avoid starting with any pre-determined theoretical ideas and being as open-minded as possible about what you might find in the data. Note, however, that it is impossible to cast off completely all of our many and varied preconceptions and assumptions about the world, so the best we can usually aim for is to be aware of how these preconceived ideas shape such things as the topic we choose to study, the questions we ask of our participants, and the areas we choose to focus on in analysis and writing-up. This idea is at the heart of the concept of reflexivity, which is central to all approaches to qualitative research (see Chapter 8).

Key definitions

Coding: An analytic technique used in many qualitative approaches, coding involves working through a transcript and noting down short comments on segments (for example, a line, or whole speaking turn) of your data, usually in the margins of your transcript.

Theme: 'A theme captures something important about the data in relation to the research question, and represents some level of patterned response or meaning within the data set' (Braun and Clarke, 2006: 82).

Theory-driven thematic analysis is particularly useful when you have a set of theoretical concepts you want to apply or test in a novel context. The aim is not to 'test' them in the statistical sense of seeing if they can withstand falsification, but is instead to see if they are of use in making sense of the situation you are interested in, and to determine if the data are consistent with the theory, or whether the theory might need to be modified in order to provide a better explanation of the data. In this respect, you might actually begin with a series of themes and look for them in your data (termed 'a priori' themes) – see Hayes (1997) for an example of such an approach. If you are interested in exploring theory-driven thematic analysis further, a particularly useful form of this approach is template analysis (King, 2004). In principle, thematic analysis can be used on data collected with a wide variety of qualitative methods. As with many approaches though, it tends to be associated with interview data.

Want to know more about thematic analysis?

Braun, V. and Clarke, V. (2006) 'Using thematic analysis in psychology', *Qualitative Research in Psychology*, 3, 77–101. (As yet there are no book-length introductions to thematic analysis in psychology, and so Braun and Clarke's article is essential reading – it is highly readable and includes lots of useful practical advice.)

Nigel King's Template Analysis website provides a useful guide to a theory-driven approach to TA: http://www.hud.ac.uk/hhs/research/template_analysis/index.htm

Interpretative phenomenological analysis

IPA focuses on individual experience and the meanings that such experience has for people. It adopts an idiographic approach to research where the aim is to arrive at a rich description of individual cases. This is in contrast to the nomothetic approach, which attempts to uncover universal laws. Thus, IPA research tends to work with either case studies or very small sample sizes. This is appropriate as the aim of IPA is not to make generalisable claims in the same way that you might want to do if you were conducting a survey or experiment. However, this does not mean that the approach is any less detailed. IPA typically involves the use of semi-structured, one-to-one interviews. Analysis proceeds on transcripts presented in a broadly playscript format (see section on transcription later in this chapter) and involves a process of coding similar to that used in thematic analysis.

The key distinguishing feature of IPA is, as its name suggests, its emphasis on phenomenology and interpretation. It can be seen as a critical realist approach insofar as it takes a cautious view of the relationship between what is said in an interview and a participant's actual experiences, but nevertheless takes the position that such experience is real, and can be made sense of by the analyst through a process of careful analysis (Shaw, 2010). This is at the heart of IPA's engagement with the concept of reflexivity, which emphasises the researcher's active role in interpreting participants' experiences.

IPA stresses the role of interpretation in two respects: (1) as people, we make sense of our phenomenological experiences; and (2) as researchers, we seek to make sense of other people who are trying to make sense of their own experiences. This two-sided approach to interpretation is known as the *double hermeneutic*. By employing such an approach, some advocates of IPA have suggested that it allows them to transcend the distinction between discourse and cognition (see, for example, Smith, 1996).

Key definition

Double hermeneutic: A process of interpretation which stresses that in the same way that people seek to make sense of (interpret) their experience, so the researcher needs to interpret people's own interpretations of those experiences.

In Chapter 8 it is argued that a research diary is useful for all research, but keeping a diary is particularly important for IPA (and grounded theory) to help the researcher to maintain a reflective diary to record impressions, hunches, and other notes on the analytic process (see Shaw, 2010). This helps to remind you that you are yourself engaged in a process of interpreting what the participant has said, something that is central to the idea of the double hermeneutic.

Want to know more about IPA?

Smith, J.A. Flowers, P. and Larkin, M. (2009) *Interpretative Phenomenological Analysis: Theory, Method and Research*. London: Sage. (A comprehensive introduction to IPA.)

Langdridge, D. (2007) *Phenomenological Psychology: Theory, Research and Method*. Harlow: Pearson. (Covers a range of approaches to phenomenology within psychology, including IPA, and is therefore particularly useful for placing IPA in a broader conceptual and methodological context.)

A useful web resource, which includes plenty of references to IPA method chapters and research papers: http://www.ipa.bbk.ac.uk

Grounded theory

Grounded theory was developed by the sociologists Glaser and Strauss (1967) as a way of developing theory inductively. By this, grounded theorists mean that, rather than starting with a theory and testing it (as is the case with hypothetico-deductivism, which underpins the experimental method) we can start with data and develop theory from it.

The central aim of grounded theory is to develop theory that is grounded in the data. Grounded theorists go as far as to suggest that you should avoid a literature review at the start of your project in case this pre-determines your course and limits the capacity for the data to truly drive theory development. Instead, a grounded theory project ideally features a delayed literature review (see Chapter 5). In this respect, grounded theory differs from approaches such as thematic analysis and IPA because of its emphasis on developing theory in order to understand processes and causal relations. It is often characterised as a realist approach, but recent developments have resulted in a specifically constructionist strand of grounded theory (see Charmaz, 2006).

Grounded theory makes use of an extended process of coding, beginning with open coding and working through focused coding, axial coding and theoretical coding (Gordon-Finlayson [2010] provides a particularly good explanation of the distinctions between these types of coding). At any point in this process you might find yourself returning to an earlier stage in the analysis, which means that different stages of the analysis feed back into each other and can be repeated several times if necessary. In this sense, grounded theory is not a straightforward linear process of analysis, but is cyclical. For example, grounded theorists emphasise the importance of continuing the process of data collection once analysis is under way. This allows you to test out hunches on cases that might provide a challenge to your emerging theory. For example, Payne (2007) provides an extended example of a study of older Chinese people living in the UK who had been treated for cancer. She describes how initially the research involved sampling participants who were members of community groups, but as the study developed the researchers began to wonder if their emerging theory would be equally applicable to people who had not joined such groups, and so conducted interviews with a sample of participants who were not members of community groups. This process is called theoretical sampling (see Chapter 3 for more on sampling).

An important process in grounded theory is memo writing, which involves frequent and systematic recording of your thoughts, ideas and reflections on your data at every stage of analysis. This is separate to coding, although it can (and should) expand upon things that you notice during coding. Gordon-Finlayson (2010: 164) describes memo writing as 'the engine of grounded theory' because it is in your memos that you will develop and refine your initial ideas that may lead you ultimately to your theory. As noted above, the grounded theory process is not linear and therefore does not have an obvious end point. However, grounded theorists recommend that you should stop your analysis when you reach the point of theoretical saturation, that is, when further data collection and analysis no longer adds anything to your theory.

Want to know more about grounded theory?

Corbin, J. and Strauss, A. (2008) *Basics of Qualitative Research* (3rd edn). London: Sage. (Despite the title, this text is devoted entirely to the grounded theory approach to qualitative research, which it outlines in a clear and accessible manner.)

Charmaz, C. (2006). *Constructing Grounded Theory: A Practical Guide Through Qualitative Analysis*. London: Sage. (Outlines Charmaz's social constructionist version of grounded theory.)

Narrative analysis

Narrative analysis, or narrative psychology, is an approach that emphasises the storied nature of our attempts to make sense of our lives. In particular, the approach focuses on how people construct a sense of self through *narrative*, and involves asking people for extended accounts of their lives, or some aspect of their lives.

Key definition

Narrative: A narrative is a story that organises some aspect of experience into a meaningful whole, usually with a beginning, a middle and an end.

As with many approaches to qualitative research, narrative analysis frequently involves the use of interviews, typically making use of open-ended questions designed to encourage participants to tell the story of their life, or of some aspect of their life in which the researcher is interested. A particularly useful form of interviewing is biographical or life-story interviewing, in which the interviewer asks the interviewee to tell them the story of their lives (see Chapter 6 for more detail). These tend to be useful in producing the level of detail needed for an in-depth narrative analysis. In principle, however, the approach can be used with a much wider range of data; for example, there is an established tradition of work exploring narrative in therapeutic consultations (see Payne, 2000). Hiles and Čermák (2008) present a useful model of what they call narrative oriented inquiry (NOI). They outline a series of steps in the research process (such as designing the interview schedule and conducting the interview), and provide illustrations of how different types of narrative analysis can be used within this framework.

In analysing narratives, it can often be useful to briefly summarise the beginning, middle and end of the narrative, as well as drawing attention to any other key features (see Murray, 2008). This process often helps to draw attention to the way in which many narratives reflect a standard form, such as a heroic or progressive narrative in which the protagonist proceeds towards their ultimate goal; or a tragedy, in which obstacles along the way impede progress, leading to a failure to achieve the goal. This helps you to begin to understand the form of the narrative you are working with, but you will also want to deal with the specific content of the narrative. In this respect, you might explore the tone of the narrative (for example, optimistic or pessimistic), the images or metaphors used to construct it, the broader themes recurring throughout the narrative, and the underlying values and principles present in the narrative (McAdams, 1993). These are only a selection of the sorts of analytic tools available in narrative analysis; there are many more subtle concepts and distinctions that you will be able to explore using the further reading below.

Want to know more about narrative?

Emerson, P. and Frosh, S. (2004) *Critical Narrative Analysis in Psychology.* Basingstoke: Palgrave MacMillan. (Introduces a critical approach to narrative, influenced by psychoanalytic perspectives.)

Crossley, M. (2000) *Introducing Narrative Psychology: Self, Trauma and the Construction of Meaning.* Buckingham: Open University Press. (Does what it says in the title! A comprehensive introduction to narrative psychology.)

Discourse analysis

Discourse analysis (DA) is the study of language (or *discourse*), and the ways in which it can be used by speakers or writers to formulate versions of 'reality'. It assumes that language can never neutrally represent 'reality' and that it is always action-oriented, by which we mean that words do things. As language users, we are all aware of how we can present different versions of things that happen depending on what impression we want to offer our listener. There are variations in the ways that discourse can be analysed, and McKinlay and McVittie (2008: 8–15) provide a good explanation of the key distinctions between these variations. Wiggins and Riley (2010) show how they contrast by analysing the same data with two different types of DA.

Despite the wide variation in approaches to DA, it is useful to begin your exploration of this approach with Potter and Wetherell (1987). They outlined three key components of DA: construction, function and variation. Discourse analysts are interested in how, through language, people construct versions of objects, events and other phenomena. We can think of this metaphorically through an analogy with house-building. In the same way that a builder would use bricks, mortar, wood and steel to construct a house, so we can think of ourselves as constantly engaged in constructing reality through the use of language. However, in place of bricks and mortar, we use raw materials such as descriptions, clichés, arguments, questions and answers to build a version of our worlds. Importantly, we have at our disposal a range of raw materials that we can put together in different ways, depending on what kind of structure we want to build. Similarly, as a house would be constructed by many builders working together – and sometimes disagreeing on how the house should be built – so we construct our world jointly with others, sometimes arguing about how best to construct it. As a result, discourse analysts emphasise that raw materials such as descriptions (for example, 'It's a bit cold in here') are not neutral statements of reality, but perform some function in the context in which they are used. For example, if someone responds to the above statement by moving to close a window, we might suggest that what was apparently a description actually functioned as a request for a window to be closed. Finally, if people use discursive raw materials to perform a range of different functions, we should expect their constructions of the world to vary depending on the function they are performing.

Taken together, these principles of DA have epistemological implications, notably challenging the notion of a singular truth or reality, and so DA can be seen as a highly relativist social constructionist perspective (see Potter and Hepburn, 2008). However, this is a source of debate as other researchers have developed alternative versions of DA that adopt a critical realist approach (see Parker, 1998; and see Chapter 1 for more discussion of these ideas). As with any qualitative approach, it is important to understand these epistemological issues *before* you begin your project – and indeed, before you decide which version of DA to adopt.

Key definition

Discourse: Any textual or linguistic material, either in spoken or written form.

Want to know more about discourse analysis?

Potter, J. and Wetherell, M. (1987) *Discourse and Social Psychology: Beyond Attitudes and Behaviour.* London: Sage. (The book that introduced DA to social psychology, and still the best starting point for exploring the approach in depth.)

McKinlay, A. and McVittie, C. (2008) *Social Psychology and Discourse.* Oxford: Wiley-Blackwell. (The first, and so far only, introductory textbook devoted exclusively to the DA approach.)
Potter, J. (2007) *Discourse and Psychology* (Vols 1–3). London: Sage. (An impressive collection of classic papers on DA in psychology. Well worth dipping into.)

Conversation analysis

Conversation analysis (CA) was developed in the 1960s by the sociologist Harvey Sacks. In recent years it has been used by a growing number of psychologists interested in the dynamics of conversational interaction. In contrast to many other qualitative approaches, CA stresses the importance of transcripts of 'naturalistic' interactions, such as telephone calls, and everyday conversations. Where interviews have been the subject of conversation analysis, it has been with a view to exploring how the interview works as a particular kind of interaction, rather than using it as a way of understanding people's views, experiences or life histories.

Instead of coding data as would be done in, for example, thematic analysis, CA involves close attention to the details of interaction (see Drew [2008: 136] for an explanation of why coding is not appropriate in CA). In order to facilitate this, a notable feature of conversation analytic work is the level of detail included in its transcripts, which ensures that minute details of intonation, overlap, timings and other features of speech delivery are included (see below). This allows conversation analysts to explore the delicate choreography of social interaction, and has led to many insights on the orderliness of conversation in a variety of informal and formal settings.

A key analytic tool in CA is the notion of participant orientation. Essentially this means that any claims you make about your data should be justifiable with reference to the way in which participants in the interaction(s) you are studying themselves treat the interaction. For example, a conversation analyst would not typically seek to suggest that gender was relevant in an interaction unless it could be demonstrated that the participants in that interaction themselves treated gender as relevant. See Stokoe and Smithson (2001) for a useful critical discussion of this issue.

Want to know more about conversation analysis?

Hutchby, I. and Wooffitt, R. (2008) *Conversation Analysis* (2nd edn). Cambridge: Polity. (A highly accessible introduction to CA.)

(Continued)

(Continued)

Wooffitt, R. (2005) *Conversation and Discourse Analysis: A Comparative and Critical Introduction.* London: Sage. (As the title implies, this book discusses both DA and CA, and as well as including readable introductions to both, it develops a series of arguments in favour of CA's attention to the minute details of interaction over some more broad-brushed DA approaches.)

A useful web resource is Charles Antaki's CA tutorial: http://www-staff.lboro. ac.uk/~ssca1/sitemenu.htm. (This website is a particularly good place to begin to get a feel for what CA looks like in practice.)

Deciding which approach to take

Now that you know a little about some of the key approaches available to you, it's time to think about how you might go about deciding which to use in your project. In Figure 7.1, we offer some guidance in decision making about which method of analysis might be most appropriate for your work. Although presented as a flowchart, what really matters is the fit between your research question(s), data collection method and analytic perspective, rather than the order in which these are selected. However, there is an important caveat here, namely that no formula should supersede a considered and personal judgement about the appropriateness of your analytic choices, and you should of course discuss these issues with your supervisor. Equally, practical criteria such as what approaches you have been taught during your degree programme and the supervisory expertise available to you are important.

In a nutshell: experience or discourse?

A useful way to begin making your decision is to think about whether or not you are primarily interested in people's experiences, or whether you are interested in the form and function of discourse. This might involve you thinking about what sort of researcher you want to be – do you value a focus on experience, or are you sceptical about treating language as reflective of experience? Whereas DA and CA involve a rejection of notions of 'experience' as a focus of enquiry, the other approaches can each be used within epistemological frameworks that assume access to experience is possible.

A related consideration concerns epistemology. Different methods of analysis take up certain epistemological positions, so your choice of method should be

What are you Interested in?	Be more specific...	Suggested approach	Most common data source	Likely epistemological framework	Example research question
What do people see as important about some activity, event or phenomena?	I'm interested in what it means to people to have certain experience	IPA	Semi-structured interviews	Critical realist	What are the experiences of parents when making food-related decisions for their children?
	I'm interested in how people tell the stories of their experiences	Narrative analysis	Life-story interviews; other biographical accounts	Critical realist or social constructionist	What do narratives of parenthood tell us about parents' experiences of feeding their children?
	I want to see what key themes are apparent, but don't necessarily want to assume a phenomenological or narrative approach	Thematic analysis	Semi-structured interviews	Realist, critical realist or social constructionist	What are the priorities for parents when making food-related decisions for their children?
What processes lead people to engage in some activity, event or phenomena?	I like the idea of developing a theory to try to explain something	Grounded Theory	Semi-structured interviews	Realist, critical realist or social constructionist	How do parents decide what to feed their children?
How is an activity, event or phenomena done in talk?	I want to explore how people construct this thing I'm interested in through language.	Discourse Analysis	Interviews or 'naturalistic' data	Critical realist or social constructionist	How do parents manage accountability concerning their food-related decisions for their children?
	I want to explore the details of interaction, and what people are doing with their talk.	Conversation Analysis	'Naturalistic' data	Social constructionist	How do parents' food-related decisions for their children get made in interaction?

Figure 7.1 Decision making chart

consistent with your epistemological stance as a researcher and with your decisions around data collection or selection. For example, if you were working with interview data you would need to consider whether you were treating language as fundamentally constructive and functional (a position sympathetic to DA or CA), or as a window to the psychological world of the participant (a position sympathetic to IPA, narrative analysis and some forms of template analysis and grounded theory), or possibly as a straightforward recounting of an event or phenomena (a position sympathetic to realist approaches in thematic analysis and grounded theory). For more on epistemology, see Chapter 1.

You might also consider whether your research question is best presented as a 'what' or a 'how' question, although often wording it either way does not alter the fundamental concern (for example, how do adoptees tell the story of their lives? What are the key themes in adoptees' accounts of their lives?). The form of data you are going to work with is also an important consideration, primarily whether it is individual or group, naturalistic or solicited, large or small. While most methods of analysis can be used with a range of data types, some are more restricted; for example, CA is so intensive that smaller amounts of data are typically examined (Forrester, 2010b), narrative analysis requires a personal narrative around isolated or life-span events (Howitt, 2010), and there is debate around the appropriateness of subjecting interview data to a discourse analysis (see, for example, Potter and Hepburn, 2005).

Top tip: take a position

Before beginning your analysis, make sure you have a clear epistemological position on what you consider your data to be (or to represent), and ensure you analyse it and write about it in a way that is consistent with that position. So, if you were using DA, you would not make claims about participants' thoughts, attitudes and feelings, but would instead attend to the nature and function of the talk. Alternatively, if you were using IPA, you would avoid writing about what the participants said as purely functional or entirely constructed, and would instead treat it as a way to understand their emotional and psychological world.

So, be clear about your epistemological position during your analysis, and write up your findings in a way that is entirely consistent with this, thus evidencing a sound understanding of these important features of qualitative research (see Chapter 1 for more on epistemology; Chapter 8 on coherence as a measure of quality and Chapter 9 for writing up).

How to analyse qualitative data

As indicated in the overviews above, there are important differences between approaches to qualitative analysis. These are not simply differences in how the analysis is done, but also involve the asking of different research questions and often the collection of different forms of data. However, it is possible to identify some broad similarities, and here we offer an overview of which analytic processes are generic across these methods, namely (1) anchoring to your research question, (2) transcription, (3) initial readings and (4) systematic analysis. These processes are interrelated, and early stages drive successive ones, like cogs in a system. This will help to make the analytic process more concrete and will facilitate the delivery of a sound, rigorous analysis (see Chapter 8).

Anchoring to your research question

It is important that your analysis addresses your specific research question(s). However, research questions can change over the course of a project as new and unexpected findings emerge (see Chapter 2 for a discussion of the cyclical nature of research question development).

In principle, any dataset can be used to address a range of research questions. For example, if you have a series of interviews with people who have chronic fatigue syndrome (CFS), you might examine the data for the way in which interviewees construct their condition in medicalised terms, or with a view to exploring how sufferers navigate the healthcare system, or how recovery from the syndrome is perceived and experienced. What you want to know shapes your analytic activity; if you were interested in the first of these questions about CFS, you would examine the entire corpus for medicalised language, whereas if you were interested in the second question, you would identify and analyse only those aspects of the data that related to interaction with community nurses, GPs and other health professionals, and ignore other parts of the data set that were not relevant. Deeming some aspects of the data as more useful than others in answering the research question is a credible and viable decision, although you must report your rationale for this.

Cautionary tale: answer the question!

Toby's research question for his final year project was 'How do young offenders account for their offending?' He collected data from three focus groups, each with five participants, who had offended. He wanted to analyse the data with discourse analysis, and phrased his research question appropriately, with the term 'accounting for' necessarily implying a focus on the function of talk. However, he encountered problems in the focus of his analysis as he was drawn to the

(Continued)

(Continued)

experiential aspects of the data (for instance, some participants reported experiences of extreme boredom, frustration and lack of purpose) and so Toby progressed his analysis by attending to the emotions, experiences and psychological states that the participants reported. His final analytic output was therefore more like what would be produced by IPA rather than discourse analysis, and did not answer his stated research question. Indeed, his output appeared to answer a somewhat different question, namely 'In what ways do young offenders experience triggers to their offending?' If you find yourself following a similar path, don't worry, all is not lost! Indeed a hallmark of a good research project is that it is flexible and can move to explore interesting findings thrown up by preliminary analysis. So, provided you recognise that your approach to the data is shifting, you may be able to switch emphasis during your project. This may involve you collecting more data, but the important thing is to:

- recognise the shift in emphasis before you get to the writing-up stage;
- learn the principles and quality criteria of any new method you need to use;
- revisit your research question so that your study is conceptually coherent.

Transcription

As noted in Chapter 6, transcription is more than merely a technical process – it involves making important analytic decisions. Transcription in qualitative research typically refers to the conversion of spoken talk (audio or video) into another representation of language, typically text (so you do not have to do transcription if your data is already text). Although transcription is time consuming (see Chapter 6), it serves many important functions; not only does it transform your data into a format suitable for analysis, it also familiarises you with your data, and stimulates your analytic thinking. It is in this sense that it can be seen as a preliminary stage of analysis.

Different analytic methods tend to favour different forms of transcription, typically distinguished as either *orthographic* (or playscript) or non-orthographic, and each varying according to the level of detail required for analysis (see Table 7.2). Playscript /orthographic transcription transforms audio data into a word-for-word (verbatim) representation in a way that focuses largely on what words were spoken, rather than how. In contrast, Jeffersonian transcription (named after its creator, Gail Jefferson) captures not only the words spoken, but also many *paralinguistic* features of the interaction, and sometimes *extra-linguistic* features. Conversation analysts typically transcribe only a portion of the data in full Jeffersonian format, as they interrogate the data at a greater level of interactional detail.

Table 7.2 Forms of transcription preferred by particular analytic methods

Analytic method	Preferred level of transcription
Thematic analysis	Orthographic/playscript
IPA	Orthographic/playscript
Grounded theory	Orthographic/playscript
Narrative analysis	Orthographic/playscript
Discourse analysis	Jeffersonian or Jefferson-Lite[a]
Conversation analysis	Jeffersonian

Note: [a]Depending on the level of detailed required by your research question and type of discourse analysis used.

A modified form of Jeffersonian transcription, called Jefferson-Lite is increasingly used (Parker, 2005), particularly in discursive work. While playscript in form, it also captures some paralinguistic features that might be seen as impacting on how the talk is understood (such as lengthy silences, shouting).

Key definitions

- Paralinguistic features include aspects of speech delivery such as pauses, overlaps, emphasis, volume and intonation.
- Extralinguistic features include gaze, body language and other non-verbal behaviours.
- Orthography is the standard spelling and punctuation system of a written language.

As well as being fit for different analytic purposes, varying forms of transcription can be understood as representing different theoretical conceptualisations of talk, with playscript forms drawing attention to the content of what was said rather than the details of interaction, and Jeffersonian transcription doing the opposite. In this sense, transcription is theory-laden. As well as being appropriate for your analytic purpose, decisions about what form of transcription to adopt should also be compatible with your epistemological and ontological position (Lapadat and Lindsay, 1999).

Transcription is not an uncomplicated activity. No form of transcription can deliver an exact replica of the original talk with all of its intricacies, and by its very nature transcription shapes the data. You will enhance the quality of your work if you can demonstrate an awareness of this. For guidance on how to format your transcript, and how to present extracts from it in your work, see Chapter 9.

Want to know more about transcription?

Lapadat, J.C. and Lindsay, A.C. (1999) 'Transcription in research and practice: from standardisation of technique to interpretive positioning', *Qualitative Inquiry*, 5, 64–86. (A broad discussion on the importance of transcription.)

Bird, C.M. (2005) 'How I stopped dreading and learned to love transcription', *Qualitative Inquiry*, 11, 226–48. (A cautionary tale about the 'dos and don'ts' of transcription.)

Jefferson, G. (2004) 'Glossary of transcript symbols with an introduction', in G.H. Lerner (ed.) *Conversation Analysis: Studies from the First Generation*. Amsterdam: John Benjamins. pp. 13–31. (A guide to symbols used in Jeffersonian transcription; available online at: http://www.liso.ucsb.edu/Jefferson.)

For an online tutorial in Jeffersonian transcription, visit Emanuel A. Schegloff's online Jeffersonian transcription tutorial: http://www.sscnet.ucla.edu/soc/faculty/schegloff/TranscriptionProject/index.html

For examples of playscript and Jeffersonian transcription of the same data, see: tinyurl.com/yayb57e

For software to assist with Jeffersonian transcription see http://audacity.source-forge.net/

Initial readings

Reading your transcripts, in a way that builds on the familiarity established during transcription, is an important early stage of every analytic method (Smith and Osborn [2008: 67], refer to it as 'free textual analysis'), and, like later stages of analysis, is driven by your research question. However, students new to qualitative methods often feel their initial reading is directionless and are unsure that they are doing it right. Table 7.3 may help to render the purpose of this first stage more tangible.

Unless you have a specific reason to begin with one in particular, it generally does not matter which transcript you begin your analysis with. This first stage of reading is as important as later stages of analysis and it helps to loosely map out in your mind the breadth and depth of the data. Once you have established this, you may feel freer to focus on more micro aspects of the data, as these will now feel *contextualised*. At this stage, it can often be useful to read your transcripts while listening to the audio recordings.

In a nutshell: contextualisation

This is a term used generally in qualitative methods to acknowledge that aspects of the data should always be understood as being part of a broader data set (such as an interview or set of extracts) which has itself been generated or collected by a researcher. In other words, nothing should be considered as existing 'in a vacuum'.

Table 7.3 Purpose of first stage reading in different analytic methods

Analytic method	Purpose
Thematic analysis, Grounded theory, IPA	Establish a holistic sense of the breadth and depth of the experiences the participant has talked about. Establish a basic sense of what appear to be the key issues, experiences or feelings that the participant reports. You may get an early sense of themes upon successive readings. Be attentive, at a preliminary level, to the way you as the interviewer are involved in shaping the data.
Narrative analysis	Establish a sense of the entire story generated by the participant, with initial identification of what appears to be the narrative tone, key images/metaphors and themes.
Discourse analysis	Establish a sense of the breadth of issues covered in the data. Be attentive, at a preliminary level, to what key issues or phenomena are being talked about. You may get a sense of what appear to be familiar and unusual ways of talking.
Conversation analysis	The initial reading might be of a Jefferson-Lite or playscript transcription alongside the audio as a way to decide what to focus on and transcribe in full Jeffersonian format. A more specific research question may be developed at this point.

Systematic analysis

Analysis, by its very nature, demands dedicated and goal-directed thinking. Carla Willig and Wendy Stainton-Rogers suggest that the challenge to qualitative researchers is to:

> go beyond what presents itself, to reveal dimensions of a phenomenon which are concealed or hidden, whilst at the same time taking care not to impose meaning upon the phenomenon, not to squeeze it into pre-conceived categories or theoretical formulations, not to reduce it to an underlying cause. (2008b: 9)

Analysis is more than summarising, rephrasing or regurgitating the data in a journalistic form, but at the same time it should not extend into over-interpretation (for example, making claims about the motives of a participant without evidence of this in the data). Reaching the right conceptual level to produce an analysis on the possible nature or function of the data that is not usually immediately obvious is a demanding endeavour, and both students and experienced qualitative researchers can struggle. These difficulties can, however, be addressed by employing a systematic analysis and recognising that qualitative analysis is a cyclical process, in which your ideas develop more conceptually over time.

Your analysis needs to be systematic so that it doesn't slip into a chaotic, haphazard, vague process that produces any output you like. As Lyons states: 'no one interpretation is the "correct" or "true" one. This does not mean *any* interpretation is a good interpretation' (2007: 5, emphasis in original). Rather, qualitative analysis is a focused and rigorous activity that seeks to impose structure on potentially quite disorganised data in ways that facilitate increasingly abstract ways of conceptualising the data in order to answer a specific question.

To facilitate this, you need a system for organising, recording and managing your analytic process. This may be in paper and pencil form, via specialist qualitative data analysis software (see in a nutshell box below), or a mixture of the two. Good organisation is not only important for keeping you on track, but will help you to evidence some markers of quality, namely transparency and rigour (see Chapter 8 for a detailed discussion of these issues). Whatever approach you take, recording your developing thoughts and hunches about your data is highly recommended. This is formalised in some approaches (for example, memos in grounded theory; reflective diaries in IPA), in which the record of your engagement in the analytic process can serve as part of the process of being reflexive about your data (for examples see Charmaz, 2008; Gordon-Finlayson, 2010).

In a nutshell: computer assisted qualitative data analysis (CAQDAS)

There are a number of computer software packages available to assist qualitative analysis (see the online QDA web link below for a comprehensive listing). If you have access to one of these through your institution you may want to explore the possibility of using it to manage your project. CAQDAS packages can be useful for organising your data, as well as for helping to clarify your analytic thinking. However, it should be noted that the packages do not do the analysis for you, just as you would not expect the paper-and-pen to do the analysis for you if you were working by hand!

If you are using CAQDAS software, make sure that you have access to some relevant training. It is perhaps still unusual for CAQDAS to be taught on undergraduate degree programmes, and if you have not been taught how to use a CAQDAS package during your course, then it might be wise not to try and get to grips with it specifically for your project. However, if this is something you are keen to explore, you could ask your supervisor if your university runs any training sessions that you could attend.

Want to know more about CAQDAS?

Lewins, A. and Silver, C. (2007) *Using Software in Qualitative Research: A Step-by-Step Guide*. London: Sage. (A classic of its kind, dealing with a range of practical and conceptual issues around the use of CAQDAS.)

The Online Qualitative Data Analysis website provides lots of useful information about the use of software in qualitative analysis: http://onlineqda.hud.ac.uk/

Analysis is an intensive process, in which you become immersed in your data. So aim to work on your analysis in substantial chunks of time, rather than an hour here and there. Otherwise you may fail to make those conceptual connections that are the hallmark of an excellent analysis. Also you waste time trying to get your thinking back to the point where you had left off.

Top tip: keeping track

If you are leaving your analysis for some time, leave a note to yourself about what you were thinking and why. This helps you pick up faster when you come back to it.

There are some commonalities between methods. For example, thematic analysis, IPA and grounded theory all involve an early stage of preliminary, open or initial coding whereby terms (usually referred to as codes) are assigned to sections of the text in a way that represents the key point, or nature, of that portion of data, or what you notice about it. While this can be done on a line-by-line basis, codes are normally applied to 'meaningful units', which are portions of data (words or paragraphs) that appear to convey something important. Such systematic scrutiny guards against haphazard or partial examination of the data and promotes a firmly evidence-based analysis (Charmaz, 1995).

As indicated in Figure 7.2, sometimes preliminary coding will generate no more than a descriptive term, but where possible, codes which represent the psychological or conceptual nature of the data (facilitated by your broader familiarity with the entire transcript) should be assigned. It is important to balance this with attempts to stay close to the data in the early stages though, so that you do not make too big a leap from it too soon. The same codes can be assigned to portions of data that appear similar, and you can return to codes later when needed, usually to refine them. Early codes are not typically reported in the write-up, but a sample can be included in your appendices if required by your department.

Initial coding in narrative analysis might generate a 'working map' of the narrative tone, imagery and themes at a preliminary level (Crossley, 2007). Coding in discourse analysis has a different meaning and typically involves the identification of all instances where the objects or phenomena under investigation are constructed in the data (Potter and Wetherell, 1987). Conversation analysis does not use the term coding but rather, once features of the talk have been selected for study, analysis focuses specifically on the details of the interactions themselves.

DEBORAH

170	DEB:	I think so, I think cos she always talks about 'oh remember our Charlotte this' and you	*shared memories!*
171		know she'll say to me 'oh I've got you on the camcorder skipping and our Charlotte's	
172		doing this' and I think it's, I don't know, I don't know if it makes her feel closer to	
173		Charlotte [INT: mm], but it makes me feel closer to her talking to her mum [INT: yeah]	*feels closer to*
174		do you know what I mean.	*lost friend talking to mum.*

175 INT: Yeah it sort of keeps that memory alive I guess as well doesn't it through her mum.

176	DEB:	Yeah, definitely, yeah, yeah, well her mum, it's quite a sad story but her other sister had	*Sadness.*
177		Cystic Fibrosis as well, her younger sister she died at like an earlier age as well, like I	
178		think she was like thirteen [INT: oh right], but it was only two years after, after Charlotte	*Death of friend's sister too.*
179		died so their mum has been through it [INT: yeah been through a lot], yeah, yeah [INT:	
180		yeah], so I mean I always feel … I don't know, I don't, I don't not wanna talk about it to	*Talks to friends*
181		her but I don't think she doesn't want me to talk about it to her so we still, we still talk	*mum.*
182		about things like that [INT: yeah] do you know what I mean [INT: yeah], so it's nice.	*"Nice".*

183 INT: And how, how, how did it feel for you when your friend died, cos that's a big thing to
184   happen, even if you've like you say grown apart, but …?

185	DEB:	Gutted, yeah, I felt dead guilty because I thought 'I haven't even been round for like a	*Gutted. Guilt.*
186		month' and I knew she was in hospital, but she was always in hospital, I spent half of my	
187		childhood life sitting in ward B3 all day with her cos you know if she had to go in and	*Time spent*
188		she had IV's and she'd be in for like two weeks. I'd come home from school and go to	*with friend in*
189		the hospital and sit with her every night and we'd you know we were into Take That and	*hospital.*
190		all that [INT: yeah] so we'd sit there listening to Take That and you know drawing	
191		pictures and stupid things like [INT: yeah], but erm I was gutted like I'd just had a little	*"Stupid things" → shared*
192		boy as well and she hadn't seen him [INT: aw] so that was quite [deep breath] kind of	*activities.*
193		thing, but I think she will have now, you know what I mean. → *Gutted*	*friend hadn't seen son.*

194 INT: She's looking down.

195 DEB: Yeah.

196 INT: Yeah, yeah, cos that must have been a real, yeah it must have been huge and like you say
197   that, it sounds like the friendship erm changed as well when you said, you're growing up
198   and you're spreading your wings.

199	DEB:	I turned into, yeah, I turned into a bit of a rebel I think as well and you know got new	*Rebellious*
200		mates [INT: yeah] and you know we hung around then we didn't play out in the street	*New mates*
201		kind of thing [INT: yeah] and we moved off, but she was still my best mate [INT: yeah]	*"We moved off"*
202		kind of thing [INT: yeah], erm I think it was when we were, when we were little, and we	
203		were like proper Take That fans and we were just, I don't know, there was something just	*Still best*
204		special, even now when I hear like Take That records and that and I go 'aw', she'd have	*mate.*
205		been made up you know what I mean [INT: yeah], she'd have been made up they got	*Special …*
206		back together [laughs] (inaudible), it was you know, it was like one of, like you said	
207		before, it was one of them special [INT: mm] friendships and it's been made even more	*"when we were little."*

Special friendship.

Music → memories
"she'd have been made up."

Figure 7.2 Sample coded transcript excerpt

Activity: have a go at coding

Watch a segment of the video-recorded semi-structured interviews available at:
tinyurl.com/yayb57e. Once you have done this, download the transcript of the
relevant interview and have a go at coding. If you are working with a friend, why
not both have a go? Discuss any differences and similarities between your codes.

Top tip: deviant case analysis

Each of the approaches discussed in this chapter make use of some form of deviant case analysis. This analytic tool involves actively seeking out cases in your dataset that contradict, or otherwise cause problems for, your analytic claims. This helps you to jettison claims that are not supported by your data, and ultimately to refine your claims so that they account for each case in your dataset (see Seale, 1999; Silverman, 2006).

Help with qualitative analysis

Qualitative data analysis is difficult, no matter how many textbooks you read, or how clearly the stages are described. Table 7.4 details some of the most common challenges and worries, with some advice on how to overcome them. It is very useful to look at good quality previous work that has used the same method of analysis that you are interested in. Examine the analysis for level of detail, use of evidence, extent of interpretative activity and how claims about the data are justified. Be aware, though, that the requirements for a final year project (especially in terms of the amount of data) may be different to those for published work. In addition, make effective use of peers (who understand your method of analysis) and your supervisor. Very few qualitative researchers work in isolation; indeed, it is deemed good practice to bring your analytic thoughts at varying stages for discussion with others (see, for example, Storey, 2007). This helps you to assess the credibility of your analysis and to see where you could be more searching, confident or creative in your thinking about the data, or indeed, where you have begun to make unjustified claims about it.

Conclusion

This chapter has introduced some of the most commonly used approaches to qualitative analysis. As will be apparent by now, however, these are not simply approaches to analysis, but provide perspectives on qualitative research in its entirety, from the type of research questions you might ask, to the type of data you collect, as well as the sorts of assumptions and claims you make about your data. Indeed, it is perhaps best to think of these approaches as providing perspectives on how we should understand psychology itself. You might now be aware that you should not approach the process of qualitative research in a piecemeal fashion; if you have a research question, you should know what approach to analysis you are going to take, what data you are going to collect, and so on. All of these things need to be decided at the start of your project.

Table 7.4 Common concerns in qualitative analysis

Concern/challenge	Ways to overcome it
Do not know where to start	For TA, IPA, GT and NA, select a transcript – any transcript – and begin with initial readings, taking it 3–5 lines at a time, and assigning a descriptive label. For DA, identify where the object or phenomena under investigation is talked about. For CA, select any 30-second portion of your data and begin to transcribe it in Jeffersonian conventions – this will help you to attend to the details of interaction.
Confused about what to focus on	Analysis should be rigorous and systematic to avoid cherry picking some aspects of the data and not others. Try to interrogate every aspect of the data for its detail, variation and complexity (Henwood and Pidgeon, 1994), and its contribution to understanding your research question. However, some data can be highly incoherent or fragmented (Storey, 2007). In such cases, remain attentive to the entire transcript or data set as well as to micro aspects of it. Be prepared to exclude some aspects of the data on the grounds that it does not shed light on the research question, and actively seek out deviant cases. Make effective use of memos/notes on your analytic decisions.
Contradictions in the data	This is not problematic as human experience, behaviour and talk is replete with apparent inconsistencies. Consider the research context which prompted the data (such as the specific conversational exchange in which it occurred), and why the account might make sense to the speaker.
Feeling stuck in your analysis	Review your progress to date, and set deadlines for the completion of different stages of the work (analysis could last a lifetime without these). Ask yourself what you are happy with as regards the the analysis so far, and what appears interesting/missing/unknown/ difficult to understand about the data. Be prepared to make some decisions about your analysis, which you can return to later if needed. Take the review and your questions to a peer or supervisor. Be encouraged that analysis tends to get quicker as you progress through the dataset.
Information overload	Return to the fundamental requirement of your research question. Be prepared to amalgamate some of your early analytic outputs (where there seems to be sufficient similarity of form or function), or to eliminate some of them (where they seem less relevant or insufficiently evidenced). Remember that analysis is an iterative process so be prepared to move backwards and forwards in the analytic process.
Feeling that you are biasing the analysis	Acknowledge that the researcher is fundamentally involved in the generation of research and its outcomes and that this can be used to promote, rather than diminish, quality. Make effective use of memos and notes to record your perceived influence on the analysis, including the decisions you are making about it. Deploy quality criteria (see Chapter 8) such as transparency, triangulation, audit trails and credibility/plausibility checks to promote rigour in your analysis.

Concern/challenge	Ways to overcome it
Over-interpretation	It is exciting to pursue possible interpretations but there must always be sufficient and credible evidence for those interpretations. Bring your doubts or concerns for peer or supervisor discussion. Consider whether you are applying psychological theory or frameworks to the data at too early a stage; these considerations should perhaps be applied at the discussion stage, leaving the analysis to be more data-driven (see, for example, Frosh and Young, 2008). Remain committed to credibility checks with others.
Lack of confidence	Remember that you are aiming for a credible, plausible account of the data and are working with likelihood rather than certainty (Crossley, 2007). Have you been systematic? Could you be more questioning of the data – what is the best possible interpretation of what it means? What are your intuitive thoughts about the data? Is there evidence for these? Be prepared to make some decisions about analysis that you can return to later if needed. Compare your work with published methods using the same methodology to assess their analytic level.
None of the above really helped ...	Remember to ask your supervisor for advice if you are really stuck – it is always better to do this than to struggle on in silence.

Note: TA = thematic analysis; IPA = interpretative phenomenological analysis; GT = grounded theory; NA = narrative analysis; DA = discourse analysis; CA = conversation analysis.

Having said that, things can, and do, change during the course of a project; new questions arise, the possibility of collecting different data might present itself, you may come across a paper that makes you think of your data in a different way. Indeed, one of the hallmarks of really good qualitative research might be said to be the extent to which it opens up new possibilities for enquiry. Equally, deciding on your analytic approach should not determine precisely what you will find: you should always be prepared to be surprised by the discoveries you generate as you analyse your data. Ultimately, the acid test of good qualitative research is the same as for good research in general: does it tell us something novel about the world, and does it do so in a scholarly and convincing way?

References

Braun, V. and Clarke, V. (2006) 'Using thematic analysis in psychology', *Qualitative Research in Psychology*, 3, 77–101.

Charmaz, K. (1995) 'Grounded theory', in J.A. Smith, R. Harre and L.V. Langenhove (eds) *Rethinking Methods in Psychology*. London: Sage. pp. 27–49.

Charmaz, C. (2006) *Constructing Grounded Theory: A Practical Guide Through Qualitative Analysis*. London: Sage.

Charmaz, K. (2008) 'Grounded theory', in J.A. Smith (ed.) *Qualitative Psychology: A Practical Guide to Research Methods* (2nd edn). London: Sage. pp. 81–110.

Crossley, M. (2007) 'Narrative analysis', in E. Lyons and A. Coyle (eds) *Analysing Qualitative Data in Psychology*. London: Sage. pp. 131–44.

Drew, P. (2008) 'Conversation analysis', in J.A. Smith (ed.) *Qualitative Psychology: A Practical Guide to Research Methods* (2nd edn). London: Sage. pp. 122–59.

Forrester, M.A. (2010a) *Doing Qualitative Research in Psychology: A Practical Guide*. London: Sage.

Forrester, M. (2010b) 'Conversation analysis', in M.A. Forrester (ed.) *Doing Qualitative Research in Psychology: A Practical Guide*. London: Sage. pp. 202–26.

Frosh, S. and Young, L.S. (2008) 'Psychoanalytic approaches to qualitative psychology', in C. Willig and W. Stainton-Rogers (eds) *The Sage Handbook of Qualitative Research in Psychology*. London: Sage. pp. 109–26.

Glaser, B.G. and Strauss, A.L. (1967) *The Discovery of Grounded Theory: Strategies for Qualitative Research*. New York: Aldine.

Gordon-Finlayson, A. (2010) 'Grounded theory', in M.A. Forrester (ed.) *Doing Qualitative Research in Psychology: A Practical Guide*. London: Sage. pp. 154–76.

Hayes, N. (1997) 'Theory-led thematic analysis: social identification in small companies', in N. Hayes (ed.) *Doing Qualitative Analysis in Psychology*. Hove: Psychology Press. pp. 93–114

Henwood, K. and Pidgeon, N. (1994) 'Beyond the qualitative paradigm: a framework for introducing diversity within qualitative psychology', *Journal of Community and Applied Social Psychology*, 4, 225–38.

Hiles, D. and Čermák, I. (2008) 'Narrative psychology', in C. Willig and W. Stainton-Rogers (eds) *The Sage Handbook of Qualitative Research in Psychology*. London: Sage. pp. 147–64.

Howitt, D. (2010) *Introduction to Qualitative Methods in Psychology*. Harlow: Prentice Hall.

King, N. (2004) 'Using templates in the thematic analysis of text', in C. Cassell and G. Symon (eds) *Essential Guide to Qualitative Methods in Organizational Research*. London: Sage.

Lapadat, J.C. and Lindsay, A.C. (1999) 'Transcription in research and practice: from standardization of technique to interpretive positioning', *Qualitative Inquiry*, 5, 64–86.

Lyons, E. (2007) 'Doing qualitative research: initial questions', in E. Lyons and A. Coyle (eds) *Analysing Qualitative Data in Psychology*. London: Sage. pp. 3–8.

Lyons, E. and Coyle, A. (2007) *Analysing Qualitative Data in Psychology*. London: Sage.

McAdams, D.P. (1993) *The Stories We Live by: Personal Myths and the Making of the Self*. New York: Guilford.

McKinlay, A. and McVittie, C. (2008) *Social Psychology and Discourse*. Oxford: Wiley-Blackwell.

Murray, M. (2008) 'Narrative psychology', in J.A. Smith (ed.) *Qualitative Psychology: A Practical Guide to Research Methods* (2nd edn). London: Sage. pp. 111–32.

Parker, I. (1998) *Social Constructionism, Discourse and Realism*. London: Sage.

Parker, I. (2005) *Qualitative Psychology: Introducing Radical Research*. Maidenhead: Open University Press.

Payne, M. (2000) *Narrative Therapy: An Introduction for Counsellors*. London: Sage.

Payne, S. (2007) 'Grounded theory', in E. Lyons and A. Coyle (eds) *Analysing Qualitative Data in Psychology*. London: Sage. pp. 65–86.

Potter, J. and Hepburn, A. (2005) 'Qualitative interviews in psychology: problems and possibilities', *Qualitative Research in Psychology*, 2, 281–307.

Potter, J. and Hepburn, A. (2008) 'Discursive constructionism', in J.A. Holstein and J.F. Gubrium (eds) *Handbook of Constructionist Research*. New York: Guilford. pp. 275–93.

Potter, J. and Wetherell, M. (1987) *Discourse and Social Psychology: Beyond Attitudes and Behaviour*. London: Sage.

Seale, C. (1999) *The Quality of Qualitative Research*. London: Sage.

Shaw, R. (2010) 'Interpretative phenomenological analysis', in M.A. Forrester (ed.) *Doing Qualitative Research in Psychology: A Practical Guide*. London: Sage. pp. 177–201.

Silverman, D. (2006) *Interpreting Qualitative Data* (3rd edn). London: Sage.

Smith, J.A. (1996) 'Beyond the divide between cognition and discourse: using interpretative phenomenological analysis in health psychology', *Psychology and Health*, 11, 261–71.

Smith, J.A. (2008) *Qualitative Psychology: A Practical Guide to Research Methods* (2nd edn). London: Sage.

Smith, J.A. and Osborn, M. (2008) 'Interpretative phenomenological analysis', in J.A. Smith (ed.) *Qualitative Psychology: A Practical Guide to Research Methods* (2nd edn). London: Sage. pp. 53–80.

Stokoe, E.H. and Smithson, J. (2001) 'Making gender relevant: conversation analysis and gender categories in interaction', *Discourse and Society*, 12, 217–44.

Storey, L. (2007) 'Doing interpretative phenomenological analysis', in E. Lyons and A. Coyle (eds) *Analysing Qualitative Data in Psychology*. London: Sage.

Wiggins, S. and Riley, S. (2010) 'Discourse analysis', in M.A. Forrester (ed.) *Doing Qualitative Research in Psychology: A Practical Guide*. London: Sage. pp. 135–53.

Willig, C. (2008) *Introducing Qualitative Research in Psychology: Adventures in Theory and Method* (2nd edn). Maidenhead: Open University Press.

Willig, C. and Stainton-Rogers, W. (2008a) *The Sage Handbook of Qualitative Research in Psychology*. London: Sage.

Willig, C. and Stainton-Rogers, W. (2008b) 'Introduction', in C. Willig and W. Stainton-Rogers (eds) *The Sage Handbook of Qualitative Research in Psychology*. London: Sage. pp. 1–12.

8

EVALUATING QUALITATIVE RESEARCH

Nollaig Frost and Kathryn Kinmond

──────── Quality criteria and why we need them ────────

Whenever you read a piece of research you probably make some form of assessment of its strengths and weaknesses. For example, a paper might offer a new perspective on your topic, but not give enough information in the method section for you to see how to apply this approach to your own work. When reading such a paper, you might have felt excited when you realised it could offer a novel way for you to work and then felt disappointed because the paper didn't fulfil this promise. These emotions are responses to your evaluation of the quality of the paper. It is useful to remember this because student projects elicit similar feelings in those who mark your work.

When considering quality, we need to bear in mind that definitions of quality are debated and there is variation in ideas about quality between different methodological traditions and between individual researchers. Your aim is to write a report that elicits positive responses from your markers, so that they feel interested and pleased to read your work. To elicit these kinds of responses and make your decisions about ensuring quality in your work, it's important to develop a good understanding about quality criteria in qualitative research. In this chapter we take you through some of the considerations that can help you to produce a high quality project and to demonstrate this quality to your reader.

In a nutshell: outline of chapter

This chapter will:

- Explain what counts as quality criteria for qualitative projects.
- Discuss quality criteria that are relevant for most qualitative student projects, these are:

o reflection and reflexivity: exploring the dynamics between researcher, participants and research context through appropriate use of reflexive practices;

o contribution to the subject: adding new and worthwhile knowledge to the field under study;

o rigour and coherence: the use and clear explanation of a strong, systematic, consistent research process;

o transparency: making clear the research process.

• Conclude by summarising what makes a credible report and providing questions for you to assess the quality of your project.

What counts as quality criteria?

In a nutshell: quality criteria

Quality criteria are ways to ensure and demonstrate that your qualitative work is high quality and therefore has validity.

All good quality research shares some quality criteria. For example, researchers have to demonstrate that they have approached their subject systematically and that they have an appropriate rationale for their sampling procedure. But, differences between projects in terms of the types of research questions asked, data collected, and analysis performed, also creates the need for specific quality criteria based on the kind of project that you're doing. For example, some qualitative researchers assess quality criteria by the degree to which a project achieves changes in social justice or social action (see for example, Denzin, 2005), while others argue that developing understanding is valuable in its own right.

There are many different kinds of qualitative research projects because 'qualitative research' is an umbrella term for a wide range of approaches to research (Gibson and Riley, 2010). Different approaches to qualitative research have their own forms of quality criteria so when thinking about your study you need to work out what sort of project you're doing and the appropriate quality criteria for this kind of project. Your first step in doing this is to identify your epistemological approach.

Your epistemological approach is about what kind of knowledge you think your project can produce. A realist stance, for example, means that you would treat your data as representing some true fact about the world. Whereas a relativist stance would consider your findings a product of the social or personal processes that were involved. Epistemology is one of those terms that students can struggle with, and if you need a reminder see Chapter 1 in this volume. Here, we're going to focus on how epistemology links to quality criteria.

If you are doing qualitative research from a realist or positivist approach, then your study is likely to be evaluated in terms of objectivity, validity, generalisability and reliability. Your training in research methods means you're probably familiar with these terms, and there is a range of text books that discuss them (for example, Robson, 2011). What is less often discussed are the quality criteria issues for the many student projects that take a more relativist approach, and so we focus on these criteria for the rest of this chapter.

Want to know more about the nature of knowledge?

See Chapter 1 of this volume and also:

Flick, U. (2009) *An Introduction to Qualitative Research*. London. Sage. (Chapters 1 and 2.)
Sullivan, C. (2010) 'Theory and method in qualitative research', in M. Forrester (ed.) (2010) *Doing Qualitative Research in Psychology*. London: Sage. pp. 15–38.

Top tip: quality basics

For a project to have quality you need to be able to answer 'yes' to the following questions.

- Do you know what you are doing and why?
- Do you know what epistemological framework you're using?
- Do you have the resources?

If you've answered 'no' to any of these, turn to Chapter 3 and see your supervisor.

The case for quality criteria

Many qualitative researchers value flexibility in research designs. This is because they believe that knowledge is a contextualised process and that researchers should be able to make judgement calls regarding their research that are appropriate for the context in which they are working. From this perspective, some qualitative researchers argue against attempts to describe generic quality criteria because such descriptions imply a straightforward, 'one size fits all' approach to qualitative research.

However, qualitative researchers cannot work with an 'anything goes' attitude if they want their work to be taken seriously. As Woolcott (2001) warns, if qualitative researchers want to avoid accusations that their work is anecdotal or merely illustrative then qualitative research projects need to be able to clearly define the quality criteria to which they are working. We are left, then, with a tension between needing quality criteria that are flexible enough to accommodate the fluidity of qualitative research, but definitive enough to be a way of assessing if something is 'good'.

The tension in trying to meet the contradictory demands of having both flexible and conventionally recognised generic quality criteria is part of larger philosophical and political debates about the nature of the knowledge produced by research. In this chapter we focus on one way of resolving this tension, which is to produce a set of guideline criteria that students can adapt for their individual projects. The aim of these criteria is to help students make informed decisions in their research, which can then be used to demonstrate to others that the work is of good quality.

Guideline criteria can be particularly useful for students and novice qualitative researchers who lack experience in developing their own quality criteria. Guidelines are also useful for students needing to demonstrate that their work addresses the qualitative research methods literature.

The criteria we suggest are taken from academic debates on quality and validity in qualitative methods and synthesised with our personal research, teaching, supervising and marking experience. They should be approached, not as a prescriptive checklist, but as an opportunity to help you reflect on your research so that you can both develop your work and demonstrate its quality to your readers.

In a nutshell: guideline quality criteria

- Reflection and Reflexivity
- Contribution to the subject
- Rigour and coherence
- Transparency

In the rest of the chapter we will explore each criterion separately, explaining what they are, why they can be considered a measure of quality, and how they might be achieved in practice.

Activity 1: identifying criteria

To help you start thinking about quality criteria, try the following activity.

- List four things you think make a qualitative research study a 'good' piece of work.
- List four things you think make a qualitative research study a 'poor' piece of work.
- Put these lists on one side and come back to them after you have finished this chapter. Review them in the light of what you have read in the chapter and think about how you will use them to address quality issues in your own project.

Activity 2: focus on an example

Next time you read an article related to your research topic pay attention to how they use the data as evidence. Does it work for you as a persuasive case? If so, how? Is there anything that doesn't work for you?

Reflexivity is a quality criterion in its own right for many qualitative projects, but done well, it can also be used to demonstrate rigour, coherence and credibility. Reflexivity is therefore an important aspect of quality and because of this we start our quality criteria guidelines with it.

Reflection and reflexivity

You are part of your research project at every stage of the process. You're the person who decides on the research question, the person who collects the data, and you're the person who analyses and interprets the data. Since you play such a significant role in the research process, what you bring to the project needs to be considered if you are to make good sense of your findings. Considering your part in your project is called 'reflexivity' and it's fundamental to excellent qualitative research.

In a nutshell: reflexivity

Reflexivity is a particular kind of reflection that involves thinking about and reviewing the whole research process in terms of the context in which the research has been conducted and the researcher's own role in that process.

Why reflect?

Objectivity is an important quality criterion for researchers who take a realist position. From this perspective, any subjectivity in the research process is seen as something that must be minimised. But other researchers, including many qualitative researchers, take a different position. They argue that research is always subjective and so the best way to deal with subjectivity is to give it an overt role in the research process.

A way to give subjectivity an overt role in research is through reflexivity. Good reflexive practice means paying careful attention to your own assumptions and biases; so that they do not overly interfere in how you understand what your participants are telling you. A reflexive section in which you write briefly about yourself and your part in the process can also help your reader to consider how subjective processes may have impacted upon the research process and your interpretation of the findings. This is important for transparency and helps your readers evaluate your work.

Reflexivity is also important because it shows awareness of the context in which the research was done and how that may have impacted upon the research process and the knowledge that is produced. This context could be understood in terms of interpersonal dynamics (for example, power relations between researcher and participants), but could also include wider social power relations that may be played out in a research project. The context may also be thought of as being about social norms and prevailing values that provide part of the research setting.

By engaging in reflexivity our subjective involvement in the research process becomes an advantage. It allows us to examine our experiences in ways that help to develop a deeper, more thoughtful and conceptual analysis.

Success story: reflexivity facilitates analysis

Lara was so pleased that a young offenders' institution had allowed her access to do a study on bullying that she did not stop to question that the inmates were put in their cells involuntarily during a break time so that she could have access to them for interviewing. When her supervisor questioned this practice Lara began to consider

(Continued)

(Continued)

how her own work could be thought of as a part of a bullying culture. Later, while Lara was writing in her research diary about rules in the institution and the context of her interviews, she realised that this was significant. First, it presented her with a key piece of information about the context in which the interviews themselves were being conducted. Second, it gave her insight into the overall culture of the institution in relation to cultural and institutional forms of bullying. This helped her to make sense of the interview data in context and deepened her analysis. This threat to the voluntariness of participation also had clear ethical implications and adopting reflection earlier on in her study may have helped Lara recognise and stop these practices sooner (for more on such issues see Chapter 3).

In a nutshell: why be reflexive?

Thoughtful, critical reflexivity allows you to show your reader that you have explored:

- the biases you have and how you understand them;
- how the context in which you did the research may have influenced the process;
- the possible impact on your findings of who you are and how you think;
- how you used your reflection to develop your analysis and develop the findings.

How to be reflexive

There are a number of strategies that you can use to put reflexivity into practice. Two important practices are reading about reflexivity to develop your understanding of what it means and keeping a reflexive research diary.

Top Tips: being reflexive

- Develop a reflexive standpoint from the beginning of your project (initially experimenting with different techniques to find one that suits you).
- Read published work that uses a similar method to you and consider the ways that reflexivity is addressed by these researchers.
- Read the literature about reflexivity from which you can develop a theoretical understanding of the approach that you want to take.
- Talk to the people around you. You can use your supervisor, your friends, your fellow students or people online who share your concerns to develop reflexivity in a collaborative way.
- Keep a research diary in which to record your reflections and document your reflexivity.

Developing a reflexive standpoint

From the beginning of a project you should try to develop and maintain a reflexive standpoint. In this context, 'standpoint' does not mean holding a particular set of opinions or beliefs (as it might in relation to epistemological or theoretical standpoints). Rather, it means training yourself to adopt a particular approach or attitude where you keep reminding yourself to reflect critically on why you have done things in the way that you have and how the context might matter.

Maintaining a reflexive standpoint will mean that you develop a habit of incorporating reflexive practice throughout the project and develop insight into the assumptions that you make about the world, its inhabitants and the relationships formed within it. In practice, this might involve asking yourself key reflective questions as you design, conduct and write up your study. These questions will help you to bring to the fore the ways that you see the world and how your thinking impacts on your research. At the design stage, such questions could include:

- Why am I interested in this topic?
- What is it about me that makes me interested in this topic?
- What will I gain from researching this topic?
- Do I care what I find out in my project and why might this be so?
- How do my values and previous experiences influence my interest in this topic?
- What assumptions do I already have about this topic?

As your project develops you may ask yourself other questions. For example, if you have conducted an interview you might want to reflect upon that specifically. To do that you could ask yourself questions like these:

- How did I feel when I was listening to that person?
- What did I think of their answers?
- How do my own experiences and attitudes relate to what they said?
- Why did I choose those questions to ask?
- What do I think I already know about those experiences?

There is no limit to how many techniques for reflexivity you can use and you may have other ideas about how you will reflect on your work.

Read up

There is a lot of literature on reflexivity and you can read this to help you to develop your understanding of the concept and how it might apply to what you are doing. Also, you will get ideas from this literature for how to put reflexivity into practice. Suggestions for reading appear later in the chapter. Some reflexivity techniques may be linked to particular research methods. So, look at how other researchers, particularly those using a similar method to you, have addressed issues of reflexivity, ask your supervisor for advice, and track down relevant readings in textbooks and academic journals.

Get collaborative

You can also develop your reflexivity skills by involving the people around you in the process. For example, use your supervisory sessions to discuss the decisions you make and the questions arising from the research process (see Chapter 4 for more on supervision).

Another way to involve those around you is to start a peer support group with fellow students, where you can get together and discuss anything from your early ideas about your research topic to the analysis of data. Some groups like to provide an opportunity each week for one member to discuss their analysis in detail with them. You could also use the Internet to create these kinds of opportunities. For example, you could set up a wiki page to discuss issues with trusted others. People can agree certain times to 'chat' on the wiki if they are unable to meet face to face because of distance or commitments at home. There are also existing online discussion groups that you could use to post queries, answer questions, join discussions or just lurk and learn! For example, see Method Space by Sage Publications (http://www.methodspace.com).

You could also use other friends or family to help you reflect, even if they are not fellow students. For example, why not arrange for a friend to interview you about being an interviewer and use the data to consider in detail the experience that you had?

Your participants may also be able to help you put reflexivity into practice. For example, you can provide your participants with your initial interpretations of their data and ask them what they think of it. This brings a useful voice to the research and also allows you to reflect on how your findings are perceived. You could also turn off the recording machine at the end of interviews or focus groups and ask people their opinion on the experience of doing the study. Reflecting on their responses can help develop your thinking about your study. This technique can also be a way of establishing research quality for studies that specifically aim to reflect or represent the voices of a particular group of people.

Research diary

Keeping a reflexive journal is probably the most common way of reflecting on the research process. The written record gives you a good aid to recall when you are developing your analysis and writing up your research. The very act of writing your diary can allow for increased reflexive awareness in your work because writing aids thinking.

In a nutshell: research diaries

In a research diary you can:

- write down what you are experiencing at different stages of the research process;
- consider sticky situations or tricky decisions you have to make as the research unfolds;
- record your analytic processes (for example, how you developed your codes and why);
- develop your analysis (for example memo writing in grounded theory – see Chapter 7).

Your diary can be a notebook, a computer file, audio recording or any other form of record that you wish. Writing a diary as you go along in your research means that you have a record when you come to writing it all up to help you remember what you did and why you did it. This enables you to start to identify important decisions made in the research process.

As the research process develops, you will find that the diary becomes a useful place for comments, thoughts, ideas and hunches that you may have about the interviewing process, the data collection and analysis, the interpretation of the data, and how you decide to write it up. As you become increasingly immersed in the data analysis process you may encounter contradictions and questions. The diary will help you to think about ways of addressing them. It can serve to clarify your thoughts and will help you to recall aspects of the research as you progress through it. The diary provides you with a useful indicator of the parts of the research that were troubling, challenging and intriguing as well as the parts that you enjoyed or were pleased about. The diary can be useful for you to identify questions that you may want to discuss with your supervisor.

Parts of a research diary though can also be private, for your eyes only. This means that you can express yourself there freely, without fear of judgement. You can refer to your diary or use extracts from it in your write up if you want to, but it's your choice in terms of what you keep private or make public.

Reflexivity in the write-up

How you include your reflexive practices in the write-up of your project will vary depending upon what these practices have consisted of and on the rules and conventions that apply to your write-up.

In some cases, researchers include a specific section in their method section that deals with issues of reflexivity (see Chapter 9). They might use this section to outline the key issues that they consider readers should be made aware of or that should be taken into account when considering the findings. For example, you might mention that you were a woman interviewing men about domestic labour and gender equity. In some reflexive accounts you might also go on to discuss how this might have influenced the dynamics of the interviews or your interpretation of the respondents' accounts.

You can also include consideration of reflexivity throughout your project, rather than in a separate specific section. Indeed, it could be argued that if you have truly developed a reflexive standpoint then this should show through the whole project in many ways.

A reflexive standpoint may also be revealed in the use of the first person to write up research – a practice that traditionally has been frowned upon, but is now quite common for qualitative studies. For more information see Chapter 9, and consult with your supervisor and any institutional rules about how to approach this issue.

Reflexivity in summary

Reflexivity is an essential part of good quality qualitative research. It means being aware of what you bring to the research process, and of how context influences this process. Being reflexive means developing sensitivity to these elements and fosters a genuinely critical approach. Reflexivity can be achieved in many ways such as keeping a reflexive diary, involving the people around you or discussing issues with your supervisor.

Want to know more about reflexivity?

Alvesson, A. and Skoldberg, K. (2009) *Reflexive Methodology: New Vistas for Qualitative Research.* London: Sage. (A useful overview of how to incorporate reflexivity into your research design.)

Bolton, G. (2010) *Reflective Practice: Writing and Professional Development.* London: Sage. (Useful when developing a reflexive diary as well as writing up your research.)

Finlay, L. and Gough, B. (2003) *Reflexivity: A Practical Guide for Researchers in Health and Social Sciences.* Oxford: Blackwell. (Several useful essays on different aspects of reflexivity.)

Flood, R. and Gill, R. (eds) (2009) *Secrecy and Silence in the Research Process.* London: Palgrave.

Forum for Qualitative Social Research, online journal, special issue on reflexivity: http://www.qualitativeresearch.net/index.php/fqs/issue/view/18

Contribution to the subject

Your project should aim to make a contribution to the subject of study, although as discussed in Chapter 10, expectations of contribution and originality are relaxed for unpublished undergraduate work. Most student projects achieve this aim by developing existing research findings, and not, as you may be pleased to read, by producing ground-breaking research (although this is expected to a greater degree in postgraduate project work). Excellent student projects often seek to add a new angle or offer a new consideration of existing studies. For example, one of our students recently explored a woman's experience of being told her son had autism. There was published research on the issues involved in parenting children with autism, but there was nothing specifically on the experience of having the news broken to you. The student was able to embed her research in the published work but then develop the study in an innovative way.

In a nutshell: contribution to the subject

To ensure that your qualitative research contributes to the area you must know your research area and how your project will offer a distinctive view on the research area or topic.

Your literature review should allow you to demonstrate that you've identified a gap in knowledge or a new approach that could further understanding. If you're taking a novel approach try to include a discussion of the possible advantages and disadvantages of taking this new approach. Such discussions can allow you to demonstrate quality in your work because it shows intellectual rigour.

Top tip: demonstrate your contribution

Carry out a thorough review of relevant literature in a way that shows that you have made a contribution to the work that you are reviewing. To do this you should show that you:

- are aware of the different approaches used by other researchers;
- understand their findings;
- can compare previous work with your own work and show how your work can contribute to the research in this area (for more on reviewing literature see Chapter 5).

It is not enough to make a contribution to the subject of study if you cannot convince your reader that your findings are credible. So as well as addressing a gap in the literature you also need to address other quality criteria, such as rigour and coherence.

Rigour and coherence

For qualitative research to be considered excellent it is vital that it is rigorous and coherent. This means being systematic and consistent throughout, and paying careful attention to the requirements of the method you're using and to ethical concerns (see Chapter 3 for further details on ethics).

In a nutshell: rigour and coherence

Rigour and coherence in qualitative research refers to the strength of the work at all stages in the research process. This means the work must be strong, systematic and consistent.

So, your project needs:

- an appropriate research question;
- a systematic, self-conscious design;
- a clear and transparent record of the research process.

A key aspect of being coherent is achieving coherence between your research questions and your methodological approach. This aspect is so important that it is also discussed in nearly all the chapters of this book!

A cautionary tale and a success story: coherence

Kara was interested in gender differences in the experiences of parents of adult children with mental illness. She ran two focus groups with husband and wife carer couples together, with a total of eight participants. Although the form of discourse analysis she used was appropriate for small sample sizes and focus group methodology, it did not fit with her research question because discourse analysis does not answer questions about such large-scale group differences. Furthermore, eight participants were too small a sample to address group differences. Kara's project therefore did not have rigour or coherence.

Amir was interested in how burglars talked about morals. At a prison where he had a work placement he interviewed 10 men convicted of burglary. Previous research with convicted burglars had used a card-sorting task to measure levels of morality. Amir asked his participants to do this task, but to talk out loud as they did it. Amir used a form of interpretative repertoire discourse analysis on the recorded talk to analyse their accounts. However, he did not report the outcomes of the card-sorting task itself because in his study the card-sorting task was a tool for generating talk, not for measuring morality. In this way Amir used a method (the card-sorting task) in a novel, but coherent way with his research question and form of analysis.

Achieving coherence is very much dependent upon sound decision making throughout your project. Conducting research requires us to make a lot of both small and large decisions, and it's important to consider the appropriateness and the consequences of these decisions. Mays and Pope (1995) argue, for example, that you need to identify, plan and execute a systematic research design in a self-conscious manner. This means knowing when you need to make a decision and being able to offer a reasoned account for why and how you made it.

Taking a systematic approach to decision making also means that the decisions you make across your project harmonise with each other. It is not appropriate to decide upon a course of action simply because you feel like it. Qualitative researchers may value flexibility, but it's not an 'anything goes' approach. Instead careful links between theory, the research question, research method and analysis need to be worked out – so that each section fits coherently (for more on decision making see Chapter 1).

One of the key ways in which decision making relates to quality is in the idea of audit trails. These are a way of ensuring that your decision making is clearly documented as you go along. Making good decisions is not enough if you do not communicate them appropriately to your readers, and to do this you first need to remember what you did and why you did it. In our experience what can feel like an obvious decision when you're deeply involved in an aspect of your project is not clear or even memorable months later when you come to write up. We strongly recommend therefore that you record your decision making as you go along.

In a nutshell: audit trails

Creating an audit trail involves recording the decisions and actions you take throughout your project and their outcomes. Audit trails are an important means of being transparent and having a 'trustworthy' analysis (Shaw, 2010) because they allow you to create, and demonstrate if necessary, a recognisable paper trail of the processes in your research. Keeping a research diary can help to construct an audit trail.

Being able to provide an audit trail for quantitative researchers is usually linked to providing the potential for others to replicate a study, but in qualitative research people rarely do exactly the same thing twice. Some methods, such as interpretative phenomenological analysis (IPA), call for independent audits to enhance quality. Here a new researcher is brought in to check that the data is credible and that the final report of the work shows a coherent and logical progression through the research study from its outset to its outcomes. Sometimes researchers use an additional method of analysis to look for convergence or divergence in the findings. This is known as methodological triangulation. Even when no actual audit takes place, preparing an audit trail so that your work could potentially be examined in such ways is a useful way of ensuring quality.

Why we provide an audit trail is usually to communicate process, so that we can let other researchers know how and why we made the decisions we did. This allows us to show transparency in our research.

Transparency

Transparency is a way of showing the rigour, coherence and credibility of your research by communicating the processes involved in your project. Readers of your research should know exactly what you did to address the research question. This means accounting for every aspect of the research, from the development of the research question (including the literature review) to the theories you use to discuss the findings.

In a nutshell: transparency

Transparency provides your audience with enough information about how you conducted the study to enable them to form their own critique of it.

Qualitative researchers often reflect on their own role in their research and such reflections may be included to demonstrate transparency (see reflexivity section above for more details). You may also need to include documentation such as interview schedules, ethics forms, consent forms and information sheets. These documents usually go in an appendix (see below and Chapter 9 for more on appendices).

Hurdles to transparency

In order to be transparent you will have to overcome a number of hurdles, for example, balancing the need to be transparent with ethical issues such as confidentiality.

In a nutshell: hurdles to transparency

Some common hurdles that must be considered when doing research that is transparent are:

- balancing confidentiality with transparency;
- writing within word limits;
- fulfilling institutional requirements for what to include;
- deciding what to include from a research diary.

Balancing confidentiality with transparency

Conflict can occur between being transparent so that your readers can judge your work and being ethical so that you do not break the confidentiality of your participants. This dilemma may be particularly acute if your participants are vulnerable (for example, children or people with mental illness) or have treated you as a confidante (Robson, 2011; Ali, 2009). In such cases you may need to do more than employ the usual ways of ensuring anonymity and confidentiality (see Chapter 3 for more on ethics). For example, you may choose not to include full transcripts in the appendices. We recommend that you explain your rationale for such decisions in your method section. If you're struggling between confidentiality and transparency talk to your supervisor while writing up.

Top tip: space saving transparency

If you want to include full interview transcripts as a form of transparency (so your reader can judge what you included and did not include in your analysis) you can save space by burning them onto a CD. Then put the CD into a paper or plastic sleeve at the back of your thesis as an appendix. Make sure your transcripts are anonymised with all potentially identifying information removed and that the inclusion of your transcripts does not contradict what you promised participants at the consent stage.

Managing with word limits

It's crucial that you know what the word limits are (maximum and possibly minimum, depending upon your institution's rules) and that you stick to them. To help you comply with word limits, identify the key processes that need to be discussed and focus on these. Be ruthless in deciding what not to include, but consult with your supervisor if you're unsure.

Use appendices to include content that is important for transparency, but not essential to the research narrative (appendices are usually not included in the word count, which can help you save your word limit for the main body of your write up).

Requirements for what to include

Your university may require you to include certain documents in your research write-up, for example:

- completed ethics forms;
- log books of supervisor's meetings;
- signed declarations of the originality of your work.

These documents add to the transparency of your work so make sure that you know what needs to be included and include it. To find out what you need to include check your relevant module or programme handbook. Often, these kinds of documents can be appendices. You can refer to these documents in the main write-up where necessary (for example, 'see Appendix A for consent form').

Deciding what to include from a research diary

It's good practice to keep a research diary that charts the progress of your project. A research diary can help you to build an audit trail (see above) and so ensure that your project is rigorous. But sometimes content in your diary that would be useful for showing transparency feels too private to share. Similarly, your research diary may have information about your participants that should not be disclosed. In such contexts you can refer to the process of using a diary without disclosing details (for example, how using a reflective diary to write down how you felt after an interview helped you to better understand the participant's feelings).

While research diaries can be used to facilitate transparency, they can also take on a deeper significance because they are associated with 'reflexivity'.

Conclusion: a credible piece of work?

We hope that our discussion of quality criteria in qualitative research has developed your understanding of qualitative research projects and that you can begin to see how you might use the criteria we have suggested, or other similar criteria, in your own work.

When thinking about your quality criteria remember that your reader needs to be able to believe in your study and its findings. Research is believable when the processes and decision making involved are clearly presented and demonstrate rigour, coherence, transparency and appropriate reflexive practice. Demonstrating these quality criteria will allow your readers to be able to trust in the processes that you've followed, accept that the findings are plausible and that the analysis is thorough and sensitive to the context in which it was produced. A good quality project should therefore allow the reader to answer 'yes' to the following questions. So make sure you can too.

- Does the project make a contribution to the area of study?
- Does it do this in a way that shows intellectual rigour and coherence?
- Are the processes involved transparent and is there appropriate reflexivity?
- Does the study address all of the above quality criteria in a way that suggests that it is a credible piece of work?

References

Ali, S. (2009) 'Black feminist praxis: some reflections on pedagogies and politics in higher education', *Race, Ethnicity and Education*, 12(1), 79–86.

Bolton, G. (2010) *Reflective Practice: Writing and Professional Development*. London: Sage.

Denzin, N.K. (2005) 'Emancipatory discourses and the ethics and politics of interpretation', in N.K. Denzin and Y.S. Lincoln (eds) *The Sage Handbook of Qualitative Research*. Thousand Oaks, CA: Sage. pp. 933–58.

Gibson, S. and Riley, S.C.E. (2010) 'Approaches to data collection in qualitative research', in M. Forrester (ed.) *Doing Qualitative Research in Psychology: A Practical Guide*. London: Sage. pp. 59–76.

Mays, N. and Pope, C. (1995) 'Qualitative research: rigour and qualitative research', *British Medical Journal*, 311(6997), 109–12.

Robson, C. (2011) *Real World Research: A Resource for Social Scientists and Practitioner-researchers.* Oxford: Blackwell.

Shaw, R. (2010) 'Interpretative phenomenological analysis', in M.A. Forrester (ed.) *Doing Qualitative Research in Psychology: A Practical Guide.* London: Sage. pp. 177–201.

Woolcott, H.F. (2001) *Writing Up Qualitative Research.* Thousand Oaks, CA: Sage.

9

WRITING UP A QUALITATIVE PROJECT

Sarah Riley

It makes sense for a chapter about writing up your project to come towards the end of the book. After all, you need to have gone through the procedures outlined in previous chapters before you have something to present. But when it comes to doing an excellent job of writing up, the best advice is to start writing early. It takes practice and time to develop your own style, and because writing forces us to put down our ideas and try to find a way of structuring arguments, the act of writing itself helps you think and develop those ideas. It therefore pays to get in the habit of writing throughout your research project – and there are plenty of opportunities for you to write. These include writing a plan (Chapter 3), a preliminary literature review (Chapter 5), an introductory letter to participants explaining your study (Chapter 3), a research diary (Chapter 7) and the report itself (the topic of this chapter).

The previous chapters in this book have focused on helping you make the right decisions so that you can conduct an excellent piece of research. But an excellent study also needs to communicate this work effectively, and this involves two further skills. First, you need to be able to meet your institution's requirements regarding the structure and content of a research report or dissertation. Second, you need to develop your own style of writing – your 'voice' so to speak – so that you can write clearly, coherently and interestingly about your work. It's often a real challenge to meet institutional requirements for content within set word counts, and developing a good writing style that is both clear and concise can also help you do this more easily. So in this chapter I focus on these two aspects of writing up, taking you through the structure and content of your qualitative research report and discussing writing styles and techniques.

In a nutshell: chapter overview

Report structure and content

- Why research reports follow a particular structure.
- Outline of a report structure and content.
- In-depth discussion of the content required for each subsection in a report.

Writing style

- How to write clearly and concisely.
- What kind of 'tone' to use and how to develop your own 'voice'.

Conclusion

- Top tips for getting the job done.

Report structure and content

Although you've done them before it's probably useful to start this section by revisiting the role of a research report and its general structure and content. It's helpful to remind ourselves about writing up requirements as regulations may change or develop as you progress through a programme of study and sometimes students have only a partial understanding of why research reports follow a particular structure. Starting with the basics is therefore a useful way of making sure you have a clear understanding of what is expected of you.

The role of the report is to communicate a study, usually from one researcher to others, but a wider audience may also need to be considered. Journalists and students, for example, are two other groups of people who may read academic work. For a student research report, your main audience is your supervisor and markers, and often your supervisor will be one of your markers. Secondary audiences might be other students who read your thesis to get ideas for their own projects and external examiners who may read your thesis as an example of the work being produced in your institution. Your potential readership is therefore likely to involve some people who know your area well, but others who may not. So what is usually recommended is that you write in a style that emulates the professional style of the journal articles in your area, while being clear enough that you may be easily understood by a potential readership that does not have specialist knowledge of the precise topic being investigated (for example, your second marker).

In a nutshell: the aim of writing a report .

Writing about your research project allows you to:

- tell your reader what you've done, why you've done it, what you've found, and how this contributes to our general pool of knowledge;
- write in a style that keeps your reader awake and interested; and
- communicate in a way that meets your institutional guidelines for report writing.

Most institutions will have guidelines for the structure they require your thesis to follow. Look them up and either keep them with you when you're writing or make notes on what's expected and refer to those regularly instead. Many institutions, for example, require particular subheadings in method sections. If your institution doesn't have specific guidelines then look up your professional body's recommendations for report or journal article writing (for example, the British Psychological Society). In general try to follow your institutional or professional body's guidelines; they are a tried and tested way of communicating research and are what your marker will be evaluating your project against.

Activity: APA style

For many students, the required structure, style and content of report writing is likely to be based on the American Psychological Association's guidelines. Look up this online tutorial of the basics: http://www.apastyle.org/learn/tutorials/basics-tutorial.aspx

---

Sometimes it's hard to translate generic regulations for research projects to the specifics of your own project. One way for you to address this problem is to see how other people have successfully resolved such problems. Usually a department will keep students' work from recent years. Ask your supervisor if they can recommend a couple of previous students' projects to read that were given good marks. You don't have to read them cover-to-cover, but flick through to get a sense of the general structure and style of presentation or focus on sections that you're having trouble with in your own write up.

At times you may find yourself in disagreement with your institution's guidelines. There is usually one of three reasons for this: students haven't fully understood the rationale behind these recommendations; the institutional guidelines haven't been updated to include requirements for qualitative as well as quantitative studies; or students are working with an unconventional method that requires a very different style of write-up. If you're struggling to meet your institution's guidelines, either because you don't understand them fully or because you think they are inappropriate for your project, see your supervisor for advice. If you think there is a case for asking for a different, more appropriate, set of guidelines ask your supervisor to negotiate this for you. Your student–staff liaison body may also be helpful here too.

Most institutions ask for a similar structure in report writing. This is because it is considered a tried and tested way of presenting the required information in a logical way. It also means that the reader can easily find specific information, such as the number of participants in the study. Below I outline a generic structure that should be appropriate for most qualitative research projects and which should also be similar to your institution's requirements. I first present this outline as a summary table, so that you can have an overview. This serves to remind you of the structure that you may be familiar with from, for example, writing previous reports. It also starts to highlight areas that may be different for students new to qualitative research.

In the next section I go through the structure of a qualitative write up in more detail by describing what is usually expected in each subsection and the rationale behind this structuring. I also discuss where you may find differences between qualitative and quantitative reports and between qualitative reports that come from different research traditions. Students often find it hard to work out where to put information, so the aim of this section is to give you an understanding of the rationale behind the structure and offer practical suggestions for how you might translate the generic requirements for each subsection into the specifics of a qualitative research project.

In a nutshell: report outline

Title page: This contains the title of your study, your name and any other administrative information required by your institution's regulations.

Acknowledgements: An optional page where you may thank people who have helped you.

Abstract: A summary of your study, between 150–300 words depending on your institution's regulations.

Introduction: An introduction to your study, which includes your literature review and your research questions. As a whole, this section should provide a rationale (i.e. a structured argument) for your study, including your research questions and methodology.

Method:	A description of your method, often with subsections such as: design, participants, procedure and ethics. It may also include headings such as: apparatus, reflexivity and quality criteria.
Analysis:	The presentation of your findings, including extracts of data, your analysis of this data and possibly links between this analysis and your literature review or research question. This section combines aspects of the 'results' and 'discussion' sections of more traditional quantitative reports.
Conclusion:	A relatively short section, drawing your project to an end, highlighting key findings, how these relate to the literature, limitations of the study and future research suggestions.
References:	Full references for all the studies referred to in body of the report. Presented in a standard format.
Appendices:	Additional information about the project that it is not necessary for the reader to know to understand the project, but which adds rigour and transparency, such as consent forms.

In-depth guidelines

Title page

Your title should be approximately 10–20 words and should describe your topic, method and possibly your participants. There is a trend to try for a catchy title, followed by a more descriptive sub-title, often with the use of a colon and a quote from a participant. For example: 'I only do it because it's there': A discourse analysis of mountain climbers' talk in online message board discussions.

Acknowledgements

Acknowledge your supervisor. It doesn't hurt to make them feel good. Even if you don't think they were that useful they probably think they were and they're likely to be the one marking your report. Other people you might want to thank include your participants, family or anyone else who has supported your studies.

Abstract

Your abstract summarises your study. Think of it as your advertisement – when looking at journal articles researchers use them to gauge if they should read the whole article – so it needs to have all the key information. What is usually required is information on the literature that your study addresses, your research question(s), your method (for example, design, participants, type of analysis), your findings and your conclusion. You have to do this within a given word length, which may be anything from 150–300 words depending on your institution's requirements. If you're struggling with this have a look at the abstracts in journal articles that are relevant to your study and see how those authors did it.

Introduction

Your title and abstract have set the scene for your reader, giving them an overview of what you did and what you found. This sets up a series of expectations for them that you should fulfil in the main body of the report. For example, try to avoid inconsistency, such as reporting different numbers of participants in your abstract and method sections.

Your job in the introduction is to take your reader back to the beginning and explain why this study is important and interesting. In general, an introduction will start with an extension of the title, summarising the key issues and explaining to the reader what you're about to tell them. Try to start this section with a short and punchy statement or question that draws your reader in. For example, rather than start your introduction with 'This project investigates how a group of "binge" drinking students made sense of government campaigns to reduce alcohol consumption' you could start with 'Extreme drinking among UK undergraduate students has been a longstanding concern for social scientists'. You can then follow this by a short outline of your study (for example, that the government has produced a series of health campaigns targeting student excessive drinking but little research has investigated how the students being targeted by these campaigns respond to the advertisements).

After this short introduction to your study your introduction will then describe your literature review. Your literature review should focus on what research has been done before in a way that presents your topic as interesting and important. The review should also highlight what kind of work is needed that could develop our knowledge on this subject. By identifying this 'gap in the literature' and showing why addressing this gap would develop our knowledge of an important issue, your introduction becomes a persuasive piece of writing which concludes logically with your research question(s).

> ## Top tip: setting the scene
>
> By outlining what you're going to say before you say it your reader will know what to expect and can settle in to you telling them your research 'story'. This is known as 'signposting'.

When writing an introduction section it might help to imagine it as a funnel shape – it should start by discussing the broad issues, developing a gradually narrower focus that leads to your research questions. You may have several relevant bodies of literature and so will need to work out a way of structuring your review so that it seems logical to go from one topic to another. When working out the structure of your introduction it can help to take a blank piece of paper and sketch out how your topics link to each other. Subheadings and 'signposting' strategies that tell your reader what they've read and what's next may help give your report a sense of coherence. For a more detailed discussion on how to conduct, structure and write a literature review see Chapter 5.

When considering the length of your introduction you need to find a balance between being able to write a concise, coherent and persuasive argument for your thesis, and having enough words left to write the rest of your report. Writing your introduction is also an iterative process. The first time you draft your introduction you may be writing it as part of a proposal, explaining and justifying what you're going to do. Towards the end of your project, when you've done your analysis, you're likely to want to re-write your introduction to highlight key areas that you now know you are going to focus on in your analysis.

Method

If the job of your introduction section was to set the scene for your study, finishing by giving your reader the questions that you want to address; then the job of your method section is to show your reader what you did to answer those questions. This is often a technical section with subheadings, and may contain quite factual statements about your method. But with qualitative research you sometimes need to give fairly detailed arguments. For example, you need to discuss in detail the procedure and rationale for doing the kind of analysis you did on your data.

Before you write your method refer to your institution's requirements for this section. These regulations often name the required subheadings, which may include: design, apparatus, participants and procedure. Try to stick to your institution's guidelines as much as possible, but if you think they are written with quantitative studies in mind you may need to negotiate a different set of headings. Examples of subheadings in qualitative projects include: design, participants (or 'data'), procedure, ethics, reflexivity and quality criteria. I discuss these in more detail below.

Design

Your design subsection should describe the structure of your method through a succinct summary that provides the reader with the characteristics of your method. For example, it could be 'an in-depth interview study using interpretative phenomenological analysis to explore the experiences of caring for an elderly relative'. If you have collected data in phases or have more than one group of participants then here is where you would explain this.

Participants

In the participants section you should give information on who your participants were. This information should focus on characteristics that are relevant to your study. Some participant sections take the form of a couple of sentences that describe the number of participants, their sex/gender, age, location or other relevant features (for instance, if your study focuses on caring, you might specify the length of time they had been a carer).

Alternatively, if participant numbers are small, qualitative researchers sometimes provide a short paragraph describing each participant. This structure is often used when the study is looking at individual experiences and wants to personalise the accounts they are giving, highlighting how different circumstances or attitudes may affect a person's experience or understanding of the topic of interest. Note that pseudonyms are always used. So for example, in Chapter 4 we met Suzy, a student from Singapore exploring overseas students' experiences of their first weeks at university. Since each of her six students were very different, it might make sense for Suzy to give a short biography of each participant, giving demographic details (age for example), but also describing other characteristics that may have structured their first experiences of university (such as when they arrived, if they had been to the country before, and what their social network was like). An example of such a biography is given below:

> Robert is an 18 year old male from Ghana, studying psychology. He has been to England on one previous occasion. He arrived two days before the first day of

university, moving straight into a room in a hall of residence on campus. One of his sisters had a friend who lived nearby and who showed him around the local town the weekend he arrived. He did not know anyone in his hall, but quickly made friends with the six people on his floor, who included home and overseas students. He described his first few weeks as 'fun'.

Data

It may be that you did not recruit participants for your study, but collected data in other ways, for example, if you recorded online discussion forum data. In this context you might substitute the subheading 'participants' with another more appropriate term such as 'data', or as in the example below 'posters', which referred to people who had 'posted' onto different weight-related websites:

Posters

During the data collection period there were 105 contributions by 46 different posters on the recovery site and 107 contributions by 24 posters on the pro-ana site. The mean number of posts per person was 2.52 for the recovery site and 4.48 for the pro-ana site. As far as we could ascertain, all posts were by females, living predominantly in the US, UK or Australia. (Riley et al., 2009: 352)

Procedure

A procedure section may follow from the participants section. This would describe in a concise way what you did. This may include information on how you recruited your participants, how you elicited data (for example, strategies for systematically accessing online data or your interview technique) and the procedure you followed to analyse your data. Given that qualitative research needs to be systematic while being flexible to the needs of the research question, there is often a need to give some details of your analytical procedure. If you want to discuss the process of your analysis in detail you may want to use the term 'analytic procedure' as a subheading.

In your analytic procedure section you may want to describe how you collected, transcribed and coded your data and how these actions meet the research methods literature descriptions of appropriate procedure for your chosen method. It's often useful to give an example. So for instance, if you are discussing codes, axial coding and categories from a grounded theory study (see Chapter 7), give one example from your findings for each of these. Alternatively, if you did something different to standard procedures, then now is the place to say what you did and why.

Ethics

Here you describe the key ethical principles that are relevant to your study and how you addressed them (see Chapter 3 for a detailed discussion on ethics).

The above sections are fairly standard for all research projects. But other subsections that you may need in your method section include apparatus, reflexivity, transcription notation or quality criteria. Include these if you feel they are relevant to your study and the theoretical and methodological approach you've taken.

Apparatus

Here you describe any technical or specialist equipment you used. This section is standard in quantitative projects and may be relevant for qualitative projects that have used specific apparatus. For example, a description of the photographs you used in a photo-elicitation study or magazine advertisements you used to stimulate a focus group discussion (and in cases like these the section heading would probably be changed to 'materials'). Similarly, if you have used an interview schedule, open-ended questionnaire or consent forms you could describe them in a 'materials' section (and refer your reader to an appendix section where you would have put copies of these documents or images). For example, 'two consent forms were developed, one for participants, and one for their parent/guardian since they were under 16 years old (see Appendix A for copies of these forms)'.

Reflexivity

Reflexivity is your thinking about your role in your study. As a qualitative researcher you need to reflect on what worked, or didn't work, the decisions you made and how your participants responded to you – and how you responded back. There are many ways to 'do' reflexivity and not all qualitative research approaches advocate a reflectivity section. Some approaches would expect reflexivity to be visible in the analysis itself (for example, including the interviewer's questions in the data extracts) or in the discussion/conclusion sections (for example, reflecting on the limitations of the study). Other approaches tend to have a separate section dedicated to reflexivity (with the assumption that it would have informed your work throughout your project).

If you want a dedicated section then one place to put it is in the method section (another might be your conclusion – see this section). The aim of such a reflexive section is to help your reader see where the knowledge you've produced has 'come from'. For example, Suzy (who we met in Chapter 4) might use the opportunity here to discuss the impact of her being an overseas student interviewing overseas students who did not come from her home country. In doing so she might have reflected on how her similarities to and differences from her participants may have affected the way her participants responded to her and how this in turn affected the data she got. (See Chapter 8 for a detailed discussion of reflexivity and how it might apply to your own work.)

Transcription notation

If you are going to present transcriptions of talk in your analysis section then it's likely that you will need to let your reader know what your transcription notation means. Transcription notation is the name for the symbols you use to describe the talk in more detail, for example, the use of an upward arrow to show rising intonation. If you're using a fairly simple form of notation you may want to put this subsection here, but if it's a detailed one you may want to save on your word count and put your notation conventions as an appendix. (For more on transcription, see Chapters 6 and 7.)

Quality criteria

Few reports have a section on quality criteria, but if you are doing more unconventional work you may benefit from including this subsection. The aim here is to clearly outline to your reader what the key components are of a good project within the approach you are using. This lets your reader/marker have a set of criteria from which to judge your study and it also allows you to make sure you're clear on the criteria you need to address so that you can check you've done so. (See Chapter 8 for further discussion on quality criteria in qualitative projects.)

Analysis

Many qualitative reports have relatively long analysis sections in which the researcher presents their analysis of their data, often supported with extracts from the data (such as quotes from participants). This section may also make links between the literature, research questions and the findings being presented. The analysis section is therefore not a 'results' section that aims to report an analysis of data without commentary. Rather, it combines aspects of results and discussion sections of more traditional reporting styles. If you are using a qualitative method and framework that employs a traditional approach to research – one that is very realist or positivistic for example, as some grounded theory studies are – then it is likely that you need to follow a traditional report writing structure of results and discussion sections. Most qualitative projects however take a different approach to knowledge generation in research, which is why in this book we would recommend combining results and discussion into an analysis section. Note though, that some approaches tend to use separate sections for analysis and discussion while others do not, so if you are not sure what framework to employ speak to your supervisor.

When making decisions about your analysis section consider first the kind of method you're using and the usual practices associated with writing up studies that use this method. Grounded theory, IPA and the various forms of discourse analysis for example (see Chapter 7) each tend to have their own ways of presenting analysis sections that may differ slightly from other methods. There is also variation within methods based on researchers' preferences or the kind of question being addressed. This variation is an advantage for qualitative researchers; it means that we can present our work in a way that best suits the specifics of our study. But this can make new qualitative researchers anxious about how to do it 'right'. Therefore below, I've outlined a generic structure for analysis sections, which may be a good starting point for structuring your own specific analysis.

Before I outline a generic structure for analysis sections in qualitative projects, it's useful to note that more unconventional or creative reports may employ a very different style, for example, imaginary conversations composed from 'real' talk (Ashmore, 1989). As with your method section, if you are using unconventional methods remember to clearly state what you're doing, why, and the quality criteria from which your work should be judged. In general, though, analysis sections often use the following structure:

In a nutshell: analysis outline

- A paragraph or two that introduces the overall pattern of your findings (naming your themes, for example).
- New subheading with the title of your first analytic unit (such as a theme, category, discourse or conversational device), depending on your method. Introduce this section with a general explanation of what this theme/category/ discourse involves.
- Give an extract as an example. Make sure you introduce it properly (for example, 'In the following extract, Jim is talking about …'). Extracts are usually indented and sometimes put in italics to show that it is a separate piece of talk from your writing. Often extracts are numbered and details about the participants may be given. For longer extracts line numbering can be useful.

- Give a detailed analysis of the extract, possibly relating this to previous findings.
- Give second extract as a further example. This should not simply repeat the point exemplified by your first extract, but should draw the reader's attention to some other aspect of the analytic unit.
- Give detailed analysis of extract, possibly relating this to previous findings.
- Summarise this first theme/category/discourse, possibly relating this to previous findings.
- Repeat this pattern for your other themes/discourses/categories.
- Finish analysis section with overall summary of main arguments and findings.

The structure outlined above allows you to develop an argument and provide evidence for that argument. This makes for a logical approach to presenting your findings and enhancing the trustworthiness of your analysis. The screen capture in Figure 9.1 below gives you an example of how I've applied this structure to my own work.

One final, but possibly most important, comment about writing an analysis: your analysis develops as you write it. It is likely that as you write up your analysis your ideas on how to analyse your data will change. This is because of the cyclical nature of qualitative research and the associations between writing and thinking. So, it is an excellent sign if, when you're writing your analysis, you can see better, more conceptual, or clearer ways of articulating your findings, or even if you begin to notice new things that you hadn't picked up on previously! If this happens, don't think of your previous work as a waste of time, you needed to do it to get to this stage. But it does mean that to do an excellent thesis you need to give yourself enough time for you to develop your analysis as you write it. As a rule of thumb, consider leaving about one-third of the time you have to do your study on your analysis. Leaving more time to do this section than you expect you will need is a good way of allowing you to write the best analysis section you can. (For more discussion on analysis see Chapter 7.)

Conclusion

This section rounds off your report. Some institutions will require that you call it a conclusion, others a discussion, but under either title the same issues should be addressed. It is normal practice to start with a summary of the findings in relation to the research questions and previous literature, to then discuss the limitations of the study and future research suggestions. A final

| Economic citizens | A subheading that is the title of a new theme |

In the 'economic citizen' repertoire participants linked controlled drug use with economic participation, constructing magic mushroom use as an occasional leisure activity, in a context in which paid work was normalised and took priority over hallucinogenic drug use.

| | A paragraph that introduces this theme |

(Extract 6, focus group 3, Joanne 38):
but I think it's got such (.) if you take them [mushrooms] (.) you've probably got about 8, 10 hours (.) depending on the quantity (.) I think that's why it's a celebration thing (.) you need to take some time out (.) if you've got anything to do the next day (..) like for example if it's mid week (.) you had to go to work the next day (.) you would not take mushrooms

| | An extract that acts as an example of the theme. Indented and titled with a number and description of where and who in the data it came from (in this case the focus group, participant's name and age) |

Joanne associates the longevity of the effects of mushrooms (*you've probably got about 8, 10 hours*) with the need to limit their use to occasions that provide time out from everyday responsibilities (*a celebration thing ... you need to take time out*). Arguing that you need to take 'time out' implies that there is something people are typically 'in', this subtly constructs economic participation as normal, an understanding then made explicit with a direct link between drug use and economic participation (*if ... you had to go to work the next day*).

| | New paragraph analysing the extract in detail |

Economic activity is thus constructed as normative and as taking priority over hallucinogenic drug use that may negatively impact on work. An alternative account was raised by some participants, but as in extract five, such apparently deviant cases were mobilised in ways that served to reinforce rather than challenge neo-liberal sense making.

| | New paragraph that links the above in-depth analysis to wider patterns in the data, it also introduces the next extract. |

(Extract 7, focus group 1, *Rebrov, age 25*):
the majority of people who take mushrooms in their lifetime (..) won't do it for any great length of time (.) for a short period (.) maybe their teenage years or (.) early adult hood and then (..) you know (.) go and get a job and (.) calm down (.) and drink beer for the rest of their lives (.) the majority (.) certainly most of my friends (.) erm have gone back to that way (.) of (.) living

| | The next extract, presented in the same way as previous extracts. |

Figure 9.1 Screen capture of a page of analysis

sentence or paragraph summing up the study with a clear take home message is often a good way to end a report.

This section then is not much different from a traditional 'discussion' section, but is likely to be shorter because much of the discussion about how the study addresses the research questions and literature will already have been done in the analysis section previously.

Sometimes students can do an excellent analysis but their conclusion lets them down. This can happen if students are too speculative or too general. Try to focus your conclusion on how your analysis allows you to address your research question(s).

Sometimes students struggle with the limitations section of the discussion. It's often hard to consider the limitations of a study in a way that is creative and constructive. Students may not be able to think of any limitations or may only think of simple suggestions for improvement, such as increasing the number of participants. Alternatively, some students can reel off so many things that they would do differently if they could start again, that they give the impression their study wasn't worth doing. Finding a balance between these two positions will allow you to show that you have reflected on your work, and that now, having come through the process of the study, you are able to identify a few key factors that affected your ability to address your research question or contribute to knowledge on the topic of your study. This is why some reports include a reflexivity section here. All studies have limitations; the key is to identify how they may have had an impact on the data you collected or the way you did your analysis. For example, you may have used focus groups because they allowed you to see how people made sense of an issue together, but in doing so, you will only have accessed information that your participants were prepared to share in this semi-public event. If you are struggling with this section speak to your supervisor or look at published work in your area for examples of how other people have addressed this issue.

The suggestions for future research may feed directly on from your limitations section because the limitations you identify can suggest the direction for the next course of study. For example, if you did an IPA study (see Chapter 7) with students who had given up smoking and identified some factors that seemed specific to the university context, it might be that you could then suggest other populations who were also institutionally based with whom you could explore the role of these factors further, thus allowing you to make a future contribution about the role of institutional identification on smoking cessation. So the limiting factor was that using a student population may have affected your findings, but the future suggestion is that this finding suggests a new area for health promotion research, that of exploring the impact of institutional identification.

Suggestions for future research do not have to be associated with the limitations that you've identified; other suggestions may come from your analysis itself. For example, if you identified a particular set of accounting practices with a group of magic mushroom users, a future suggestion may be to look at online discussions so that you can analyse a much large data set to see if these patterns are particularly common among this group of drug users.

References

As with all reports list all the references for anything you've cited in the main text. This includes: journal articles, books, book chapters and web-pages. Make sure you follow your institutional guidelines for how to format these. There are several variations and since a sign of an excellent thesis is attention to detail make sure you're consistent and are using the right one. Your course handbook may specify and give you examples. In general, English-speaking psychology departments use the formatting recommended by the American Psychological Association, the Australian Psychological Society, the British Psychological Society or the New Zealand Psychological Society. These organisations provide examples of formatting on their institution's websites. You may also want to use reference managing software such as EndNote.

Appendices

In the last section of your report are your appendices. This houses all the extra bits of your project that are not essential for your reader to understand your study, but may help your reader if, for example, they wanted to follow up your study or wanted to critically evaluate aspects of your study, such as seeing if your interview questions closely match the themes of your analysis – a sign that you only found what you were looking for. Appendices tend to include documents such as: consent forms, information sent to participants, interview schedules or other relevant materials (for example, the photographs used in a photo-elicitation study). As such, appendices may not take on the same formatting structure as the rest of your report. Appendices may also contain the raw data, for example, anonymised transcripts of interviews. Often this would be a significant amount of paper and so not all institutions require this. One solution is to include a CD with the transcripts on them in a paper envelope bound into the thesis as an appendix.

Each document in your appendices should be given its own heading and labelled accordingly, for example 'Appendix A: Consent forms used for first phase of data collection'. Note that all appendices should be referred to in the main text, and if you have several appendices make sure that you refer to the right one!

In a nutshell: what each section 'does'

Abstract:	summarises your whole study, sets the scene for your reader.
Introduction:	explains why your study is important and interesting and logically leads to your research question(s).
Method:	through a range of subheadings this section shows your reader what you did to answer your research question(s).
Analysis:	a mixture of results and discussion that allows you to describe the patterns you have found in your data, give evidence of these patterns and possibly relate this analysis to your research questions/literature review.
Discussion/conclusion:	this section rounds off your report; it focuses on highlighting the key points of your findings, limitations of the study and future research recommendations.
References:	this lists all the sources you have referred to so your reader can look up anything that interested them.
Appendices:	house all the extra bits of your project that are not essential for your reader to understand your study, but may help your reader if, for example, they wanted to follow up your study or wanted to critically evaluate aspects of your study.

Writing style

Qualitative research is an umbrella term for a wide range of research practices. Some qualitative researchers take a traditional approach to research, both in terms of how to make sense of the knowledge they produce (see discussion on ontology and epistemology in Chapter 1) and how to communicate it. Traditionally researchers write in the third person and imperfect past tense. An example being: 'the results showed a reduction in metabolism between the two test periods'. In this example the researcher is absent and the events described are in the past tense. If you are taking a traditional approach in your research project a traditional approach to writing up will keep your project consistent.

But for other kinds of qualitative projects a different style may be more appropriate. Some strands of qualitative research come from a historical tradition that sought to challenge traditional positivist writing styles. For example, some qualitative researchers argued that by writing in the third person researchers hid the fact that there was a decision maker behind the research, creating an illusion of objectivity. This critique led to some researchers arguing that academics could challenge this illusion by writing in first person. For example, 'in this paper I argue that ...'. Other qualitative researchers, while equally critical of traditional approaches, do not consider using the first person as a way of making research more 'authentic' or 'transparent'. Such researchers argue that using the first person is simply another form of presenting the research and is no more or less transparent than any other. As Watson notes, 'plain speaking is simply a rhetorical alternative, not a turning away from rhetoric' (1995: 806). So when you're deciding whether to write in third or first person you need to consider the tradition that you're working in and your own personal preferences. Whatever you choose, make sure you're consistent throughout.

Requirements on whether to write in past or present tense are also relatively fluid in qualitative research, with some researchers using the past tense and other researchers writing predominantly in the present tense. Again, pick the tense you want to write in and keep to that tense unless it would be illogical to do so. For example, your method section is usually written in the past tense as you are writing about what you have done.

Writing a good research project requires you to both develop your own style and meet your institutional requirements. So be familiar with what's required from you and try to pay attention to how you present your arguments – so that you can communicate the content of your project clearly and with style.

Writing that has style usually has clarity, structure and a 'turn of phrase' that keeps the reader interested. Academics are well known for writing dense prose that is abstract and high-sounding, but hard to understand (see Billig [2011] for an interesting discussion of this issue). It's tempting to try and emulate this style. But think about how you feel when you read these kinds of texts. Reading dense, turgid, unclear, ambiguous and overly complicated writing is hard work, and often leaves a reader feeling irritated. And this is not what you want your reader-and marker- to feel when reading your report.

Top tip: writing style

If you find yourself enjoying reading an article, try to notice what it is about the author's style that has made it a pleasant read. Then you can emulate it in your own work.

When someone writes clearly the reader stops noticing that they are reading and instead they become focused on taking in the content of the document. Clear writing therefore allows reading to become an enjoyable activity because the reader can immerse themselves into the content of the writing. Writing clearly is a skill that develops with time, practice and a bit of know-how. Here are some writing tips aimed to help you develop an understanding of good writing skills.

Clear writing tips

- Use clear and concise sentences. Avoid repetition, waffle, labouring a point or having so many points in a sentence that the reader gets lost in what you're trying to say.
- Cut unnecessary words that do not add to your argument. For example, in the sentence 'a very important study' the 'very' is unnecessary because the word 'important' tells the reader that this is an issue that needs consideration.
- Use the simplest word with the same meaning. For example, for 'utilised' write 'used'; 'before' works for 'prior to' and 'during' means the same as 'in the course of'.
- Use a mixture of short and long sentences. Short sentences can add punch. Very long sentences are hard to follow, so try breaking up sentences that are longer than 25 words. To reduce overly long sentences try replacing a comma, semi-colon or connecting word (and, but, because, although, since, however) with a full stop.
- Write your arguments in a logical order, 'signposting' them on the way (telling your reader what you're going to say, saying it, saying what you've told them).
- Explain your thinking. Don't assume your reader knows what you're talking about, or understands why one concept should be linked to another or what your results mean if you don't tell them.
- Where possible, write in the active tense following a sentence structure of: subject, verb and object/noun. For example, in the sentence 'the researcher applied her coding plan to one transcript' – we know who did what to what. The 'researcher' is the subject, the verb is 'applied' and the object is her 'coding plan'. If we write this information in a passive way: 'the coding plan was applied to one transcript', we don't have information on the subject (that is, who did the applying of the coding plan) and we've used two words for the verb 'was applied' when we could have used one. Writing that is in the active tense often has a more logical order, has less ambiguity because you know who's doing the deed; and may make your writing sharper because it can use less words. To identify 'passive' writing that needs 'activating' look for the following things in your own writing:
  o The verb 'to be' (am, is, was, were, are, be, been, being) alongside another verb, such as in the 'was applied' example above.
  o The subject is missing or is after the word 'by'.

Conclusion

Many people find writing up their research project a daunting prospect. And considered as a whole it may be. But the process of writing can be an enjoyable experience that can let you feel creative and give you a sense of achievement – both in what you've done and how you've communicated it. The aim of this chapter has been to guide you through the process of writing so that it can be a good experience for you. So I finish with a final set of top tips for getting the job done and wish you happy writing!

Top tips: getting the job done

- Write throughout your project to develop your style. Writing is a craft that takes time, practice and attention to learn.
- Apply your planning skills (see Chapter 3) to know what your institutional requirements are for the content and structure of a write-up. Plan how you might meet them. And keep a note of any decisions you made so you can incorporate them into your writing when you need to.
- Read your writing aloud to yourself– it will let you 'hear' where the problems are in your writing. For example, you may notice that you need to make a clearer link between arguments, or that a sentence has two points that would be better presented in two separate sentences.
- Think of your report as a story – it should have a beginning, a middle and an end, taking your reader on an interesting journey that is regularly signposted on the way.
- Writing is a cyclical process. Get your ideas out in a draft form, rather than aim for perfection first time round. Once a significant section has been written, then return to it to do cycles of polishing up.
- If you cannot remember something then leave a box where the information should go and look it up later.
- You think as you write. Give yourself enough time to be able to develop these ideas as you write up.
- Leave even more time than that. Things always take longer than you think and it's harder to be creative when you're anxious about deadlines.
- Don't write your report in the order that you are going to present it. Write the more straightforward bits first – such as the method. Your abstract should be written last. You write your method first to remind you what you did and because it's usually the most straightforward part of a project writing it will often give you a sense of achievement, getting you in the mood to carry on writing and face the more difficult aspects. You write your abstract last, because it's only once you've written a full draft of your thesis that you will be most clear about what you did and found.
- When writing keep a clear note of where the information you're using came from. Otherwise you may spend unhappy hours looking for lost references, or worse, find yourself accused of plagiarism. You are especially vulnerable to producing plagiarised work if you cut and paste from other documents you've accessed from the web. If you are using electronic sources it is advisable to clearly mark such texts to yourself in your draft writing so that when you come back to it you know it's not yours, or avoid cutting-and-pasting altogether and type in the idea you want to discuss in your own words.

- If you're having difficulty writing find a strategy for getting you started. Once you begin writing it's usually much easier to carry on. At other times you might need motivation to carry on or strategies for helping keep you focused or giving you new energy. The following strategies may be useful:

  - Keep your energies up. Try to eat healthily, avoiding the highs and lows of sugar/caffeine if you can help it.
  - Go for a short walk. Movement and fresh air can help.
  - Do the straightforward bits first to get you started.
  - Get rid of distractions (turn off your email and phone).
  - Start the day with writing (not, for example, emails, reading, or the television).
  - Apply psychology to yourself: what are the motivations and strategies that work best for you? If you find getting started difficult because it seems such a big thing to do, tell yourself you only have to write for five minutes, then you can do something else. Once you've written for five minutes, you'll probably be happy to do more.
  - Set yourself goals, such as writing a specific number of words a day (for example, 700) and stop when you've done them.
  - Reward yourself.
  - Read this chapter for inspiration – remember you can do it!

- Do not use reading this chapter as a way of avoiding writing your thesis.

Want to know more about writing up?

Denman, T. (2007) *How Not to Write*. London: Piatkus Books.
Lyons, E. and Coyle, A. (2007) *Analysing Qualitative Data in Psychology*. London: Sage. (This book has examples of project write-ups with author commentaries on them.)

References

Ashmore, M. (1989) *The Reflexive Thesis*. Chicago: Chicago University Press.

Billig, M. (2011) 'Writing social psychology: fictional things and unpopulated texts', *British Journal of Social Psychology*, 50, 4–20.

Riley, S., Rodham, K. and Gavin, J. (2009) 'Doing weight: pro-ana and recovery identities in cyberspace', *Journal of Community and Applied Social Psychology*, 19, 348–59.

Riley, S.C.E., Thompson, J. and Griffin, C. (2010) 'Turn on, tune in, but don't drop out: the impact of neo-liberalism on magic mushroom users (in)ability to imagine collectivist social worlds', *International Journal of Drug Policy*, 21(6): 445–51.

Watson, T.J. (1995) 'Rhetoric, discourse and argument in organizational sense-making: a reflexive tale', *Organizational Studies*, 16, 805–21.

10

WHAT NEXT?

Cath Sullivan

The previous chapter focused on producing an excellent write-up and you might think that once you have done that your dissertation is finished. Getting to that stage is a big achievement, but in this chapter I will show you that it isn't necessarily the end of things. There are three key ways in which you can extend the research work that you do as a student. These are:

- using your student research as evidence of what you can do (your transferable skills) when applying for jobs or other courses;
- publishing your dissertation as a journal article; and
- using your dissertation as the basis for a proposal for subsequent research.

Demonstrating skills

Doing research as a student will have helped you to develop a number of skills that will be useful in many areas after graduation, in employment, further study or just in general everyday situations. When you go on to apply for other courses or jobs you will need to give good examples of the skills you have and some of these examples may come from your experience of doing research. So, this first part of the chapter will highlight some of the skills that are developed and practiced in this work and show how you can use your experience as evidence that you have these skills.

You use a large range of different skills when doing research as a student and coming up with examples of things you did while planning, conducting or writing up the research can provide really good examples of your skills. When applying for a job, it is easy to say that you have got the skills that are asked for, but what you really need to do is provide evidence of this. Genuine, concrete examples from your experience can be used to demonstrate that you possess certain skills and have used them successfully in the past. This will take you much further than just saying you've got the skills and hoping that people will take your word for it.

In a nutshell: your research is evidence of ...

- Critical evaluation
- Time management
- General research methods skills
- Qualitative data collection, data management and analysis skills
- The ability to work independently
- Interpersonal skills
- Communication and presentation skills – for example, clear writing, argumentation, use of appropriate technical language and possibly also verbal presentation skills if you also did an oral exam as part of your assessment

---

Critical evaluation

In completing your work you examined a body of literature and evaluated this in terms of what gaps there were in the literature. You also had to consider how your findings fitted in with previous literature and theories, which involves thinking critically about your findings and about those of others. You also identified and considered limitations of your research and this provides another piece of evidence of critical evaluation.

Time management

A key part of completing a student research project is being able to manage your time properly. So, the fact that you had to produce a timetable as part of your planning provides a useful example of this. You might also want to think of examples of where you had to adjust your timetable as the process went along. Describing, for example, how you modified your timetable to accommodate an event, such as a delay in getting your data collected, can show that you are able to timetable flexibly and be adaptable. You could also show that you are able to create sub-goals in order to break a larger task down into smaller, more manageable sections with their own individual goals. And discussing how you strategically planned your project (see Chapter 3) might allow you to demonstrate that you have the skills to manage the responsibilities of a new job.

General research methods skills

There are many basic research methods skills that you have practiced while doing your project. You could talk about how you went through the literature and devised a good research question or how you wrote your ethics application. In an interview you could specifically talk about how your decisions were shaped by what you'd read in the literature.

Qualitative data collection and analysis skills

You can show that you were able to collect and analyse data with a qualitative technique. As many students still do quantitative work in many areas, this could put you at a particular advantage as it shows that you have a broader range of skills (assuming that you will also have done some quantitative practical work). This will be especially useful if applying for a course or job where qualitative skills are sought, and you can use examples from your experience to show that you have the skills that they are asking for and make a strong link between your experience and the job.

The ability to work independently

Your experience of doing research as a student provides a concrete example of your ability to work independently on a big project. You could talk here about how you set your own deadlines or targets to help progress towards your goals or how you shaped the project to make it your own piece of work that reflected your interests. Obviously, you didn't work entirely unsupervised but you could also use this as a strength here, by giving examples of how you made decisions that allowed you to put into practice your supervisor's advice. You could describe, for example, how you made changes to your interview schedule in order to include a greater number of prompts in response to your supervisor's advice on an early draft.

Interpersonal skills

Various aspects of your skills in dealing with other people will have been applied to your student research work. You may, for example, have had to negotiate access to organisations or groups of people to recruit participants, you may have had to deal with 'gatekeepers' (see the discussion of recruitment in Chapter 3). You might want to draw upon examples of how you have answered queries from prospective participants or had to deal with the communication of technical ideas in everyday language. Also, managing the relationship with your supervisor could provide examples of how your inter-personal skills have been practiced and enhanced by doing a dissertation (see Chapter 4 for more on this).

Communication and presentation skills

A key component of your project is writing. You can use various different parts of this to show that you have skills in a number of areas of communication (also, see Chapter 9 to prompt you for ideas on how your work shows good writing).

Top tips: excellent evidence of communication skills

- You have written successfully for different audiences – for example, writing information for your participants and also writing in a more academic style for your ethics submission.
- You will have used technical terminology appropriately. For example, you can show that you were able to use technical terms in your write-up, but that you either explained or avoided them when you wrote for your participants.
- If you also did a viva (oral examination) you can use this to show that you have good skills of verbal presentation and maybe also as an example of your ability to produce good visual aids (like slides or a handout).
- A successful write-up includes clear and persuasive arguments that are based on evidence. This ability to write arguments is another communication skill that could be useful elsewhere, and that is evidenced by your written accounts of student research.

This section has illustrated a key way in which your experience will be useful in the future. You can draw upon this (the practical things you did to plan and conduct your research and the write-up itself) to come up with good practical evidence of some of the skills you have practiced or acquired on your course.

Activity: identifying skills and examples

Find a job description for a job that you would like to do, or a set of criteria for a course that interests you. If you don't have either of these to hand, you could search on the Internet for something suitable or look in a newspaper. Write out a list of the skills that are required and, for those that are relevant, write down a practical example of something you did as student researcher that shows that you have this skill.

Being able to use your student research experience to give tangible evidence of your skills, is important because many of these skills are particularly valued by employers of graduates, especially the interpersonal and communication skills (Landrum, 2003; Biesma et al., 2008).

Success story: dissertation work as evidence of skills

As an undergraduate Baljit did an interview study with British Asian students about their attitudes to marriage, using thematic analysis to analyse the data. After leaving university, she applied for a job with a national charity as a research assistant. They were looking for somebody with qualitative research skills to work on a project interviewing women about domestic violence. Baljit wrote in her application that she had the ability to work independently and that she had skills and experience in qualitative research (as these were highlighted on the job description). She was very pleased when she was offered an interview for the job. In the interview, she was asked to provide an example of her qualitative research skills and she was also asked to talk about her ability to work independently. Baljit drew briefly on two practical examples to show evidence of her experience in these areas.

First, she talked about how she had written a semi-structured interview schedule and had taken care to ensure that she followed certain principles of good practice in doing so – for example, checking informed consent at the start of the interview, using easy and non-threatening 'ice-breaker' questions to ease rapport, using open questions later on to elicit a fuller account and preparing prompts to help with this. She then talked briefly about how she had managed her project partly by identifying small achievable sub-goals for herself as she went along (writing participant materials, transcribing two interviews this week, writing the method section), checking them with her supervisor, to make sure she was on track to meet her deadline. Baljit was told later that she had interviewed very well and was offered the job.

There are also ways in which your dissertation might be presented and published to a wider audience and the next section considers the most common of these – publishing a journal article.

Publishing your dissertation

Although doing a dissertation is a useful thing in its own right, sometimes the write-up can be developed further and lead to its content being published or disseminated in other ways. The most common way to publish research findings is in the form of a journal article. In the next sections, I will outline how academic publishing works, consider the possible benefits of publishing your dissertation in this way and give some practical advice on how to make the most of this if you do get the chance to give it a go.

Most dissertation work does not get published, and it would be a mistake to think that your work isn't good if it's not published. The most important criteria for deciding if your dissertation is publishable is the quality of the data, and not the quality of your write-up or even analysis (Wood et al., 2009). It is possible to do an excellent dissertation that is well planned, executed and written up, but that does not have data that is publishable. For example, your sample size may be perfectly acceptable for a dissertation but considered too small for publication in many journals. Or, you may have done a project that largely replicates previous research, which made a good dissertation but would not be of interest to journal editors.

An excellent dissertation involves you doing something that is appropriate for the task in hand – that is, something that is practical in the time available, that applies and extends your research skills and meets the educational goals that correspond to it. One way to end up doing a poor dissertation is to try and over-extend yourself, or to become too fixated on the idea of doing something that might end up being publishable or makes a unique contribution to the literature (this is something expected that may be of postgraduate students but seldom is a requirement for undergraduates). Remember that those students who have aspects of their dissertation work published have not necessarily done a better dissertation than those who haven't.

Having said that, some of you may be approached by your supervisor about the possibility of publication. If you are in this position, it is important for you to know how academic publishing works so that you can think through carefully what your options are and make a decision that is best for you. Even if you are not considering having any of your dissertation work published the next section will provide you with useful information about publishing that may be of use to you in the future (for example, if you are applying for a job involving research).

The process of publishing journal articles

The most common way for research findings to be disseminated is as articles that are published in academic journals. You should already be familiar with journal articles, but what you may be less familiar with is the process of publication. In this section, I will explain how a finished study can eventually (if you're lucky!) turn into a published journal article.

In a nutshell: publishing a journal article

- The authors decide what work needs to be done to produce the article and begin discussing the order of authors' names (will it be 'Smith and Jones' or 'Jones and Smith'?).
- The authors write various drafts of the article until it is ready to submit to a journal.
- The finished article is submitted to a journal for consideration.
- The editor(s) of the journal read the article and decide whether it fits in with the aims and scope of the journal.
- If the editor(s) think the article is suitable they send it out to appropriate academics to be peer-reviewed.
- Once the reviews are done the editor(s) decide whether the article will be published (in its current form or a modified form) or not.
- The editor(s) communicate the decision to the authors.
- If the paper has been accepted in a modified form, the authors will have a certain amount of time to change it and resubmit.
- The editor(s) return the modified article back to the reviewers to check that the changes are satisfactory.
- The article may then be accepted or further revisions may be requested.
- Once all revisions are made the article will be considered to be 'in press' and will eventually appear in print.

As you can see, academic publishing can be a very drawn-out affair. Writing an article (or 'paper' as they are often known) can take some time, but this is really only the start of a very long process. It can take many months for papers to be reviewed and amended and then the time between them being finally accepted and actually appearing in print can be lengthy. The editors of this book, for example, have experienced this time to be as short as four months or as long as two years. So, this is the first thing to note – if you do decide that you want to go down this road, don't expect to get there very quickly. Also, bear in mind that many articles are rejected by journals or are accepted only on the condition that very major revisions are made. Competition is fierce, even for experienced researchers, so remember that you may not actually succeed in publishing your work even if you decide to try. This is a difficulty all researchers face – and even very experienced people have their work rejected by journals – so if you want to do research you will have to get used to it and it is not necessarily something that should put you off trying.

As the above suggests, deciding to try to publish something based on your dissertation work is likely to be time-consuming and could be a frustrating experience. So, why do it? There are some potential benefits as well as some drawbacks and these are as follows:

> ## In a nutshell: why try to publish dissertation work?
>
> - Writing a paper allows you to extend your experience of research work. Even if it is not published, this is a useful addition to your skills and experience and may be useful when applying for jobs or courses.
> - You will also gain a fuller insight into how publishing works, which will help whenever you need to develop understanding of a body of knowledge (you will be much better placed to know how this body of knowledge came into being).
> - If your attempt to publish is successful then you will find it useful to have a publication on your curriculum vitae.
> - Working on the journal article, even if it doesn't get published, may help you to establish potentially useful networks with academics (you might find out about funding or job opportunities, for example).

Writing the article

Writing for a journal is different from writing up the research you do as a student – papers are shorter, more concise, more technical and written with the specific purpose of disseminating research findings to other researchers (rather than to meet educational goals). So there will often be a substantial amount of work to do in order to turn the dissertation work into a journal article. Bits of the dissertation write-up might be used, but it is more common to produce an entirely new piece of writing and also sometimes to re-analyse the data. One issue that you should begin contemplating before the article is written is who is likely to be named as authors and in what order their names might appear. This issue may seem simple but it can be contentious and considering it early on can help to avoid disappointment and conflict at a later stage.

> ## In a nutshell: why does the order of authors matter?
>
> Generally, the order of authors on a paper indicates the extent to which each person has contributed to the writing of that paper. So, if somebody else's name appears before yours, this indicates that they have done more work or made a more important contribution. Also, as you will already know, when there are a number of authors we often shorten the reference, so that only the first named author appears in the text (so, Jones, Wright and Albatross, 2009, will tend to be referred to as Jones et al., 2009).

In some disciplines author names are always presented in alphabetical order of surname, but it is common (and standard in psychology) to stick to the principle that the order of names reflects the extent of the contribution. This is a simple idea, but it can be difficult to determine in practice. In some cases, there may be a number of authors who agree that they have all contributed equally. In such cases authors may simply use alphabetical order (bad luck if your name begins with a Z!). Authors who commonly work together may simply take it in turns to go first – and this can work fairly well when there are frequent and regular collaborations. Alternatively, researchers might decide to ensure that somebody does more of the work on the paper before they start writing, so that they can more easily determine the order of names.

So, what does this mean for you as a student? First, it is important to remember that the order of names is significant and that it is advantageous for an author if their name appears first. Second, you should be aware that the convention about name order is that it should reflect the relative contributions that each author has made to the article – and so if you write the article yourself with some guidance and help from your supervisor then your name should probably go first. If, on the other hand, the article is mostly written by your supervisor then it would make more sense for you to go second. It will be useful to you in negotiating this issue with co-authors to be aware of some of the relevant issues and conventions. If your supervisor doesn't bring up the issue, you may want to raise it yourself so that you know what to expect. It is common for dissertation work to need substantial rewriting to be suitable for publication and so ex-supervisors often make a very major contribution. Therefore, it is more common for the student's name to be second and having a publication as second author is a major achievement, especially at the start of a publishing career. What matters the most is that the order of names is a fair reflection of the distribution of effort and that everyone is in agreement. Also, although it's a good idea to start thinking about and discussing this early on, it isn't always possible to determine who has contributed what until the paper is finished – so some flexibility and re-negotiation may be needed.

Deciding what counts as a contribution and how to judge the size or importance of a contribution is, of course, something that can be difficult. To help sort out these issues, you can refer to existing guidelines on the determination of authorship in research publications, for example the British Psychological Society's (Game and West, 2002), which include the following points:

- Authors should have made a significant contribution to the article and/or the research project.

- Significant contributions can include research design, conducting analysis, interpreting findings and writing sections of the article.
- More minor contributions (for example, data collection, supervised analysis, recruiting participants or giving advice on methodology) should be acknowledged with a footnote.
- If all authors have made an equal contribution then a note to this effect can be included at the start.
- Neither the inclusion of names nor their order should be influenced by the status, degree of experience or standing of the individuals concerned.

They go on to give some specific guidelines for the publication of student–supervisor research, which include the following:

- Students should normally be the first author, providing the article is 'substantially based on' their work.
- Supervisors should ensure that they create a situation where it is possible for the student to do what is necessary to be credited as first author.
- Exceptions can be made to this (for example, when the supervisor devised the entire design, when very close supervision was needed in writing the article).

In order to create a journal article you will have to think carefully about how this differs in format from your dissertation write-up. It is useful to try and decide at the start what journal you will be aiming for. To do this, you will need to think about things like the 'aims and scope' of the journals you are considering. Do they fit with your intended article? Try and find journals that publish similar work to yours – both in terms of methodology and in terms of topic areas. At this stage of a publishing career, you may want to try and go for journals that are somewhat less prestigious as there may be less competition and you could get a decision much more quickly. It might be possible to identify a journal that publishes work by students – again read the information about the journal carefully to try and work out things like this.

Once you have decided on a journal, you should look up the instructions for authors for that journal (they normally appear on the journal's website and they tell you things like how to format the text, how many words to include and what to include). Also, it is important to think about the aims and scope of that journal (again, you can find these on the website of the journal or inside the cover of a printed copy) and to try to tailor your article to fit as well as you can. Read published journal articles (especially those that are very similar to your own in terms of methodology) and examine them for their structure and style so you can use these to model your own article. You may also find it useful to read and reference articles from the journal that you are aiming for.

Top tips: turning a dissertation into a journal article

- Decide on a journal before you start writing and tailor your article to match the aims and scope.
- Make sure you find and follow the instructions for authors for the journal you aim to submit to (for example, about word length, format).
- Be aware that your article, like many other pieces of writing, will probably go through many stages before being ready – get feedback from as many people as you can on the drafts and try your best to use it when revising.
- Use similar published work as a guide to the length, format and style that you are trying to aim for (and remember that journal articles are different from dissertation write-ups).

Submitting your article

Once the article is finished you will need to submit it. These days the majority of journals use online submission systems. The instructions for authors should give you full details of how to do this. It is very important to closely follow the directions, which can sometimes be long and a bit complex. You will probably need to have your document files saved in a particular format and complete an online form giving information such as contact details and key words that related to the article. You may also be asked to save and upload any diagrams as separate files (sometimes as graphics files such as jpegs).

You will also find that there are specific instructions for creating an anonymous version of the paper that will be sent to review. The editors of the journal will know who the authors are but when they send the paper on to be reviewed this is done anonymously. The idea is that the review process is more objective if the reviewers do not know who has written the paper. It is therefore important that you follow any instructions for anonymising your paper carefully.

The editor(s) will read your paper when they receive it and they will make an initial decision about whether they think it is suitable for the journal. At this stage, they may reply to you and say that they don't think it is suitable. When this happens it can be quite disheartening but at least this kind of decision is usually made and communicated quite swiftly, so you don't lose too much time. Also, the fact that your paper doesn't fit in with the aims and scope of a particular journal doesn't necessarily mean that it is poor quality. If this happens, you will need to identify another journal and make any necessary modifications to the paper (so that it fits the author instruction and aims of that journal) and try again.

If the editor(s) feel your paper is potentially suitable for the journal, they will send it out to be reviewed. This is done anonymously and the editor(s) will send the article to other academics who are working in the same or a closely related field. The reviewers will be asked to judge the article in terms of its suitability for that journal and its quality according to criteria that are specified by the journal (these commonly include things like the quality of the research design, the way it was conducted, the usefulness of the research and whether it makes a contribution to knowledge, the quality of the writing, the level of appropriate critical analysis). It is usual for an article to go to two or three reviewers for consideration.

The reviewers' decision

When the reviews are completed, these are sent back to the editor for consideration and a final decision. The decision generally will consist of one of these options:

- Rejecting the paper as not suitable for publication (or for that journal).
- Accepting the paper with major amendments. This might include re-analysis of data or the collection of more data and very substantial changes to the writing. When this decision is made the paper is often treated as an entirely new submission when it is resubmitted.
- Accepting the paper with minor revisions. This would involve making less substantial changes to the paper – smaller amounts of rewriting, or perhaps just correcting some typographical errors, clarifying small sections of the writing or adding in a little more evidence to strengthen a particular argument. When this decision is made the editor(s) will often send the revised version back to the same reviewers to simply check that you have done what was asked.
- Accepting the paper as it is. This is very unusual but remember that the process of having a paper reviewed and amending it is not a failure, but an important way in which we draw upon the views of others to help improve our writing and ideas.

It is very important to remember that the first three are the most common outcomes and many journals only ever accept a small proportion of those papers that are submitted. The average rejection rate for all journals published by the American Psychological Association in 2009, for example, was 77 per cent and some individual journals had much higher rates – such as the *Journal of Applied Psychology* with 91 per cent of submitted papers being rejected (APA, 2010). Having a paper accepted with major revisions is a good achievement and, if this happens, you ought to be very pleased. In reality, even very experienced researchers are sometimes daunted by making major revisions and can feel hurt by the negative feedback (whether tactfully expressed or not). It's important to remember that these reactions are quite normal, but that it is essential to try and find a way to manage them if you wish to have a publishing career. Although we all need a little time to lick our wounds at times like this, it is important to try to force yourself (sooner, rather than later) to get to grips with the comments, whether you agree with them or not, and try to make the changes that are asked for. This can be hard, but many researchers feel that once made, the changes make for a better paper – even if initially they feel affronted and disagree with the reviewers' comments. Try to stick with it!

When making changes in response to a reviewer's comments, it is essential that you keep track of the changes that you have made. When you resubmit, you will need to explain in writing what changes you have made and how they address the reviews. There are times when authors can actually argue with the points made by reviewers by appealing to the editor directly (as it is the editor who has the final say). This is potentially a risky strategy and one that does not always work and it may be one that is best avoided by less experienced researchers or saved for those occasions where you are totally at a loss as to how to do what a reviewer has asked you to do.

Success story: responding to a review

For her psychology dissertation, Helen did a thematic analysis of patients' experiences of an intervention designed to help coping with chronic pain. Later, Helen's supervisor suggested they write up some aspects of the findings as a journal article. Helen and her supervisor worked together to write an article presenting the findings in relation to three of the five themes that were included in the original dissertation write-up. They sent this off to a journal and eight months later they got a reply saying that the paper would only be accepted after major revisions. The reviewers asked for several key things:

1 Reduce the paper from 5500 words to 2000.
2 That they either present all five of the original themes or 'discuss in the limitations the problems with omitting them from the paper'.
3 Extend the discussion and method sections in a number of ways.

Dealing with these reviews was daunting and difficult, not least because the request to extend the paper seemed to directly contradict the instruction to reduce its size. The authors gritted their teeth and set about trying to make the changes. In order to reduce the size, they decided to focus on only one theme. This was not a simple decision because the reviewers seemed unhappy with the exclusion of themes, but it seemed the only way to reduce the paper. So, they added a section justifying this focus by using evidence from the data and other clinical research to show that this theme was most clinically relevant. Even after doing this, the paper was still longer than the requested 2000 words but they decided to resubmit anyway and explain in a covering letter that they felt it was impossible to further reduce the paper without leading to problems in its logic, coherence and the quality of the evidence presented for the analysis. The editor accepted this longer version and the paper was eventually published.

Managing the process

In some ways managing the process of preparing a journal article is very similar to managing the process of doing your dissertation. So, you will find that you can use many of the chapters from this book to help you with aspects of this (for example, planning and timetabling, managing the relationship with your co-author(s), reviewing relevant literature). However, I would also offer the following additional tips for the first time journal article author.

Top tips: surviving your first journal article

- Agree at the outset which co-authors will do what, and discuss authorship (although be prepared to be flexible about this too).
- Remind yourself that many articles get rejected, or are accepted subject to major changes and try not to be too disheartened.
- Pick a journal before starting to write and tailor your paper to it.
- Consider whether you have the time to do the necessary work to produce a journal article and whether it is the right choice for you.
- Bear in mind the advantages of gaining experience of publication and remember that these are not all dependent upon actually getting your article published (especially as you're starting out).
- Celebrate if you get published! The long process leading to publication can drain the sense of success out of you. Remember to step back and recognise your success.
- Be patient – publications take a very long time to get into print.

So far, I have considered transferable skills and writing for publication. A third way in which your dissertation work might provide a useful springboard for the future is by forming the basis for developing a proposal for future research work. This is considered in the next section.

Developing a proposal from your dissertation

Some graduates may be interested in going on to do further study – either at masters (for example, MSc, MA, MRes, MPhil) or doctoral level (for example, PhD, DClinPsy). There is a fairly large range of such courses but most of them have at least some element where you need to conduct an independent research project. In many cases, this will involve you having to develop, in conjunction with a supervisor, a proposal for this research project.

Also, you may find that you apply for jobs that involve doing some research and being ready to come up with ideas, or having some ideas in store, may be useful.

In a nutshell: why build on your undergraduate dissertation

- You will be quite familiar with current knowledge in that area.
- You should have good familiarity with relevant theories.
- Doing your dissertation will probably have given you some good insight into how to examine the relevant area with particular research methods.
- The findings from your dissertation may provide you with some insight into gaps in the area, as in the suggestions for future research that you included in your project write-up.
- You will already have worked with an academic who knows about that area and they may help you with networking and gaining information in that area (such as looking for funding) or may be able to supervise your further research themselves.

If you go on to do a postgraduate course that involves an independent research project, you don't have to do something that is related to what you did for your undergraduate dissertation; you may not wish to, or it might not be feasible for the course you're applying for. But for those of you who want to develop your dissertation further, I offer the following advice.

The earlier chapters of this book describe many processes that will be the same for developing research ideas and proposals at any level. So, you can use these to help you with proposals that you might do after your undergraduate work.

Some key things that you can do to build upon the dissertation for future research plans are as follows.

- Talk to your (ex-)supervisor about other future possibilities.
- Go over the dissertation write-up carefully and think about the areas you have identified for future research. These may be things that you can turn into a proposal – as part of your rationale will already be there.
- Think about what you have learned about the methodology that you used – how can you improve on this in the future? What methodological choices would you make differently in the future? Again, some of this will be there in your write-up.
- Incorporate any feedback that you obtained on your project (either at the draft stage, at the final stage or in relation to a viva or presentation if you did one) as you develop your ideas.

Success story: dissertation to PhD proposal

John used discourse analysis in his undergraduate dissertation to analyse how fatherhood is constructed in newspapers in the UK. One of his findings was that 'ideal fatherhood' tended to be constructed with emphasis on both economic provision and emotional care in some newspapers (those with a more middle-class, liberal readership). In writing up his dissertation, he noted that a limitation of his study was that it didn't reveal anything about how men themselves construct fatherhood, or respond to the constructions they encounter in the media. John made the point that studies addressing this had been conducted but not very recently and that this was problematic because it is an area affected very much by rapid changes in social attitudes and policies. He therefore recommended that future research address this issue. After graduating, John was interested in doing a PhD and he approached potential supervisors, emailing researchers with interests in parenting and discourse to explain this aspect of his undergraduate dissertation. This led to a discussion with one academic, during which they developed a proposal to interview men about their understandings of fatherhood and their perspectives on media representations of fatherhood. The proposal was submitted to a highly competitive Postgraduate Funding Programme that ran at the academic's university. The combination of a good proposal, a good fit between the academic's research profile and John's dissertation experience led the panel to award John funding to do the study.

Conclusion

In this chapter I have considered three main ways in which your dissertation work can be useful for future activities. A key benefit to doing a dissertation is that you can use this in the future as a concrete example of transferable skills that are useful across a range of occupational and educational settings. Dissertations sometimes form the basis of academic papers and it is useful for you to arm yourself with information about this process if it is something that happens for you. Even if it doesn't, remember that dissertations that are not published are not necessarily less good than those that are and you can still draw upon many aspects of what you've learned and apply them to future situations. Finally, some of you may use your dissertation work as a basis for writing future proposals for research – for a job or in applying for a future course. All of these three ways of taking your dissertation work further will work best for you if you understand the system as well as you can, and this chapter has provided some key information that will help you to do this and to make the very best of your experience of doing a qualitative dissertation.

---------------------------------- **References** ----------------------------------

American Psychological Association (APA) (2010) 'Summary report of journal operations, 2009', *American Psychologist*, 65, 524–5.

Biesma, R.G., Pavlova, M., Vaatstra, R.,van Merode, G.G., Czabanowska, K., Smith, T. and Groot, W. (2008) 'Generic versus specific competencies of entry-level public health graduates: employers' perceptions in Poland, the UK, and the Netherlands', *Advances in Health Sciences Education*, 13, 325–43.

Game, A. and West, M.A. (2002) 'Principles of publishing', *The Psychologist*, 15, 126–9.

Landrum, R. (2003) 'What employers want from psychology graduates', *Teaching of Psychology*, 30, 131–3.

Wood, C., Giles, D. and Percy, C. (2009) *Your Psychology Project Handbook: Becoming A Researcher*. Harlow: Pearson Education.

11

OVERVIEW AND CONCLUSION: BE A SCHOLAR

Stephen Gibson, Cath Sullivan and Sarah Riley

In this concluding chapter we provide an overview of the key themes of this book, draw some conclusions about the process of doing a qualitative project, and consider some of the joys and frustrations of doing academic research.

In Chapter 1, we highlighted three key themes of the book – decision making, critical thinking and methodology – before using the subsequent chapters to explore the processes of doing good qualitative research. These processes included how to formulate research questions, how to plan and manage your project, how to work with your supervisor, the ethical issues involved in qualitative research, how to undertake a literature review, the various options for data collection and analysis that are open to you, how to evaluate your analysis according to appropriate quality criteria, how to write up your work and what your project might lead on to. Here, in our concluding chapter, we return to the three key themes of decision making, critical thinking and methodology to show how they're related across the different processes of doing a qualitative research project. We also highlight some of the other quality issues that have been recurring themes throughout the chapters in this book.

In a nutshell: key themes of the book

- Decision making: Making timely and informed decisions will help you to steer your project in the right direction, and prepare for the unexpected.
- Critical thinking: Evaluating your own and others' work according to appropriate criteria will help to demonstrate your grasp of the core principles of good scholarship.
- Methodology: Appreciating the links between epistemology, ontology, your research question(s), data collection and analysis will ensure that your project 'gets off the ground' and remains airborne.

As you will perhaps appreciate by now, these key themes are related. You'll now have a sense of just how many decisions you have to make over the course of your project – and you may already have made some of them. There are many options available to you, and knowing which ones to take can be daunting. This is where a good grasp of methodology is helpful, and central to being able to make decisions informed by your methodological reading are your critical thinking skills. As we noted back in Chapter 1, you probably underestimate how good you are at thinking critically, and it's a skill that you can develop as you progress through your project.

In our experience, students often struggle with the idea that they are allowed (indeed, expected) to take a position on a debate. Often, there is a vaguely misguided attempt to sit on the fence in the name of 'fairness', something that can lead to banal conclusions along the lines of 'every approach has something to offer'. What your markers are looking for is a scholarly, well-argued position – so tell them why you used the approach you did, why you interpreted your findings in the way that you did and why your work is important. Enjoy the chance you have to be an apprentice academic.

In a nutshell: be a scholar

While you're doing your project you should be thinking of yourself as an academic-in-training, as a junior member of a scholarly community. What goes on in universities is important because, at its best, academic research has the power to show us new ways of thinking about the world and new ways of being in the world. Don't lose sight of that even if this is your first or only foray into the world of academic research.

While decision making, critical thinking and methodology are key themes in this book, you may have noticed other recurring themes around good practice in qualitative research that have run through the chapters. In the following section we draw these themes together as our final list of tips, highlighting how they relate to the various stages of the research process.

- Being systematic: whether you're planning your project, conducting your literature review, collecting or analysing your data, being systematic is crucial. If you're not sure what this means think back to previous chapters. In Chapter 3 on planning, we talked about taking time early on in your project to produce a plan that spells out what you will do and when you will need to do it. This is being systematic. Chapter 5, on literature reviewing, described making rigorous notes on the articles you read using key questions for identifying relevance. This is being systematic. Chapter 6, on data collection, recommended that you make sure you are aware of the possibilities available to you for data collection, and that you have a rationale for the approach you select. This is being systematic. And Chapter 7, on analysis, discussed keeping a record of the process of analysis (for example, a research diary). This is being systematic.

- Quality: if you're new to qualitative research, the standards for assessing the quality of your work might initially seem unclear. This is because, ultimately, there is no single unified entity called 'qualitative research'. Instead, as you will have gleaned from Chapters 6 and 7, there are a multitude of perspectives on qualitative data collection and analysis, some of which contrast with one another as sharply as they do with quantitative research. As noted in Chapter 8, there are some common indicators of quality (for example, reflexivity), but even these tend to be treated differently in different approaches. You therefore need to get to know your chosen approach so that you can evaluate it appropriately. So, for example, if you're doing interpretative phenomenological analysis (IPA), evaluate it according to the criteria for evaluating IPA, but if you're doing discourse analysis (DA), evaluate it according to the criteria for evaluating DA.

- Get to know your approach: don't rely only on textbooks! As much as we hope this book has been useful in helping you to think about the process of doing your research project, the actual substance of that project will come from elsewhere. In particular, once you've settled on a methodology for your project (for example, grounded theory or conversation analysis), you need to immerse yourself in it – see Chapter 7 for further reading suggestions. Immersing yourself in your method and methodology becomes increasingly important as you progress through academia, and essential for postgraduate work or an excellent mark for a final-year undergraduate project. Knowing your approach by reading enough so that you have a good working knowledge of both the methodology and how it has been applied in previous research will allow you to write confidently and with skill at all levels of study.

- Ethics: as in any research project, ethics are central to the design, conduct and analysis of a qualitative project. They are also implicit in how you relate to your supervisor and others involved in your project. There is a temptation to think of ethics as a box-ticking exercise that you go through before getting on with the business of doing the research, but being ethical is integral to being a researcher at all stages of the process.

- Make it your own: it's your project! Take control, relish the opportunity you have to find out about something that interests you, and don't sit back and wait for your supervisor to start pushing you. You'll get much more out of it if you can feel like it really is *your* project.

- Ask for help: yes, it's yours, but you're not on your own. A student project is an independent piece of work with supervision. Those last two words are crucial – your supervisor is the best resource you have for your project, so make the most of them! If you feel you are struggling, don't shy away from them – tell them, and ask for their suggestions on how to get over your difficulties. Similarly, make sure you draw on the expertise of other people who you may have access to for assistance in your research (for example, technical staff, librarians).

- Flexibility: one of the most important things to bear in mind as you are planning and conducting your research is to remain flexible. There is no question that good planning at the outset – as outlined in Chapter 3 – will greatly enhance your chances of producing an excellent project, but a plan should always allow room for manoeuvre so that you can respond flexibly to developments in the project. As explained in several of the chapters, it is perfectly okay for your project to evolve in unanticipated directions as you go along. Indeed, it might well be suggested that the capacity to be surprised and to be led where the project takes you is one of the hallmarks of excellence. If you hadn't anticipated your project going in a particular direction, then it probably indicates that you haven't forced the research to conform to your own views of the issue, event or phenomena that you are investigating. Nevertheless, this can lead to some anxiety, and highlights two differing types of uncertainty, which we will (imaginatively) call Bad Uncertainty and Good Uncertainty.

In a nutshell: good and bad uncertainty

Bad uncertainty: Something crops up unexpectedly that you really could (and should) have planned for!

Good uncertainty: Your research throws up something (such as a finding or a possible avenue for further data collection) that you simply hadn't (and couldn't) have anticipated.

Getting to grips with bad uncertainty and learning to embrace good uncertainty is central to the success of your project, so let's say a bit more about them.

Managing uncertainty

There are some unexpected events that you really should expect – for example, you should expect that not all the people you invite to participate in your research will agree to do so. If you haven't prepared adequately for this kind of thing, then your project may suffer. However, there are other unexpected events that might well indicate that your project is a well-designed and interesting piece of work. Think about it like this: if we could plan every last detail of a study to the point where there was nothing that could surprise us, then would there be any point in conducting the research in the first place? A good project will strike a balance between those aspects of the research process that you can – and should – prepare for, and those that you simply can't. Indeed, it is one of the most satisfying and exciting aspects of qualitative research when your findings open up possibilities that you hadn't previously considered. This is not to suggest that every student will have this experience with every project – even seasoned academic researchers don't feel this way about every project they're involved in – but you can at least feel relaxed about the possibility of being surprised.

So, what sorts of things can we anticipate – or, what things shouldn't be unexpected? Well, you will have gleaned from many of the chapters that the links between the assumptions you make about the nature of knowledge (epistemology) and reality (ontology), the research question(s) you ask, and the way in which you collect and analyse your data are inextricably connected. In Chapter 1 we used the metaphor of the methodological kite to try and capture the way in which these elements of the research process are mutually reinforcing (see Figure 11.1).

So, if you realise that your findings are inconsistent with the epistemological position that you had in mind, or that your analysis isn't addressing your research question(s), then you are most likely coming across something unexpected that you really should have expected. As you will appreciate by now, good planning from an early stage will help you to avoid this.

However, if you begin to analyse your data and find that a new research question springs to mind, which potentially takes you down a different path, then this is an encouraging sign because it shows a development in your

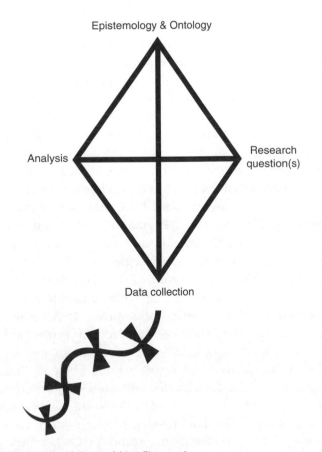

Figure 11.1   The methodological kite flies again

thinking that could only have come about by engaging in the processes of qualitative research. This is an example of how qualitative research is cyclical.

Qualitative research: going round in circles

Qualitative research can be thought of as being cyclical in two ways. First, each stage of research, such as developing your research question, producing your literature review, or doing your analysis, is an iterative process. For example, when analysing data qualitative researchers usually engage in several rounds of analysis before moving on to the next stage. These cyclical processes allow researchers to develop deeper and more conceptual ways of thinking about their project.

The second way in which qualitative research is cyclical is the conceptual thinking produced by approaching each research stage iteratively, which may ultimately lead you to take a different path from that which you originally planned. This will often require you to go back to earlier stages in your project with a new perspective or a more knowledgeable standpoint.

Re-visiting early stages in your project with a new perspective can be a very exciting aspect of qualitative research, but it can also be daunting, leaving you faced with some important decisions about the ways in which you develop your project.

New ideas can lead to you wanting to collect more data, or to re-assess some of your assumptions. They might even lead you to wish you'd done a completely different project altogether! This is where Chapter 10 is particularly useful in reminding you that your project needn't be just an endpoint, but can be the starting point for so much more. Nevertheless, you may have to deal with the potentially tricky issue of managing the cyclical nature of qualitative research – with its associated heavy toll on your time – and the necessity of having to produce a piece of work by a specified deadline.

One way to manage the cyclical nature of doing qualitative research with a limited time frame is to remember that while qualitative research can be thought of as cyclical, these cycles take place over a set period of time and reach an endpoint. You might therefore think of your project as both cyclical and linear at the same time (see Figure 11.2), with several cycles of, for example, data collection and analysis, taking place along a broadly linear trajectory.

It can be useful to build these cycles into your project timetable by, for example, planning double the amount of time you think it will take you to do an activity (see Chapter 3 on planning your project). But, since it can be difficult – if not impossible – to identify in advance precisely where your project is going to take you, you also need to draw on your critical thinking and

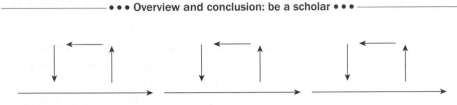

Figure 11.2 The process of a qualitative research project

decision-making skills. In consultation with your supervisor, you should have the confidence to say 'enough is enough' and move on at appropriate points.

You may feel that you have yet to fully mine your project for all its varied and rich possibilities, but at some point you will need to switch from exploratory-researcher-mode to deadline-chasing-student-mode. Remember, if you are so wrapped up in your project that you feel as though there's still so much more to be done, then it sounds like you've caught the research bug – maybe you should stick around academia a while longer?

Success story: catching the bug

Not all students who undertake a research project as part of a degree course will go on to further study, let alone a career in academia, but the authors of the chapters in this book have tried to convey the excitement of research, and particularly qualitative research. We all caught the bug at some stage – some of us as undergraduates, some much later on – but we're infected beyond all hope now regardless. We've tried to leave traces of the bug all over this book in the hope that some of you might catch it too.

It's worth emphasising again that high quality projects tend to involve, among other things, wide reading and thorough knowledge. So, our final tip concerns something that we've found to mark out the most impressive projects from all the rest – the importance of reading.

Top tip: read, read and read some more!

The very best student projects will demonstrate engagement with a broad array of sources, so make sure that you keep your reading going throughout your project. It sounds so simple, doesn't it? The more you read, the more you will grow in confidence as you begin to consider the options available to you from a position of expertise. So try to build in time for regular reading throughout your project.

We conclude this book by pointing out that if you've gone to the trouble of reading this book you're most likely doing things the right way already. We wish you the very best in your journey through the world of qualitative research and hope that this book has given you an idea of the routes available to you, what the terrain might be like and where you can catch a lift along the way.

INDEX

Page numbers in **Bold** represent Figures. Page numbers in *Italics* represent Tables